AUTOMATION AND THE FUTURE OF MAN

AUTOMATION
AND THE
FUTURE OF MAN

S. DEMCZYNSKI

London
GEORGE ALLEN & UNWIN LTD
RUSKIN HOUSE . MUSEUM STREET

PRINTED IN GREAT BRITAIN
in 11 *point Times New Roman type*
BY EAST MIDLAND PRINTING CO. LTD
BURY ST EDMUNDS

To the memory of my parents

INTRODUCTION

AT all times the main preoccupation of man has been his daily survival and the satisfaction of his basic needs. To these ends he has had to concentrate nearly all his mental and physical powers, leaving little time to ponder on more basic and farther-reaching issues. Yet ultimately the latter may prove more important for survival than the satisfaction of more apparent needs.

This seems particularly true in the case of our own civilization. In spite of all our tremendous scientific and technological advances the human lot on this planet does not seem to be, in general, very much better than it was thousands of years ago. It is not only a question of the unequal distribution of benefits derived from modern technology, which permits the greater part of the world's population to live at starvation level while others nearly choke themselves with an over-abundance of goods. Even in economically privileged societies life does not seem to be an image of an earthly paradise. Some would say it resembles rather a mechanized version of hell. The feeling of the emptiness and futility of modern industrial civilization is widespread. Mental illness is on the increase. The mass-man of today seems unable to benefit from the powers he has won through science and technology. He seems to be growing alienated from the world and from himself. It almost looks as if the gods permitted man to gain new knowledge in order that he should destroy himself and perhaps all other higher forms of life.

The rise of fanatical ideologies, the anti-rationalism and anti-intellectualism of the present epoch, do not encourage attempts to find the answers to the problems confronting us today. The conformism of the masses, the decline of art and the split between science and the humanities, the utilitarian outlook on life, and the heavy conditioning to which we are all subjected, do not create an atmosphere conducive to creative thinking. Yet the answers must be found it we are to survive.

It is fairly obvious that the old ideologies which guided us successfully through the millenia of pre-industrial civilized life can no longer serve as sign-posts in an age of automation and atomic power. While ideological decay apparently begins in the West, it would not seem that the virile ideology of the East, spreading under the protection of totalitarian regimes, has really found a solution of the problems facing the human race today.

It is easy to blame our troubles on industrialism and mechanization, with consequent departure from the more 'natural' ways of living. But can such criticism be justified? Can the machine which augments man's natural powers a thousand-fold and frees him from incessant drudgery really be so intrinsically evil? Need it be true that our mechanical slaves are bound in turn to enslave us and bring us to destruction? Or is it rather our stupidity and shortsightedness in the application of these machines that brings disastrous consequences, otherwise avoidable?

The influence of machines now permeates all aspects of our lives. Our whole civilization is built on an industrial base and in view of the spectacular advances in automation and automatic data processing it is certain that our dependence on machines will show a further sharp increase in the near future. Hence it is illuminating to analyse the ideological and sociological problems of our times by considering the interaction of man and machine.

In order to comprehend the various effects of mechanization today we must examine the influence of machines on the growth of industrial societies in the past. To discuss future developments in this field we must first become thoroughly acquainted with the most advanced machines of today. This involves the study of cybernetics, information and communication theory, automatic controls, electronic computers and various other fields of modern science and technology. Consideration of the ultimate potential of the machine poses certain serious philosophical questions and involves the problems of the basic properties of life, brain and mind, man's position in the universe and the purpose of his existence. The study of the interaction of man and machine takes one into the fields of psychology and sociology. In a survey covering so many issues, the method of exposition must necessarily be cursory; an extensive bibliography has been listed for the reader interested in pursuing a more detailed course of study.

ACKNOWLEDGEMENT

For constructive criticism and encouragement, my thanks go first to Mr R. Ruddock, Staff Tutor in Social Studies at Manchester University. Other people who contributed in a similar manner and whose help is gratefully acknowledged are: Mr M. C. Bonney, Mr R. W. Crossland, Lecturer of Education at the University of Manchester, Dr S. Eilon of Imperial College of Science and Technology, Mr P. Holland of The English Electric Company Limited, Mr R. W. Paterson, Staff Tutor in Philosophy, University of Hull, Miss B. Pearson, Mr R. D. Waldron of Research Laboratories, Marconi's Wireless Company and Mr J. Yarnell of The de Havilland Aircraft Company Limited.

I would like, however, to stress that none of them should be in any way associated with or held responsible for the views expressed in this book. I am also very much indebted to Mrs A. Boydell and Mr J. Howarth for linguistic correction of the original manuscript, which task took a great deal of their time and effort, and to Mrs J. Airey, Miss M. Fish and M. J. Turner for their gallant efforts in typing my almost illegible handwriting.

I am also grateful to The de Havilland Aircraft Company Limited for providing the facilities for typing and duplicating the manuscript and for generally helpful and encouraging attitude towards the present work.

S. DEMCZYNSKI

CONTENTS

PART ONE

PART ONE

CHAPTER 1

The First
Industrial Revolution

CIVILIZED man has a tendency to see himself as essentially different from all other creatures on this planet. This belief has often been explicitly stated or indirectly implied by various thinkers, living at different historical times and belonging to different civilizations, although of course, not everyone has always subscribed to it. Whether Paleolithic man already had dim notions about his intrinsic superiority over the great beasts of his time, we can only guess, but it is rather doubtful. In pitched battles, when he was matching his puny strength, aided only by primitive stone tools, against the teeth and claws of large carnivoras, man was certainly not always the winner. Thus, the idea of man as lord of creation was unlikely to have developed in those remote times. In the primitive totemic customs, which according to some scholars are likely to be as old as the human race itself, there is little to suggest the existence of a belief in a sharp line dividing human beings from the rest of the living world; there is much which points to the contrary. However, with the advent of agriculture and animal husbandry the early human civilizations developed. The more complex they became, the more vividly men began to realize that their ways were very different from those of animals.

Men could make tools, use them, and with their help make more elaborate tools. Men could form abstract ideas in their minds, and because they could speak they were able to communicate these ideas to other men. Men could form societies based on close and complicated collaboration, involving the division of labour. With the progressive development of societies, the apparent distinction between men and animals continued to increase. This difference was later endorsed by

B

some religions, which by attributing the immortal soul to men alone, created in the minds of the faithful an unbridgeable gap between man and the rest of life. It may be pointed out that even on an advanced philosophical and theological level the notion of the intrinsic distinctiveness of man has by no means been universally accepted. Indian thought, for example, rejected it, seeing man as a part of nature and merely a step in the long and thorny chain of successive reincarnations towards perfection, the latter being the complete dissolution of personality and the merging with the eternal Mind of the World or Nirvana. The sharp distinction between man and the rest of life is also lacking in the Taoism of Lao-Tse.

However, our own Western Civilization, based on Christianity, accepted in general the complete division between man and animals. The founder of modern philosophy, Descartes, with his sharp division between mind and matter, considered animals as automata, basically different from rationally thinking, free-willed human beings. Even now, the view that perhaps we are just a species of animals really began to spread after Darwin published his views but his idea of the descent of man is still far from general acceptance.

For the sake of argument, however, let us assume that man is in fact not essentially different from other living creatures and let us try to describe the human animal. What is really his most obviously distinguishing feature? The 'thinking' or the 'rational animal' are flattering names but experiments with animals demonstrate with increasing clarity that they too must be credited with some measure of rationality. They can certainly learn some uncomplicated tasks. It is easy to dismiss their feats as simple conditioning, but what about the chimpanzee, confronted for the first time with some fruit hanging from the ceiling and two boxes, each too low in itself to enable him to reach the fruit, who reaped the reward by placing one box on top of the other? Anybody who ever observed a sheep-dog in action must admit that its behaviour seemed rational and certainly effective for the purpose of herding sheep.

The ability to form abstract ideas also does not seem to be an exclusively human prerogative. It has been convincingly demonstrated that a raven can produce in its mind the idea of a number although this concept must in his case, of course, remain in the averbal state.

Somebody described man as a gregarious animal, but this definition does not seem to be very revealing, as many species exhibit gregariousness in a much greater degree. It is, of course, perfectly true that man needs contact with other men in order to develop to a truly human level. The few known examples of humans who survived from early childhood among animals without contact with other people convincingly demonstrate the point. These unfortunate creatures were not only definitely animal-like when first caught, but, if the capture did not occur earlier than at the stage of late puberty, they remained forever in a sub-human state in spite of all educational efforts. However, once developed, man at least has the choice of staying alone. How does this compare with social insects like ants or bees, which do not have to learn to live together but possess the inborn, infallible instincts to co-operate, so that they simply cannot help being gregarious?

There is, however, one trait which is exclusively and typically human: the making of tools. We can see man-made tools wherever men have existed. From the stone axe to the inter-planetary rocket, man lives with and by his tools. From the dawn of human civilization up to our technical age tools have been indispensable for human survival, they have conditioned the progress of societies and made a tremendous impact on every aspect of human life.

The ability to make tools is so important that it is generally accepted as a first step over the border line dividing men from animals. It is the membership card of the human race. Of course, strictly speaking, there is also no sharp dividing line in this field. Animals too can use extremely simple tools, e.g. monkeys do throw stones at their enemies and they are known to reach fruits with the aid of sticks, and a chimpanzee can even 'make' the tool, in a way, by joining together two rods in order to reach a fruit. Also the tool-making activity is obviously the outcome of complicated, more general mental processes which, if they were only better known, would probably be considered as an even more typically human trait than the tool-making itself. In the absence of this knowledge, the creativeness in the field of making and using tools seems to be the most apparent typically human propensity.

All living forms, other than man, have only one general method to secure their survival. It is adaptation to the environment. If, due to the massive activities of the species, the environment itself changes that is purely accidental and certainly unplanned. Owing to his tools and techniques in their use man can, within limits, change the environment to suit himself. Through prehistoric times and the relatively short period of recorded history there has been continuous interaction between cultural, social and technical developments of the human race. Although one does not necessarily subscribe to the thesis that the means of production existing at a given historic period condition every other sphere of human activity, and one may consider the development of ideas as the primary factor, it cannot be denied that the tools existing in any age had profound effects on human culture and civilization. This book attempts to discuss some social and philosophical consequences of the most advanced tools man has created so far: the mechanically-powered, fully-automatic manufacturing machines and the machines which can perform the equivalent of certain lower mental functions of the human brain. The present chapter concerns itself with the immediate precursors of these advanced machines and their consequences. These precursors are, of course, the mechanically-powered, non-automatic, manufacturing and transportation machines.

Starting with the stone axe the tools of man had been growing increasingly complex. This process was very slow at first, measured by intervals of hundreds of thousands of years, then by tens of thousands, and it finally gathered momentum with the rise of the first civilizations. The use of metals was an enormous step forward. The wheel rotating on an axle was perhaps one of the greatest of human inventions, second only to the discovery of fire. It was certainly a triumph of human ability for abstract thinking. Nature failed to develop the wheel in any of its living creatures and so there was no working model to suggest this idea to early man.

However, we observe that prior to our epoch, no matter how complicated and diverse the tools became through the ages of creative inventiveness, they all had one feature in common. The motive power driving them was almost universally the human or animal muscle.

The employment of draught animals like the ox and the horse was undoubtedly helpful but these animals have strength of roughly the same order as humans and thus the picture was not really changed. They demand a lot of care and they feed on the fields where food for human consumption can be grown. Also the manner in which their strength can be applied is very inflexible compared, for instance, with electrical energy. As far as power-sources to drive manufacturing and processing tools are concerned, only the wind-mill and the water-mill made substantial contributions, but these represented a small fraction of the total power-consumption of the community. Among the tools serving as means of transporation, the wind-driven sailing ship held a place of honour accounting for a sizeable portion of the total tonnage transported by any means. For us who freely employ machines endowed with powers equal to large herds of strong beasts, this power-hunger of earlier civilizations seems remote.

The clock mechanisms of the eighteenth century were marvels of ingenuity, complexity and precision. But even they were driven by a human hand, which had to wind the spring.

Due to this fundamental limitation in the amount of power per head of population, the standard of living was inevitably low so far as common man was concerned. Assuming that the density of the population was such that the existence of the food-gatherers and the hunters was out of the question and that everything had to be grown or made, man had to work hard and for long hours just to keep himself and his offspring fed and sheltered and clothed. He could produce little surplus food and other articles to support the relatively very small minority not directly engaged in production. So the number of people who could afford an education was small and progress was slow. The life of the great majority of the human race was hard and short. We must not forget that the intellectual and artistic glory of Pericles' Athens was built on foundations of slave labour. So was the grandeur of Imperial Rome. For every Chinese mandarin, Indian yogi or our own philosopher or monk there were many labourers toiling without relief in the fields through almost every hour of their waking life.

Ours is the first civilization which has managed to exploit, on a large scale, the power resources present in nature. The development of the steam engine in the second half of the eighteenth century and of the internal combustion engine in the nineteenth made it possible to use tremendous amounts of energy, stored over millions of years in fossil fuels, like coal and natural oil. The hydro-electric power station can convert the energy of running water into its electrical equivalent, easily transferable wherever required. Consequently it became possible to exploit the enormous power reservoirs of mountain waterfalls and rivers, remote from populated centres, on a scale inconceivable in water-mill times.

Finally, during the last two decades, the forces within the atomic nucleus have been tapped to provide energy for human use.

All these tremendous technological advances are the results of the practical application of scientific method, the latter being perhaps the greatest and most distinctive achievement of Western Civilization. Hence it may at this point be useful to say a few words about the essential features of that method and how it came into being. The majority of people who are not scientists themselves regard the natural sciences with feelings bordering on superstition. Scientific theories and experiments seem to them fantastically complicated, remote and incomprehensible. The terminology is baffling and the scientists who can think with these apparently strange notions and produce sometimes almost miraculous results are often thought of as extremely clever but odd. And so the common man views them with awe or suspicion. The specialized jargon developed by nearly every branch of science does not help to explain matters. Now, while it is true that through centuries of progress many sciences reached a very complex level, the method underlying all these developments is really so simple that it can almost be called extended common sense, and it cannot be too strongly emphasized that this method matters more for the long-term development of science and technology than the body of facts actually known at any given time. Once the scientific method had become firmly established the advances of the last few centuries were almost the natural consequences. The essence of scientific method is simply this:

A certain group of observable phenomena is first described in terms of measurable quantities. As almost all phenomena occurring spontaneously in nature are very complex and difficult to describe, the experiment is performed, when possible, under artificial laboratory conditions. By these means the phenomena are simplified, and the number of quantities involved are reduced to a manageable number, permitting easier measurement and control. In short, we start with the controllable and measurable experiment. When the body of experimental facts is known, an attempt is made to describe the relationship between the quantities involved in deterministic or statistical terms. That is, a theory is proposed explaining why things happened as they did. This theory must satisfy two main conditions: it must be compatible with all known facts and it must permit the prediction of the outcome of future experiments. Hence the validity of the theory can be checked by further experimentation. Of course, the above sequence is often reversed. In observing the phenomena in nature somebody suggests a possible explanation; controllable experiments are then conducted to check the theory.

This description is necessarily an extremely simplified one. During actual scientific investigations many other factors make their contribution and progress is usually far from straightforward. In his work the scientist depends a great deal on those intangible factors known as imagination, insight and inspiration. The conceptual elegance and the aesthetic quality of a new theory are also not a matter of indifference. The religious and ideological background of the investigator has a bearing on the course of his thoughts. The desire to prove one's view right; or demonstrate that another man's was wrong can give strong if unconscious bias to the investigations. But the final confirmation of the theory is always an experiment, not a purely logical argument. Again, no claim for the final and absolute truth is ever made. Any scientific theory is only a tool, the best means to predict the outcome of experiments. As soon as facts which contradict the theory come to light, the theory is discarded and a new hypothesis that fits the facts better is sought. Another important feature of scientific method is that no personal authority, even of the most eminent man, is sufficient in itself. As a rule, the results are only acceptable if it is possible for any qualified investigator to confirm them by repeating the original experiment.

What could be, then, a more obvious and common-sense method for investigating the world around us? To rely on actual experiments, to confront continuously the results of one's thinking with observable facts, and, in case of discrepancy, to trust the latter. Yet it took thousands of years of civilized life before scientific method was developed and firmly established.

Many tentative explanations have been suggested as to why this happened. One is that the intellectual classes of past civilizations were, to put it crudely, too snobbish. They did not themselves work manually but nevertheless enjoyed the products of the work of others, and they may have grown uneasy about it. Modern psychology would say that their feeling of self-importance was threatened. A simple self-defence mechanism may have offered the explanation that manual work is not worthy of nobly-born men. As experiment seemed suspiciously similar to manual work it was rejected as undignified and unworthy of the philosopher, who was supposed to reach the truth by meditation alone. Unfortunately, the results of medi- tation, if unchecked by experimentation, proved repeatedly quite unsuitable for investigating the physical world.

Religious dogmatism also did not create a favourable atmos- phere for the incubation of scientific method. Insisting that the final truth is already known did not encourage an inquiring attitude of mind. Also, all new investigations, if conducted on a fundamental level, were always potentially dangerous as they could lead to theories contradicting the orthodox views. Some religions put such an emphasis on purely spiritual life, or on life after death, that investigations of the physical world appeared trivial and unimportant by comparison.

The second factor that must be mentioned is that the absence of swift means of communication prevented any real contact with other cultures. Many other explanations had been sug- gested but none of them seems to be sufficient to explain why it was that only Western Civilization stumbled on the development of scientific method.

The substitution of mechanical power for that of the human muscle is undoubtedly one of the greatest and potentially most beneficial of developments. It was of the same order as the dis- covery of fire, agriculture, the domestication of animals or the introduction of metals. The mechanically-powered machine multiplied the power available to the community by hundreds or even thousands of times. This phenomenal increase brought two main consequences: firstly, it enormously increased the production of goods per head; secondly, it relieved men from the task of serving as mere power-generators, so that for the first time in human history the common man ceased to be a beast of burden. Prosperity could be increased, life could become easier and pleasanter and a great amount of human energy could be released for education and research, leading in turn to further improvements. The power barrier, decisively limiting the economical development of past civilizations, was at last broken and the sky became the limit. It is obvious now, looking back through the perspective of more than a century, that the change brought by the machine was so tremendous that it could not be dealt with on a purely technical and economical plane. Everything else had to be changed in consequence if harmonious growth was to be achieved. But our social system had grown up in the ages of agriculture, of craft industry and of mercantilism and was ill-prepared to do so.

The machine depreciated the market value of physical strength. It was so much more powerful and economical that any human being who had nothing but the strength of his muscles to sell, found that he had little to offer. The sensible and humane way would have been to teach him to perform some task for which a machine had not yet been built. It cannot be too strongly emphasized that the human energy freed by the introduction of machines was fundamentally an asset for the community. Only by absence of foresight did it become wasted energy and lead to so much personal degradation and social misery.

With artisans displaced by the faster and more economical machines, the matter became even more serious. It was no longer a problem of unemployment alone; the loss was even deeper. The machine-made products were simple and of purely utilitarian value. They were more plentiful and cheaper, and thus could be enjoyed by much greater numbers of men. But the beauty of the objects produced by craftsmen of old had gone. This was much more serious than it may sound to the utilitarian-minded twentieth century man. It is not merely a case of sympathizing with the intellectual and artistic crust of the society that regrets the charm of bygone days. The feeling of beauty is an essential part of human nature, however primitive. Men had worn necklaces, carved their huntings spears and drawn pictures of great artistic quality on the walls of their caves, long before the first corn was grown. Beauty is one of the factors which make life worth living; men do not live by bread alone.

There is no fundamental reason why industrialized society must live in an ugly world. On the contrary, as more high-quality human energy is liberated from crude tasks, there is more time and there are more resources for general education; thus things should become more beautiful. What, then, went wrong? Why do we live in an uglier, although immensely richer, world? Is it perhaps because the growing importance and influence of the machines conditioned our minds to think in purely utilitarian terms, leaving no room for beauty? The multitude of standardized, mass-produced goods surrounding us at all times cannot fail to standardize the categories of our imagination and perceptive appreciation. This does not mean that our minds have been conditioned to be satisfied with the purely utilitarian aspect of the goods. The vague restlessness and dissatisfaction of our time seems to indicate that the urge for something more than bread alone is still deeply rooted in human minds. But to be able to satisfy this urge the mind has to be developed and given other nourishment besides purely technical education. Industrial civilization has failed to achieve this so far, but it did not have to happen this way. It is our own fault if we let the machine impoverish our artistic sensitivity.

The rising industrialism of the nineteenth century had gradually drawn a great part of the rural population into the towns. The life of the country village was governed by a well-developed body of customs and traditions. This code might have been far from the optimum for the given environment, but at least it was there, so that everybody knew what to do and how to behave in a given situation. Relationships in the community were well-defined, everybody had a sense of belonging and because he was watched by his friends and relations, whom, by necessity, he could not ignore, gross misbehaviour was restricted. As the conditions were, broadly speaking, stable over a long period of time a way of living developed which suited these conditions fairly well.

This was not so when the young men or women moved to the industrial centre. The surroundings and the work were be-wilderingly new. Old ways of behaviour did not suit them, the new code of life was unknown to the newcomer, and, at the early period of industrialization, simply did not exist. Old ties were broken, thousands of new attitudes had to be developed and learnt. In a village community everybody's position was defined. In an industrial centre men became hands to be taken on or rejected as necessary. The rootless, shifting, swelling masses of the early industrial proletariat were not defended against the employers by any laws, because there were yet none applicable to this new situation and they had to be won in the teeth of stiff opposition. The defensive mechanism of trade unionism developed very slowly, being continuously impeded by any means that the newly-risen ruling class of industrial entrepreneurs could muster. Profit was the ruling motive, and ruthlessly pursued. In its name the factories were built with hardly a thought to the fact that human beings were to work in them. The towns were developed exclusively as shelters for masses of industrial workers.

In time the great stone deserts arose—an insult to the people who had to inhabit them. Although the prophecies of Karl Marx about the rich getting richer and the poor getting poorer were contradicted by the facts, largely due to the intervention of other than economic factors, the situation at the time when he was preparing *Das Kapital* was grim indeed.

In spite of all blunders, the output of mechanically-powered machines was so great that the nations of Western Europe could not help but become steadily richer. With the rising standard of living the education of the masses improved, and aided by improved means of communication, it was easier for the workers to combine in nation-wide trade unions. In time, these powerful organizations could not only negotiate with employers on equal terms but, in many cases, dictate to them the conditions. Apart from direct economic pressure, organised labour could exercise great political pressure. Thus the rich have not become richer, as Marx professed. The lot of the common man in Western Europe improved enormously and it is largely true to say that in economical terms, he now gets a fair share of the national cake.

On the ideological plane, the victorious machine helped the spread of the utilitarian view of life. It is true that work started in remote times simply as the means of satisfying urgent needs. It is difficult to imagine that the ape-man chipped stones with any other purpose in mind but to make much-needed hunting tools. The bulk of human energy was spent in those days on hunting, food gathering and fighting. Staying alive was a full-time job, requiring every ounce of physical energy and stretching the wits to the utmost. Gradually the work became the predominant activity, satisfying not only man's immediate physical needs but also permitting him to discharge his mental energies. It gave a feeling of achievement, self esteem, a place in the group, and it satisfied human creative abilities. With the advent of mass production all this was gone. The method of production was designed from the point of maximum efficiency, completely disregarding the psychological needs of the worker. It culminated in line-production where the worker is a mere cog in a complex manufacturing process. Line-production may be a marvel of efficiency, but it is not possible to have a feeling of achievement by repeatedly knocking the same kind of bolt into the same kind of hole. Work came to be considered purely as a means of earning a living and nothing else, an unavoidable evil to be done with and forgotten.

With the increased mechanization of almost all trades this attitude spread progressively further. When the satisfaction of achievement had gone from work, the only visible sign of success was the financial reward. The combination of dehumanized work, the disappearance of a sense of beauty, the collapse of the old ways of living and old values under the impact of changes bought by industrial revolution, the emphasis placed on the economic aspect of production, on profit, on making more and more goods, created the atmosphere where everything is measured in terms of utility. It is hardly surprising that to have a bigger television, newer refrigerator or more modern electric cooker has become the main aim in life for many people, as if human happiness was directly proportional to the number of these gadgets. But it would be unfair to blame the machine-builders for that.

Religion ceased to play a really significant part in the life of the highly industrialized societies. The triumphant progress of science wrested from nature a continuously increasing number of secrets. Nineteenth century science was, on the whole, rigidly deterministic. Everything seemed to be explainable, and Divine intervention did not appear to be necessary. The universe was thought of as a gigantic mechanism, completely predictable, working according to immutable laws. It was widely believed in the second half of that century that the great majority, if not all, of the major physical laws were already known. Thus, with a little patience and time, everything would sooner or later be explained in terms of basic theories. The work of future generations of scientists promised to be monotonous and unexciting.

Such uninspired optimism was swept away by quantum mechanics, relativity theory, the wave theory of the structure of matter and other epoch-making discoveries of the twentieth century. Today we are far less sure of ourselves. We feel again that we are, as Newton put it, 'boys playing with pebbles at the shores of an enormous ocean of knowledge'. Although we know much more, we realize even more acutely the extent of our ignorance. The rigid determinism gave way to the statistical approach that permeates modern science and we are no longer certain about the nature of the basic laws of the universe. But the prevalent materialistic outlook was scarcely shaken, although there is a strong reaction against it among the modern philosophical schools on the Continent.

The other reason why religion lost its hold on the great masses of people in highly industrialized countries can be found, perhaps, in the attitude of Christian Churches during the Industrial Revolution. In general, it was always the policy of the Church to support the existing order, and during the terrific class-struggle in the early industrial societies the workers got little more from the Church than the spiritual guidance centred on life after death, and charity. Charity, often carried out with heroic self-sacrifice by churchmen and other religious people was only a drop in the ocean of human misery. The real need was for large-scale social reforms, for fundamental changes in the existing systems. The Church was not prepared to go so far and consequently the workers felt themselves let down. They badly needed ideological leadership and, not having received it from religious organisations, they found it in all brands of socialist theories. The Marxist idea of the dictatorship of the proletariat is of course incredibly naive and has in practice been proved impossible, nowhere more convincingly than in the communist states themselves. Dictatorship can only be exercised by an individual or by a relatively very small group of individuals. Any attempt to circumvent this difficulty, which was clearly realized by the early Marxist leaders, who said that the communist party is a living essence and embodiment of the proletariat and as such expresses its will, is equally unacceptable. The party, if it seizes power, is simply a new ruling class, a new aristocracy. It may rule in a way more beneficial to the worker than the old masters did or it may not, but this is another story and in either case does not lend support to the idea of proletarian dictatorship. However, to an exploited worker the Marxist ideology had probably as strong an appeal as Christianity to an oriental slave working for his Roman masters. The proletariat itself was to be the Saviour, Marx his prophet and millenium was soon to follow. Today, although by long and large the worker in Western communities gets his full share, the alienation from the Church remains.

On the political plane industrialization contributed to worldwide tension due to the competition for raw materials and for the markets for mass-produced goods. The machines were consuming growing amounts of coal, oil, metallic ores, and a great variety of other raw materials, not all of which were to be found in the industrialized countries themselves. Many of them had to be bought from abroad, or better, taken away from the under-developed communities which happened to possess them. So the industrial empires spread all over the world in search of food for their hungry machines. Under the pretext of bringing superior civilization, the peoples of other continents, some primitive, some of ancient cultural heritage, were conquered and the riches of their countries exploited with hardly any substantial repayment to the natives. It is very true that Western missionaries, teachers and doctors did great work in those distant lands but their activity was on far too small a scale and was really incidental. The industrialized nations made the conquests for their own benefit and the avantgarde were adventurers, professional soldiers and entrepreneurs. The doctors came later, partly because a healthy colony was more efficient than a sick one.

The arguments that the non-industrialized races were not able at the time to exploit the mineral deposits of their countries is substantially correct, but this did not entitle the Europeans to take these riches for little more than nothing. The European very rarely approached the coloured man as a brother, ready to teach and to help. The aim was the quick enrichment, not the long-sighted policy beneficial to both sides. As a result, the white man created a sea of hatred and has been ejected from nearly every country as soon as the natives felt themselves strong enough to oppose him. Do some people never learn that the superior technical development of Western nations was primarily due to the combination of favourable factors of geographical, economical, political, and ideological character and not due to the intrinsic racial superiority of the white man?

The competition for raw materials and markets stands large among the causes of both world wars. Industrial power became synonymous with military power and war became a matter of technical research, production and provisioning. Personal bravery still mattered but it was essentially a war of machines; the science and industry behind the army became the decisive factors in the struggle. Now with the advent of nuclear weapons the very existence of civilization and maybe even the human race itself, has been threatened. But who would be silly enough to blame the machines or their designers for these disastrous developments?

This review of the large-scale effects brought by mechanically powered manufacturing and transportation tools concentrated mainly on the undesirable consequences of the industrial revolution. It has been done not with the view to show the machine as an apocalyptic beast, but because the harmful features of industrialization are perhaps less apparent to the eyes of twentieth century man than the good ones. The latter are obvious: the standard of living has increased enormously and work has become less exhausting. As a result, more educational facilities and more spare energy and time are available for the pursuit of higher, more human aims in life. The people in industrial societies are healthier and live longer today than any previous generation in history. Hunger, cold and lack of proper shelter are largely abolished in such societies. We are not oppressed by plagues and many diseases connected with mass poverty have almost disappeared. To advocate a return to pre-industrial conditions because of some harmful consequences of industrialization discussed before is folly. It would mean the death of hundreds of millions of human beings. This country, for example, could hardly maintain half of its population, even on starvation level, if it returned to a non-mechanical, agricultural and pastoral way of living.

There is no way back. It does little good to blame it all on the machine which supposedly leads to a break with nature. We achieved this break very long before anybody even dreamt about mechanical power. Agriculture, domestication of other species of animals, the making of tools are all unnatural. And what about the making of the first fire? No, we broke with nature hundreds of thousands of years ago and since we can no longer ask her for help, we are on our own. We have to master the knowledge of what is good for us, of how should we live in harmony with ourselves and with our environment, or we must perish. There is no alternative. It is contention of this book that although we have not yet mastered the consequences of the First Industrial Revolution, we are already facing another revolution brought about by the fully automatic manufacturing machines, and the machines which can perform the equivalents of certain mental functions.

The tools of the first type represent the development of mechanically-powered machines carried to its logical conclusion. The tools of the second type, the 'thinking machines', can perform the equivalents of certain lower mental operations with tremendous speed and accuracy. This means that the machine is invading the field which until now had been regarded as the exclusive domain of living and thinking creatures. One might point out that the abacus, the slide rule and the desk calculator are also the mechanical means of performing certain mental operations. This is true but the new machines, the digital computers, are more powerful by many orders.

This will be explained more amply in the following chapters. The discussion of whether the machine will ever be able to perform the higher mental functions, that is the creative, artistic or scientific activities, is also left to the later chapters. It suffices now to say that the automation of manufacturing and the mechanization of lower mental tasks is bound to have tremendous consequences. On a purely economic plane, the latter will be comparable with those of the first Industrial Revolution. But, in the long run, the mechanization of thought processes will have even more profound effects. It is bound to make a great impact on our basic outlook on the world and to multiply our mental powers as mechanical power multiplied our physical strength. And everything that man created, from the hand axe to the interplanetary rocket, he achieved by virtue of his mental abilities. If the latter are increased, so will be increased man's power to control nature, for better or worse. Let us hope that this time the advance will be more planned and that more attention will be given to the social consequences of introducing the new machines. If the greatest care is not exercised in this direction we are likely to face bigger disasters than ever before in the history of our species.

CHAPTER 2

The Tools of the
Second Industrial Revolution

IT has already been stated that until the invention of an efficient steam engine, a hydro-electric power generator and an internal combustion engine, the tools of man, although already very complex, shared one feature in common, namely, they were generally driven by human or animal power. Considering next the mechanically-powered tools, created in great variety from the beginning of the first industrial revolution until the second world war, it is again possible to distinguish one very important feature which was, generally speaking, shared by all of them: that, although the driving power was that of steam, oil or electricity, control was exercised by human beings. The mechanically-powered machine could be compared, very roughly, to a great tank full of water under heavy pressure, with one human hand on the tap and the other holding a short length of rubber pipe connected to the tap. By spending a little energy on turning the tap much greater energy is released in the jet of water and is applied where necessary by directing the rubber hose. This principle of power amplification did not apply, in general, to the machines of the pre-industrial era. The pulley and the lever magnify the strength applied, but their output power is actually always smaller than the input power, due to the inevitable dissipation of energy by friction in the machine. In contrast, the mechanically-operated machine can amplify the small human power applied at the input, into the huge output power. But human control of the input is still indispensable.

Suppose that we have a machine of the following type. If the input tracer of the machine is moved by the human hand along a certain contour, a similar contour is cut by the output cutting-tool in a thick steel-plate. The latter operation requires, of course, great amplification of a very small input power.

Supposing now that although high dimensional accuracy is required in the cutting of steel plate, the contour is of an uncomplicated shape and it would be easy to move the input tracer along the curve by mechanical means. In this way the human contribution would be rendered unnecessary and the machine could operate in an entirely automatic way. However, difficulties immediately appear. Assuming that the input tracer follows the curve precisely, we have to rely on the utmost precision of all parts of the machine to produce the correct output shape. A complex machine of such precision would be uneconomical. Further, even if it were built, it would have to work in conditions of nearly constant temperature and humidity, isolated from wind, dust, etc., as all these factors could effect the output. In more general terms, such a machine would require great internal precision and must work in a constant, or at least strictly predictable environment. The first condition makes the machine prohibitively expensive: the second very severely limits its application. Imagine an air plane in flight with all control levers moving accordingly to a pre-calculated plan, but without the instruments measuring the actual performance of the plane. Such a plane would never arrive at its destination because the slightest gust of wind would put it out of balance.

Now let us ask how the human operator controls the hypothetical machine described above. The answer is that he continuously observes the results produced by the output cutting-tool and applies the necessary corrections at the input. Hence the machine itself is open-looped, in the sense that the input affects the output, but the output does not affect the input. The loop is then closed by the human operator. Thus by means of a backward transmission consisting, in this case, of a human eye, a nervous system and a hand, the output now affects the input. It has been realized that it would be possible to build this backward transmission as a part of the machine itself. Such a closed-loop machine would measure its own output, compare it with the input and use the error as the actuating signal for correcting the output. Thus the machine could correct its own errors and, in doing so, could dispense with the human operator and with the high internal precision. It would also be able to cope with the disturbing effects of the environment.

Many ingenious gadgets have been built on these lines without at first realising clearly all the implications of the principle involved. As a matter of fact, the early steam engines already had automatic speed regulators working on the above principle, but it was not until the nineteen-thirties that the full importance of the feedback in controls of all kinds was recognized. It has been realized that feedback has been fully employed by all animals since time immemorial and is one of the basic features in the behaviour of living organisms. When I pick up a pencil from the table my eyes are continuously observing the movement of my hand and my brain corrects the hand's movement by sending appropriate signals to the muscles. This corrective process is mostly subconscious in the adult, but watch a baby learning to grasp objects. He often misses them until he learns to control the movement of his tiny hand by estimating the decreasing gap between the latter and the desired object. Watch him learning to walk. His sense of balance, the vestibular organ in the middle ear, continuously informs him about the position of his head and proper corrective action is taken by the muscles. The eyes continuously register the horizon, thus providing the reference for orientation in space. The senses in the muscles send signals to the spinal cord and to the brain about the tension in these muscles and about the position of the members of the body. Without constantly measuring the output, which in this case is the position of the head and the body resulting from the movements of the legs, no human being or animal could ever walk properly. The results must be continuously sensed and the correction applied.

By using the more sophisticated forms of feedback the trends in output can be sensed and measured and corrective action can be taken before the actual errors occur. In certain kinds of feedback-controlled machines or servomechanisms it is possible to keep the error within almost any desired limits. The principle of feedback can be used in the construction of a great variety of systems of mechanical, electrical or hydraulic character. It can also be applied to studies in various other fields, often apparently unrelated to biology or technology, such as economics.

By constructing the complex feedback loops controlling the performance of mechanically-powered machines, the tools have been created which are able to perform an incredible variety of complicated tasks without any human intervention at all.

Control technology required the development of accurate sensing elements or instruments capable of taking precise measurements of various physical quantities, and the creation of building blocks permitting the construction of complex and versatile systems. Here the techniques of modern electronics made themselves indispensable. Without the electronic valve and other devices of electronic or electrical character the development of control systems would be very severely limited.

Automatic feedback controls can be much faster than the human operator, immensely more precise and capable of uninterrupted performance without getting tired. They can work in conditions unhealthy or lethal for human beings and are expendable.

The combination of knowledge and experience accumulated during the centuries in the field of mechanical design with modern electronic techniques and the principle of feedback, has resulted in the creation of the versatile and completely automatic cutting tools. When these are connected by automatic transfer machines to manufacturing stations, the automatic production line comes into being. This can produce highly complex final products from raw materials without human assistance, apart from maintenance and fault repairing.

Although the fundamentals of the general theory of closed-loop automatic controls were fairly well known before the second world war, some of the first practical applications of servomechanisms on a large scale took place during that war. One of these was the automatic control of anti-aircraft fire, where human operators were found to be too slow and unreliable. Servomechanisms spread to the control of planes, rockets and manufacturing tools. Today, fully automatic production lines have been built and the automatic factory is now more an economic than a technological problem.

Alongside these developments other advances were taking place in the field of communication. Radar installations and systems transmitting coded signals or human speech were growing continuously more complex and more difficult to build. The need for a general quantitative theory of communication was growing progressively more urgent and the first question to be asked was: What is the thing being transmitted or communicated? Thus the idea of information content of the message has been born and has given rise to the development of highly mathematical information theory applicable to all sorts of communication systems.

It was soon realized that the general theory of control and its twin sister, the general theory of communication, were applicable not only to machines but also to studies in the behaviour of living beings, animals or man. The consequences of realizing this fact have been tremendous, both scientifically and ideologically. Living and non-living things were until then thought to be quite dissimilar. Now at least one of the separating barriers was broken down. This gave rise to the science of cybernetics, which concerns itself with the general principles of control and communication in machines and animals. The similarity of certain features in the performance of large scale, complex systems, living and non-living, has its parallel on a micro-level where studies of viruses, proteins and nucleic acids led to a gradual dimming of the once sharp line that divided living from dead matter.

Let us limit ourselves for the moment to the effects of the above ideas on technological development. The general principles of cybernetics are being applied in the construction of machines capable of carrying out the majority of routine physical tasks, and machines which transmit, store and process information. The latter are of particular importance, because their properties allow them to perform some tasks equivalent to certain, relatively lower, mental functions of the human brain. Hence the means exist which will enable the worker of tomorrow to be equipped with the machines that multiply his mental powers by a similar ratio as the mechanically powered tools on the shop floor multiplied the physical powers of an artisan. Gigantic data-processing systems are now being planned, which will not only perform the work of millions of clerks, but will be able to execute calculations and clerical procedures impossible by any system, other than electronic, because of the sheer bulk involved. This second point is particularly important because it will enable the leaders of great and complex organizations to have at their disposal, perhaps for the first time, sufficient data for making rational decisions, instead of ruling mainly by sheer guesswork as at present. The scientists and the engineers working on large technical projects are already being aided by powerful data-processing machines. This help will become immensely greater in the future.

As the electronic computer is always the heart of any advanced, large scale data-processing installation, it is useful to describe the salient features of the machine in more detail. Electronic computers can be divided into two main types: analogue and digital.

The analogue computer can be used to represent the relationships between variables describing certain mathematical (symbolical) or physical systems, by the analogous relationships of currents and voltages. So, instead of solving the problems by mathematical techniques, which may be very difficult, or at present impossible, or instead of experimenting with the actual hardware, which may be too expensive, the system is simulated by the equivalent behaviour of its electronic analogue. This method is extremely helpful but it is not without serious drawbacks. The machine is not very flexible; in general it has to be built for the solution of problems of a particular type and is not easily adaptable for the study of other classes of problems. Secondly, in the simulation of a very complex system it is difficult to produce the required over-all accuracy.

Feedback techniques are widely employed but in scientific computations we are often dealing with accuracy of a different and much higher order than compared to that required from manufacturing or transportation tools. Also certain types of error are not readily amenable to feedback controls. It is true to say that there is a definite limit in the accuracy of analogue simulators, beyond which their construction becomes prohibitively expensive or even technically impossible. Such computers are used almost exclusively for the study of problems of a scientific or technological character, or become themselves parts of automatic control systems of an advanced character. Their use in the field of large-scale processing of clerical data is negligible. It may also be added that the analogue simulators may be constructed without recourse to electronic techniques; the first ones were, in fact, of a mechanical character.

Digital computers are built on an entirely different principle. It has been realized for a long time that vast classes of mathematical and logical processes can be represented by long chains of yes-no statements. The physical counterpart of such an elementary logical unit is a device capable of two distinct stages, e.g. an on-off relay. If a sufficiently versatile system of such devices is available, then the mental problem expressible in yes-no or binary notation can be translated into a corresponding state of this physical system. Subsequently, the physical system can be manipulated according to the rules, which again is the translation of the principles of logic, applicable to the original problem, into the physical operations of the system.

The final stage of the relay system is then translated back into the language of the original problem and constitutes the solution of the latter. In this way many mathematical and logical problems can be solved by purely mechanical means. However, there are difficulties in this technique. When the procedure for solving a given mathematical problem is expressed in binary notation the number of elementary steps is usually very large. Owing to this great 'logical depth' and the fact that even a slight inaccuracy at any point in the calculations may be amplified into a gross error during many successive steps, the system must perform all arithmetical operations with great precision, implying the use of numbers with many decimal or binary places. The great number of steps and the high level of accuracy required at each step necessitates the employment of an enormous number of two-state relays. Hence this technique is only practical if one has a physical relay which is very fast, reliable, long-lived and not prohibitive in price. Although electro-mechanical relays were initially used for the purpose, there were hardly adequate building blocks for large scale digital systems.

With the advent of the electronic valve, an electronic relay or bi-stable element came into being, which could change its state thousands of times faster than any mechanical device. This has led in the last two decades to the development of computers capable of performing various methematical and logical computations at fantastic speeds. The main parts of the digital computer are: input and output units, arithmetic unit, control unit and memory unit. The input unit accepts the data fed into the computer. The translation from human to machine language is performed as a rule, by human operators and their comparative slowness and unreliability is one of the chief weaknesses of the system if a huge amount of input data has to be fed in, as for example in commercial applications of Automatic Data Processing. It is hoped that an automatic reader will eventually be developed, capable of directly translating any kind of standard print or even reasonably good handwriting into machine language.

The output unit delivers the results and here the situation is much more satisfactory, because the translation from machine into human language is done by the machine itself, with the result that the speed of this operation, using extremely fast xerographic printers if necessary, matches the internal speed of the machine.

The arithmetic unit performs the actual processing of the data contained in the various memory or storage units. The speed with which elementary steps are performed by the arithmetic unit is measured in advanced computers in micro-seconds, or even in millimicro-seconds in experimental models.

The memory unit serves as a store for the data, and many bi-stable devices of a magnetic, electronic, or electrostatic character are employed as elements of memory storage. Thus we have magnetic drums, magnetic tapes, ultrasonic lines, electronic tubes, transistors, magnetic cores, electrostatic tubes, low-temperature devices employing the phenomena of super-conductivity, and so on. The basic features of the memory unit are the amount of information which can be stored in it and the time of retrieving or storing a unit of information, called the access time. The latter quantity is usually specified on the assumption that the information will be retrieved in a random fashion. For the fastest memory units the access time is comparable with the speed corresponding to that of the arithmetic units. In general, the faster the memory the more expensive is each unit of information storage. Hence a large computer usually has several memory storages in a hierarchy of increasing volumes, and associated with them, larger access times. The fastest and least voluminous of them is actually directly used during calculations at a given moment. It is being progressively replenished from the second fast memory with the information to be used during the next steps of the programme.

The control unit directs the operations of the machine during any particular application, on the basis of a set of instructions known as the programme. This programme is stored in the memory unit and must be immensely detailed, taking into account every possible eventuality pertaining to the operations. Present-day machines are unable to show any degree of initiative or intuition, even of the sort that lower animals are perfectly capable of. The machine must be instructed in the minutest detail about everything it is required to do. In mathematical applications this is not an insuperable hindrance, apart from the long time it takes to write a programme. In business applications this means, however, that only procedures which can be completely specified by chains of logical steps can be mechanized. Other procedures, which contain elements of human intuitive decision, must be re-designed, with decision criterion rigidly specified, or left to human clerks. The machine is perfectly capable of making a choice at certain points in the calculations between alternative courses of action, depending on the results so far obtained, if a complete set of decision rules is given. In the early computers, the programme was stored in a plugboard wired according to a set of consecutive steps, which the machine was to perform. Hence although the facilities to make the decision about alternative courses of action at branching points was available, the programme itself was unalterable during a given run. With programmes stored in the same way as any other information, provision can be made for modifying the instructions themselves during the progress of the calculations. This gives the programmer much more flexibility.

The ability of a digital computer to perform, with tremendous speed and accuracy, the long chains of logical steps employing enormous amounts of stored data, has obviously great potential for applications in both scientific and business fields. The digital computer was developed during the last war under the pressing need to execute the voluminous and repetitive calculations required for the solution of urgent mathematical problems. Like many other major technical advances, the construction of a digital computer had been possible a long time before that, but the creation of a suitable technological and scientific climate was first needed to make the necessary effort available. At first, the computer was used exclusively for the solution of scientific problems, particularly in the realms of non-linear mechanics, statistical studies, astronomy etc., where often the solutions of a set of equations describing the problem in mathematical language cannot be found by analytical methods, but can only be arrived at by painstaking numerical analysis. This latter technique requires a mass of repetitive calculations, often prohibitive in bulk, even for a large team equipped with ordinary desk calculators. Thus many problems, which were never tackled before for these reasons, have been successfully solved by digital computers. Scientists and engineers could now embark on many investigations which previously had been barred by the sheer bulk of the necessary calculations. New methods of design, hitherto impossible, have been developed. Deeper insight into the nature of many purely mathematical problems has also been achieved.

In time, computers themselves became parts of complicated systems, performing controlling functions of the type considered up to then to be the exclusive sphere of the human operator. In cases where these decision-making tasks could be completely defined, as in a chain of logical operations on data available through artificial sensing elements, they have been found vastly superior to human beings on the grounds of speed, reliability, amount of data taken into account, endurance in adverse environmental conditions and expendability. On the other hand, the enormously superior flexibility and self-organizing ability of human thinking, makes even the most powerful, present-day computer look, by comparison, a moron, in all situations which cannot be foreseen in every essential detail.

The salient features of a computer, employed for the solution of scientific problems of a type which requires enormous numbers of repetitive calculations and uses relatively few basic data, are: the speed of the arithmetic unit, short access time to a relatively small memory store and ease in programming. With the increasing use of computers in science, the idea of applying them to processing routine clerical work gradually gained acceptance. Here, for the first time, was the machine which could execute a long chain of successive data-processing steps, make the choice of alternative ways of proceedings, employ an enormous amount of data stored in its memory, and do all this at a speed millions-fold greater than the human clerk. At the same time, the machine had to be instructed in the greatest possible detail about every step, was entirely incapable of coping with even the most trivial of unforeseen events and departures from the standard scheme, and was very expensive in capital cost, depreciation and operational cost. The obvious choice was to use it first in cases where great volumes of repetitive and well-defined data processing was involved, as in insurance companies, banking, pay-roll accounting, inventory-keeping and so on. It was quickly recognized that, for business applications, it was essential for a computer to have a large memory storage, input facilities permitting rapid feeding of data, and a fast output printer to prepare the mass of issuing documentation. The utmost reliability and ease of maintenance was also required. These differences in the desirable features of scientific and business computers are disappearing now with the application of the former in such fields as meteorology, the continuous simulation of guided weapons, space guidance, large scale statistical studies etc., where large memories and good input-output facilities are essential, and with the increasing employment of business computers to the solution of mathematical problems arising from operation research techniques applied to business.

CHAPTER 3

Automatic Data Processing in Business

DURING the last two hundred years we have witnessed spectacular improvements in manufacturing methods. Successive types of machines have been able to produce goods at an increasing rate and with a decreasing amount of human supervision. The culmination of this process, the fully automatic factory, is an easy idea to grasp on a descriptive level. However, the real meaning of the automation of clerical functions by means of digital computers is perhaps less familiar to people outside the specialists' circle and for this reason a few words will be said about it here.

The advances in manufacturing techniques during the first industrial revolution, which can be truly described as fantastic when compared with the thousand-years-old manual methods, have not been matched by comparable advances in techniques used in clerical and administrative procedures. The output of a modern machine shop is hundreds or thousands of times greater than it would be if the same number of highly-skilled artisans worked using purely manual methods. In comparison, the techniques of the modern clerk, employing pen and ink are not basically different from those employed by his predecessor in the early civilizations of China or Egypt.

Although typically modern data processing aids, like accounting machines, duplicators, punched cards etc., are now widely employed, the pen and ink methods still account for the bulk of clerical work in many businesses. This is because none of these aids can perform a chain of logical operations without human intervention. Due to the necessity of translating repeatedly from human to machine language and vice versa, and due to the need of human aid at various stages, the speed of partly mechanical procedures is limited.

The backwardness of clerical techniques is only matched by the equally embryonic stage of our knowledge of organizational problems arising when large numbers of human beings work towards a common aim. In a very small manufacturing unit, it is possible for one human being to service a given job in all its aspects, such as receiving a customer's order, ordering raw materials, costing the work, invoicing the final product, etc. In a large organization, because of the increasing complexity of work and consequently the specialist knowledge required, because of the physical impossibility of simultaneous accessibility to every file by every clerk, because of the limited number of people who can be supervised by one man, and so on, the work is functionalized, with every clerk performing only the most minute and fixed part of the total clerical services for every job. It should also be noted here that clerical servicing for any job is not, in general, functional by its nature.

The establishment of such a vast and complicated clerical network, typical for almost any kind of large enterprise, creates a tremendous flood of internal communications, necessary for controlling and synchronizing all parts of the system, but basically unnecessary from the point of services required for the given manufacturing process. Although human beings are enormously versatile in comparison with any kind of available data-processing machinery, they are by the same standard slow and unreliable. Hence the whole system invariably lacks the power to perform all data processing required for the basis of sound managerial decisions. This combination of ultra-modern manufacturing techniques with antiquated clerical methods, which could be compared to a tractor and an ox pulling together in the same harness, is now reaching the breaking point. The most obvious adverse result is that the relative cost of clerical services per unit manufactured is steadily increasing, in many cases far outstripping the direct manufacturing cost. Thus the situation arises where great advances in manufacturing techniques, lowering the direct manufacturing cost, say, by half, result in only a small drop in the final price per unit.

This state of affairs is obviously undesirable, but it is still not the worst consequence of present data processing methods.

Far worse is the fact that these methods are entirely inadequate tools for policy making and general administration. With the increasing complexity of activities and structure, the amount of information required for rational administrative decisions (as opposed to sheer guessing) is growing rapidly. The manager vitally needs more and more information, of a kind he would not require at a more primitive stage of industry. Not only does he want to receive this information rapidly, in step with actual physical manufacturing processes, but he wants it suitably pre-digested, with the outstanding summary results clearly stated.

A trolley load of unprocessed data delivered every hour is not much use to anybody. However, even the basic requirements of the unlucky administrator are rarely satisfied in any more complex enterprise. He receives the data quantitatively in-adequate, unprepared, and usually too late. Hence in general his decisions can only be inspired guesses. Even if these happen to be right, it takes too long, due to the sluggishness of a pen and ink clerical system, to translate them into actual physical events. In desperation, decentralization is employed, either officially by splitting into smaller, largely independent units, or by quietly tolerating the high degree of autonomy of departmental heads. In the end, the business gets out of hand, and in many cases develops and grows, or withers, in an uncontrollable manner.

Instead of controlling the stream of events the managerial aim becomes a desperate exercise in swimming the stream, concentrating more on keeping the head above water than on guiding it. The same can be said not only of industrial concerns but whole modern communities. To control and guide modern society, with its ever-increasing complexity of internal and ex-ternal relations, the enormous mass of data, delivered promptly in a suitably condensed form, is an essential prerequisite. This can hardly be done by pen-and-ink alone.

In such a situation the advent of digital computers seems to offer the first real ray of hope. These modern electronic machines, which are capable of performing long chains of logical opera-tions at a speed millions of times faster than that of a clerk, herald the advent of a new era in the development of in-dustrial societies.

There is a growing tendency to view both the machine shop and the office as analogous processing units, but, while the former processes metal or some other physical material, the stuff which is processed by the latter is information. Because the degree of mechanization is far more advanced in manufacturing than clerical methods, advances in production automation are made to sound hollow. There is therefore much to be said for the slogan: A.D.P. first, automation afterwards.

Considered in this way, automatic data processing is seen as part of an irresistible historic process. Hundreds of millions of human beings are today wholly or partially employed in performing mental tasks far below human dignity. Their minds grow progressively arid, wasting their tremendous potential. The data they produce is very inadequate for coping with the complexity of modern life. It is all very well to argue the economic and organizational pros and cons of substituting a digital computer for a group of clerks, but on a large scale such discussion simply misses the point. The automating of progressively complex mental tasks is bound to happen, just as surely as the motor car, once invented, was bound to supersede the horse. In the end the clerical and administrative work, and part also of the designing and scientific work, will be as automized as that of any machine shop. The cost of automatic data processing as compared with manual labour will steadily decrease. The procedures, where human decision-making power seems indispensable, will be re-designed to suit the machine, just as furniture or shoes or anything else has to be re-designed when changing from artisan techniques to mechanical production. The data delivered from an A.D.P. installation will be so much more suitable for managerial use that businesses which do not apply these techniques will quietly die out as thousands of artisan trades disappeared when faced with mechanical competition. The businesses which introduce the new techniques skilfully and at the right time will flourish. All this is inevitable and only the timetable cannot be accurately predicted. Let us hope, however, that this time the development will be more controlled than during its power-phase counterpart. The industrial revolution was inevitable in the ideological climate of the eighteenth century, once the necessary technical level had been achieved, but the consequent slum dwellings, the incredible ugliness of the industrial areas, child labour, the creation of a rootless proletariat, the destruction of cherished educational, cultural and social values, mass unemployment, and unlimited human misery, was not.

The first applications of digital computers in business consisted of the substitution of a machine for a group of people engaged on certain repetitive and voluminous procedures, e.g. preparation of the payroll. The machine was to do something previously performed satisfactorily by human beings, but at a lower cost, (or so at least it was hoped). Great disappointments resulted in many cases, because the cost of installing the computer, including all preparatory organizational and technical work, and the total running cost was usually higher than originally expected. Today it is recognized that with the present prices for computers, the break-even on a direct clerical cost basis ought in many cases to be considered a lucky event. It has also been realized that to use the computer for one or two particular applications, just as a substitute for a group of people, is entirely missing the point. Modern computers are capable of much more than that, and, like any other machine, can be profitably applied only if their true potentials are exploited to the maximum.

It has already been pointed out that one of the weaknesses of modern organizations is their excessive degree of functionalization, unavoidable in the presence of primitive data processing techniques. A computer is powerful enough to permit the re-integration of the whole administrative network and it ought to be regarded able to perform all, or at least the majority, of essential clerical services for all physical jobs. Thus, with the computer the flood of internal communications should largely disappear, together with duplication of work by certain separate departments. The information will flow in one integrated stream through a network containing the computer at its centre, with everything else attached to it. The system will become more controllable, more definable, and its response will be more predictable. Although the idea of integrating clerical and accounting procedures is nothing new, the digital computer enables it, for the first time, to become a practical possibility and to achieve full growth.

The potentialities of a computer are exploited to the fullest by making it perform data-processing jobs, which, while highly valuable for purposes of supervision and policy making, could not be done by any other means because of the sheer bulk and the time-limits involved. Thus the aim is to deliver the masses of data, suitably processed into condensed reports, to the managers and supervisors in step with the actual physical processes, in order to enable the superior planning and control of the whole enterprise. Hence, the indirect benefits in terms of capital saving, more economical allocation of resources, better throughput due to more effective production planning, reduction of inventories, and improved sales due to better market analysis, and many others, are considered the main advantages.

Even more important gains will follow. It has been realized for a long time that all problems in business are closely interrelated. The division into buying, production, sales, personnel departments, and so on, is largely artificial and mainly due to the fact that no human brain can take all the relevant factors into account simultaneously. The advantages of using the computer, which can appreciate the thousands of different aspects of a business simultaneously, analyse them and arrive at the optimum compromise, are obvious. Further, it will be possible to simulate many alternative courses of action and choose the best, a task usually completely prohibitive for people aided by desk calculators only.

Thus, starting from the general principle of maximum rate of return on capital employed, it will be possible to allocate the resources optimally. Much research is still needed on what the real information needs of an executive are, depending on his position and type of business. The flow of production, especially in jobbing shops, will be effectively controlled, perhaps for the first time. As a result, the working capital will be reduced and the inventory will decrease in size. Accountancy will become less historical and will concentrate more on the predictions of future developments from past trends, which (apart from legal requirements) is its true purpose, as an aid to top managerial control. The overheads will be split into much more detail to establish more accurately the economics of each product and procedure. The task of the operational researcher will be made easier because more numerous and more reliable data will be available, because the functioning of the system will be more predictable and because a powerful tool for complex, statistical calculations will also be available in the organization.

It is well known from the theory of servo-mechanisms that, broadly speaking, the basic source of trouble in closed-loop systems is delays in the loop, which may lead to instability and other undesirable effects. Almost any business organization, including executives, operators and machines, can be thought of as an extremely complex closed-loop system. This system performs certain actions to achieve some aims, observes the results, estimates the differences between plans and achievements, and takes further corrective measures. To make overall control effective, the results must be accurately measured and promptly reported to executives. Their orders must be transmitted without delay to those organs which will transduce them into physical actions, delays in any part of the system being detrimental. Moreover, by observing the trends, all kinds of troubles should be anticipated before they actually happen, so that preventative action can be taken, analogously to phase-advance control in servo-mechanisms.

The difficulties contained in the practical implementation of such an advanced project, are, of course, immense. One is fully aware of the innumerable obstacles which have to be overcome in the much simpler present-day applications of digital computers. However, it is my contention that those difficulties are not insurmountable, provided proper resources in manpower and money are allocated for the task. Although the establishment of the A.D.P. installation of an advanced character will be much more expensive than the simple substitution of men by a machine, the rewards will be immeasurably greater. In fact, this seems to be the only way of making the introduction of a digital computer really economical. Half-hearted attempts incur the grave risk of financial losses.

On the technical side, computers will become progressively faster, more reliable, and equipped with larger memories. The ratio of the cost of the equipment to its data processing powers should decrease, and through the use of solid state devices the size and power consumption will be drastically reduced. This trend will presumably continue, until we arrive at a stage of molecular relays, permitting us to employ, in a reasonable-sized computer, as many of the basic elements as there are in the human brain.

Reliability will be improved not only by progress in purely engineering techniques, but also by a more sophisticated network of relationships between elements of the computer or its logical design. It must be remembered that the human mind is still capable of performing its basic tasks even if millions of its elements are put out of action by some form of damage. Our present computers are out of action when a single element fails. However, certain methods already exist for designing a reliable system from unreliable components and these techniques, it is hoped, will be further developed.

The necessity of constructing an automatic reader has been pointed out previously.

At present, the programming of a large computer for business applications, involving thousands of elementary steps, is a major task. To facilitate this work the technique of automatic programming has been devised, enabling a programmer to state the basic steps of the task and to leave the computer to produce the corresponding detailed instructions, according to pre-established rules. Eventually, it is hoped, it will be sufficient to describe the task unequivocally in a language similar to ordinary English. The creation of a suitable language for communication between machine and human beings is, however very difficult, not only because they employ, in general, different physical signals, e.g. electrical impulses on the one hand and voice or writing on the other. Human language is greatly redundant, meaning that any letter or word is partly pre-determined by previous letters and words. Because of this redundancy we are able to correct errors and reconstruct in our minds those parts which are distorted or missing due to imperfect pronunciation, transmission or hearing. On the other hand, economy demands that machine language be as little redundant as possible. Unfortunately human beings cannot express themselves in a non-redundant language without committing numerous mistakes. Furthermore, the meaning of words in everyday language is hopelessly vague, from a machine's point of view. When a machine is instructed every word must have a precise and definite meaning, but again, human beings find it very difficult to phrase their instructions in such a language.

All these advances are not a matter of years but of decades. However, they are well on the way and their impact on every facet of human life in industrial societies will be tremendous. If we want to avoid being caught again in a web of an overwhelming and uncontrollable process, as happened during the power-revolution, a lot of long-range, hard thinking has to be done now.

CHAPTER 4

The Second
Industrial Revolution

HAVING reviewed very briefly in the previous two chapters the
salient features of the tools of the second industrial revolution
and the techniques of their use, let us now consider the effects
which the introduction of these tools is likely to have on
industrial societies. In this chapter we limit ourselves to rather
more obvious and direct consequences, which the large-scale
applications of automation and A.D.P. are bound to have.

Automation of the physical and clerical tasks cannot take
place overnight but will be a gradual and lengthy process. The
first obvious limitation of its rate is the economic one. Automatic machines are very expensive and require an enormous
capital outlay. The fact that the capital thus allocated on the
national scale would bring excellent returns will not in itself
provide the required resources. Great increase in capital
expenditure demands large-scale savings, which cannot be
achieved without affecting adversely the present standard of
living. Western societies are unwilling to do this and totalitarian countries, to which the above solution may be acceptable,
have in general much smaller capital resources per head, and
even they cannot, for obvious reasons, depress the standard of
living of their citizens below a certain limit. As one would
expect, the process of automation proceeds at the fastest rate
in the U.S.A. and U.S.S.R., the two giants of our times. Although the former is more advanced at present, there are visible
signs that automation in the Soviet Union is gathering momentum at a higher rate. The ultimate economic justification of
automation is that in the long run automatic production is
cheaper, provided the volumes are large enough. In other
words, the cost per unit manufactured will decrease, even when

the initial high cost of the automatic machine is included, if a sufficiently large number of units can be made and sold. This problem has been faced continuously since the beginning of the first industrial revolution, and, viewed from that angle, automation is merely the culmination of the age-long process of substitution of machines for men. The rate of this process depends, as far as the economic side is concerned, on the availability of capital, the cost of labour, the supply of raw materials, and the size of accessible markets. Hence, in the regions where a plentiful supply of cheap labour exists, automation will progress at a slow pace. In the countries where the cost of labour is high, the economics of the introduction of automatic machines are obviously more favourable. The continuously increasing cost of labour (in real terms) in the industrial societies expresses the prevailing attitude that the progressively higher reward for the same amount of work is something to be taken for granted. But, apart from more efficient administrative methods, this can only be achieved by the introduction of more machines, and in particular, those which will produce with a decreased amount of human contribution. Automation is clearly in the line of the historical development of industrial societies, and it is bound to develop just as surely as the power revolution did in the past.

The other fundamental factor limiting the rate of progress of automation is the technical manpower required. Automatic machines are obviously very complex in design and make heavy demands on the knowledge of their makers. The maintenance and fault repairing, let alone the designing, become themselves jobs for the highly-qualified technicians, instead of being routine work done by a man with a screwdriver and an oil-can.

These technologists and technicians of tomorrow cannot be trained in a day. First of all, there are not enough teachers suitably qualified to instruct them. These must be trained first, which makes the whole business rather long. According to many experts who have studied the problem in detail, the limitation imposed by the availability of technical man-power, both at present and in the foreseeable future, is even more fundamental and severe as far as automation is concerned, than the availability of the capital.

There are many other factors having a strong bearing on the progress of automation, but they are, perhaps, less fundamental than either of the two discussed above. The level of demand for mass-produced goods, the fluctuations in the world economic situation, the political scene, the attitudes of powerful social factions (like the groups controlling the capital or the trade unions), all have their contributions to make. But these are not quite so basic and would all become of minor importance in the event, for instance, of a major war requiring very large armies in the field and enormous quantities of provisions. As this could be achieved only by decreasing the manpower in the factories, automation would become essential for national survival, sweeping away all other considerations. Then all the limitations, except that of total capital and of technical manpower available, would be disregarded. The capital investment could be increased by enforced savings, but there is an obvious limit here. And although technical training could be accelerated there is a maximum rate at which human beings can learn. The above example is purely hypothetical as any real future war would almost certainly involve the massive use of nuclear weapons with resulting universal destruction. Thus a return to the bow and arrow would be more likely than the construction of automatic factories. The example quoted is intended merely to point out that many features of the present societies are less immutable than one is accustomed to think, and that the large-scale political or social upheavals can easily change the foreseeable rate of development of new technology.

As an automatic production line becomes an attractive economical proposition mainly if a very large number of identical items is to be made, one would expect that the degree of automation in a given industry will be proportional, other things being equal, to the size of the market for which this industry is working. Thus the large markets for standardized products existing in the North American continent or inside the Communist bloc create particularly favourable conditions for the development of automation. The smaller and generally more diversified markets of Western Europe require more flexibility in design and production. It is easier to build an automatic factory manufacturing only one type of product than a factory capable of producing many types of a given class of goods, although the second proposition is still technically feasible. Perhaps the best way is to manufacture limited numbers of types of standard parts which can then be assembled into many different final products. The production of motor cars has already progressed far on these lines; it is quite astonishing for an uninitiated person to realise how many common parts are contained in the cars of apparently different makes. The spread of this tendency will necessitate a lot of changes in the methods of design. However, as far as the latter is concerned, even greater changes will be needed because the capabilities of automatic machines are different from those of manually controlled machines. There are many types of operations which are easy for the human operator to perform but which would require the construction of a complicated and expensive automaton for their successful execution. For instance, an automatic cutting machine can follow a smooth contour with great speed and accuracy, but the construction of a mechanical hand, comparable in versatility and precision of movement to the human hand is still a technical impossibility. The mechanical hands designed for the remote handling of dangerous radio-active materials, although marvels of ingenuity, are still very clumsy as compared with the human equivalent. Another example may be taken from the field of electronics. The completely automatic manufacture of ordinary radio receivers would be impossible if one adhered to a conventional design involving a complicated mesh of wires. For automatic production the design must be fundamentally changed. The components must be made so that they can be assembled without wiring and other operations difficult for an automaton.

The change in design to suit the new manufacturing tools is, of course, as old as human industry itself and has taken place at a greatly accelerated rate during the first industrial revolution, as mentioned before.

The tendency towards standardization, desirable for technical and economic reasons, is likely to increase in the automatic age, with all the accompanying detrimental effects discussed already. However, it is contended that this trend and all its consequences are not unavoidable and can be successfully combated if we really wish to do so. There is no fundamental reason why the goods made by the automaton should be less pleasing to the eye than goods mass-produced by any other method. However, the decision must be taken on whether we want purely utilitarian products or require something more. If anything, the production of truly artistic goods could be stepped up in the automation age by liberating more people from lower manual and mental tasks, and by providing for a higher general standard of education. It is up to the community, or its rulers, to decide how the wealth, increased by automation, is going to be used.

The large resources required for the creation of an automatic production line means that in every instance automation must be considered from a long-term point of view. The capital commitments will necessarily be large so, one has to be sure that the desired return on this capital will be maintained for a long time. Consequently, predictions of long-term market trends increase in significance. The build up of necessary technical knowledge, the training of supervisory and maintenance staff, and the adjustments in existing distributive networks according to the new conditions, will all require a long time. Hence the importance of planning for the future will be unquestionably increased by automation. The decisions taken today will make their consequences felt ten or more years later and whole organizations will be committed in that period to the course chosen at the beginning of the venture. Every major action will have to be co-ordinated and streamlined with the basic policy. As progress continues, it will be increasingly difficult to make major changes in this policy, so the correctness of the initial decisions will be all-important. The increasingly stringent requirements on policy-making, covering longer time intervals and operating in the progressively more complex environment of modern society, require new methods of administrative techniques. While the businessman of old could rely on experience and intuition only, the adequacy of these mental tools alone in the age of automation is very seriously questioned. In fact, the necessity of introducing more scientific and quantitative methods into administration and policy-making is now generally accepted. The questions which are still not settled are how much of the traditional field can be covered by these new techniques, how to infuse the latter into the minds of people accustomed to the old intuitional approach, and what is the optimum blend of new and old managerial ways.

Long-term planning at company or group level is now accepted as indispensable and great efforts are being made by almost every large enterprise to develop this vital activity. The substantial capital resources required for the successful introduction of automation, and the need for accuracy in predictions of future developments, favour the big industrial units. Although the medium to small company can improve its competitive position by the skilful introduction of auto- mation, it seems probable that the big concerns will gain relatively more from them per unit of the capital employed. This is so, firstly because the large capital necessary will be more likely accessible to the big company than to a small one, and the former will be able to afford to wait longer for the amorti- zation of the capital expenditure. Secondly, mass-production creates favourable conditions for the introduction of auto- mation. Thirdly, the big company can more easily attract the scarce, highly-qualified technical man-power by virtue of its name, connections with universities and professional societies, support of research scholarships or establishment of internal training courses. Fourthly, it is easier to predict the developments of the market when one controls a sizeable portion of it. Many other arguments could be advanced but they all can be reduced to the fact that the larger the industrial unit the bigger its resources, and that it operates on a bigger scale and plans in terms of longer periods of time. All these factors are favourable to automation, which will thus increase the tendency for mergers and for the creation of powerful concerns.

Machines which can wholly or partly perform the work of human beings, or even merely increase the efficiency of the latter, have always been viewed with greatest suspicion: first by the artisans and then by machine operators themselves. The former were under-sold and outpaced by the power machines, until the artisan trades, as known before the first industrial revolution, largely disappeared. It is a fair guess that the first machine operators cared little about the artisans whom they displaced by augmenting their forces with mechanical power. However, they were themselves soon threatened by more efficient machines which needed a smaller human contribution for the same product. Finally, a fully automatic machine dispenses with the human operator altogether.

Unemployment is perhaps one of the most terrible things that can happen to a working man. Before the advent of the welfare state, the more or less developed version of which is now generally accepted in industrial communities, unemployment simply meant starvation. But even if the worst consequences are avoided by subsidies, permitting the jobless worker to exist without actual physical hardship, his situation is not really much better. Men do not live by bread alone, and the fact that in certain countries the unemployed have a higher standard of living than the full-time working people in other countries does not mean that unemployment can therefore be tolerated, or even that it is a desirable feature of the economy, provided that it is kept within certain limits. Men are, on the whole, an active and enterprising race. This is particularly true of people living in a temperate zone: because of climatic reasons perhaps, the tropical races developed a less active type. In prehistoric times mere survival was a full-time job and hard work with primitive tools demanded a heavy expenditure of energy. This state lasted for countless generations, and by the selective process of evolution the type of human being capable of considerable power output, both physically and mentally, had to become predominant. To such a being inactivity is unnatural and, therefore, harmful. It is true that in some communities a slower pace of living and a low level of activity are generally accepted, but the opposite is true of the industrial country. Work and an active life are placed very high on the scale of values and this ideology is stressed in the schools, the press, the churches and so on. The jobless worker not only suffers from the lack of a natural outlet for his energies which his body and mind, accustomed to regular activity continue to supply, but he also feels himself an outcast. The mind, finding the stress produced by accumulating energy unbearable, becomes confused as if trying to cease to function altogether. All this is confirmed by factual observation. It is well known that a long period of unemployment leads often to serious mental and emotional disintegration. After many frustrations the initial frantic search for alternative work changes into a stupor of laziness. Despair creeps in and real attempts to get another job become progressively rarer. Self-discipline disappears and it becomes increasingly difficult to keep a job even if one gets it. So much for the theories which maintain that unemployment actually increases productivity because the fear of it drives workers to a greater effort and better discipline.

Must, then, the mechanical substitutes for human workers create unemployment? The answer is a definite 'no'. Automatic or power machines, or in fact any tool increasing the efficiency of labour, would indeed render some people jobless, if the total level of manufacturing and servicing reached by the community were fixed. Any tool or machine is designed to increase productivity per amount of work performed by the operator, and the automatic machine is the outstanding example as it needs no operator at all (or almost none). It releases the worker from his job, but this does not mean that he must remain idle. The machine increases the total productive powers of the community taken as a whole, therefore makes it richer and permits its members to engage in activities which the community could not afford before.

Besides, it is well known that although a machine displaces some workers it also creates new jobs for others. Somebody must be engaged on the construction of this very machine. The latter needs maintenance and repairs, the increased output requires more effort from the transportation and distribution network, and so on. In existing highly mechanized societies the level of employment is actually higher than in the less technically advanced communities of today or yesterday. Consideration of the detailed process by which machines abolish some jobs and make in their places new jobs available leads to very complex theories. Fortunately, there is really no need to go through all that. All that matters is that in the long run these machines will increase the productive powers of the society tremendously and they will make it richer. How this increased wealth is divided between the members of the community is up to the internal system. If the latter is adequate for the occasion then everybody should be better off in the end. If this does not happen then the economic system must be changed accordingly, but it does not mean that the introduction of automation should be abandoned or delayed. An economic or social system which cannot accommodate advances in technology which increase the wealth of the community is simply a bad system. It is madness to insist that the advances which make society wealthier as a whole must be rejected because some fraction of this society will actually be poorer as a result. If the latter is really the foreseeable consequence then the only sane answer is to change or modify the economic system.

The machines could only produce real scarcity of work if there was a complete abundance of every imaginable product and service so that nobody desired anything more. If, in such an economic paradise further automation was introduced, some people would indeed have nothing to do. The example is, of course, unrealistic and is used to show that to blame unemployment on automation or any other form of mechanization is muddled thinking.

Having arrived at the conclusion that automation is bound to increase the total wealth of the community, the question still remains: what about the transition period when large amounts of capital expenditure are needed, when new machines are substituted for old ones, and many people lose their former jobs and have to change to other occupations?

It may be observed that the transition period is really more important than the final state, because the latter will never materialize. The industrial society progresses continuously from one technical innovation to another and is always in a state of transition. There is no final state but only a period of lull, when a major step has just been accomplished and work towards the next one has not yet got into full swing.

The transition, even with perfect planning and the best will in the world, offers some real difficulties. Even if the worker is fully subsidized during the training for another job his problems are not yet solved. It is easy for a youngster to learn another trade but what about the old people who, have become masters in their profession? They may be unwilling or simply unable to learn an entirely new trade. They would be at an obvious disadvantage with the young men who are more adaptable and quicker to learn. They would lose in one step all the seniority and respect which their hard-won mastery of the former trade gave them. It is almost certain that only in exceptional cases would they ever rise to their former status in the new situation.

In general automation will create more technical jobs, requiring a higher mental standard than those occupations which will be made redundant. Some people are more adaptable than the others, some learn more quickly and some more slowly. The latter categories, young and old, will find the change a trying period, even if they are cushioned economically. Here is the obvious analogy to the lower caste of labourers displaced by the power machines. There are also people who genuinely like doing a certain kind of work and would be very upset if a machine was invented to perform the job faster and cheaper. The fact that the new jobs offered may be even more challenging and difficult and that full training would be given, together with an adequate financial compensation, may not always be a satisfactory answer.

Although the appalling working conditions prevailing in the factories during the early stages of industrialization are now much improved, there are still many occupations which are inherently unhealthy for human beings. Nobody would seriously suggest that coal mining is a healthy job. To spend a great part of one's working hours in dark underground passages, often in great heat and humidity, breathing dust, cannot be beneficial for the human body. At most, it can be said that some people can stand up to these conditions for many years without becoming ill. Many jobs involve working under arduous conditions; others are dangerous, for example, dealing with corrosive acids, flames, high explosives, etc. A great number of these unhealthy or dangerous occupations could be performed by suitably designed automata—sparing human bodies and minds.

The latter are particularly threatened by many kinds of work arising in industrial civilization when the principle of division of labour is carried to the extreme. As mentioned before, the worker on the production line becomes a part of a complicated machine. He performs strictly defined and simple functions at the pace dictated by the conveyor belt. There is no need for him to understand how his work fits in with that of the others, why it is being done at all, or what is the final product. Those things are taken care of by the designers and supervisors and all that is left for him is to execute certain simple movements repeatedly, methodically, accurately, and in rhythm with the machine. The only reason he is there is that he can perform these movements better and cheaper than the machine could at the given stage of technological progress. Considered as a part of a machine he is simply more economical when all factors are taken into account.

There are millions of manufacturing jobs outside the proper mass-production lines which come wholly or partly within the above description. They cannot possibly engage even a small portion of the vast mental capabilities of an average human being, as they do not require any intelligence and consequently cannot give any satisfaction. The excessive simplicity of the tasks, the vanished comprehension of the final aim of the activity, the removal of initiative and decision-making powers, the pace dictated by the machines, all turn at present a sizeable portion of the working population into semi-automata. It is curious to hear, while this state of affairs prevails that automation should be opposed because it threatens to turn men into robots. Such criticism is based on a fundamental misconception. It is a highly developed power-machine or a semi-automatic manufacturing facility which turns a man into a robot, just because such a machine requires continuous human contribution, thus making man work as an integral part of a mechanical system. Fully automatic machines will free men from the burden of low manual and mental tasks. The human cogs from the production line will have to become skilled technicians capable of understanding the intricacies of the complex machines so that they can maintain them. Broadly speaking, the more advanced the level of automation the more technical knowledge will be required for almost any work left to men. Hence the more human their work will become. Ideally, all the tasks which can be mechanized should be performed by the machines, leaving only those where typically human attributes, like a high level of abstract thinking, intuition, creative ability, artistic talent, quality of leadership, great manual dexterity etc., are absolutely indispensable. It must be clearly realized that the very fact that the job can be mechanized means that the man who does it manually is reduced to the level of a robot. Hence to use a machine as a substitute is to free him from the work which, by definition, is a task fit for an automaton. Such a liberated man can now occupy himself in a way that corresponds more closely to his potentials. This may sound extravagant when we look at the millions of wretched human beings performing simple stultyfying tasks in the modern industrial world, apparently not being able to do anything else and not even wanting to. Yet the majority of them are not intrinsically much different from those at the top of the social line. In fact, some of these human robots have been born with greater natural endowment than some company directors. But at the present time, the majority of industrial tasks are simple and somebody has to do them. Because of a rank at birth and later, because of many environmental factors outside the control of the given individual, only a few reach the positions where they can exercise their human capabilities. This is not to deny the great importance of natural endowment, personal effort and hard work, but even if everybody were a genius trying to do his best, the great majority still would have to remain doing monotonous, simple, tasks because at the present level of technical progress such is the bulk of available work, which simply has to be performed.

This is so not only as far as the manual or semi-manual tasks are concerned. An inquiring look at the modern office would quickly convince that the above statements apply even more to the 'white collar' jobs. As pointed out beforehand, because of the continuously improving efficiency of manufacturing techniques but basically ancient clerical methods, and because of the increasing administrative complexity of modern enterprises, the ratio of clerks to machine operators is steadily increasing. Thus the social importance of clerical work is assuming very large proportions. Now what are all these millions of clerks really doing? To begin with, some of the clerical services performed in any community are the result of traditional business customs or legal requirements which are basically unnecessary. It includes jobs like keeping records which nobody ever uses or sending memos which are promptly put into waste baskets by the recipients with hardly more than a cursory glance over the contents. But let us disregard this sort of direct wastage of effort and consider only the work which is being done for valid reasons. The bulk of such clerical work consists in taking data from one piece of paper, adding something to it from another and putting it all together on the third piece. The keeping of files, the copying of records, translating the spoken word into written symbols, the issuing of standard instructions and orders according to strict rules, these constitute the major volume of office work. The simple arithmetical and logical functions performed during these occupations would not challenge the intelligence of a child. A tremendous wastage of human talent is allowed to occur.

Even if we assume that the relatively few people who manage to make their way towards more intelligent occupations do so because of superior mental endowment, which is manifestly not always true, it would still not say anything about the average. It would merely indicate that the men at the top are better than the average, but it would give no indication about the true potentialities of the latter. Man must be given a chance to develop his abilities to the fullest; it is no use putting him first into the environmental straight-jacket of dullness and then complaining that he is not very bright.

Lest somebody finds this rather fanciful let us go back to prehistoric times. As is well known, men of, shall we say, the late paleolithic period differed little, if at all, in their natural endowments from the modern man. So there must have been Shakespeares, Beethovens and Newtons among them too. But how could the potential musical genius express himself in those days? Probably by emitting weird cries and playing the drum; hardly adequate means for the creation of the Ninth Symphony. The potential Newton may have gained much esteem by chipping off sharper flints than anybody else: but he had been given no mental tools for the creation of the gravitation theory. How can a man, doing a repetitive, simple job for thirty years, help becoming a semi-automaton? He has to grow into one if he is going to stay sane while performing the same routine every day. The better jobs are taken by the smarter or luckier; the rest are dull. And yet as soon as mechanization of offices is proposed the cry arises: what about the displaced clerks? But does anybody seriously propose to keep for ever an increasing proportion of the population doing unhuman work if we have the technical means of avoiding it?

The other consequence of large-scale automation stems from the fact that automatic machines require such a vast capital expenditure that they must be kept running all the time to provide the necessary return. This would mean shiftwork for a large part of the population, with consequent far-reaching changes in living and social habits. It follows inevitably that all public services, shops, places of entertainment, almost everything in fact, must be run on a day and night basis. Additional difficulties in maintaining a condition of quiet in dormitory areas would arise. Shall we end with daily and nocturnal family life, changing alternately? Perhaps not, although on physiological grounds it is quite possible to shift the schedule without producing harmful effects. Provided the schedule is kept to regularly over a considerable period of time, it matters little whether one sleeps during the night or during the day, always assuming the proper conditions of rest in either case.

In the late middle ages and in the modern era work has been

E

built up into a mythical concept and reinforced with religious beliefs. Work, as an activity in itself, became the most highly valued thing in modern times. To keep on working, to do the work well, to avoid laziness and negligence, this has been the ideology of progressive Western societies. Unfortunately, the attitude towards work, proper to times when almost the only real work was done with pick and shovel, persists still in industrial accountancy, and causes a lot of difficulties. Only the 'direct work', meaning the actual machining or processing by the operators is approved of as a really necessary contribution in the making of the product. Everything else is an overhead. This is so, probably because it is difficult to split many kinds of expenditure product-wise and to attribute a part of them to every item. But it is also partly because the top managements do not see the other functions on the same level of importance as the direct machining or manual operations, intimately connected with the making of the product. They know very well that many, although perhaps not all, of those other indirect jobs are absolutely necessary, but somehow they cannot help considering them as something they would dearly like to get rid of. To keep the overheads at a relatively low figure becomes a major task for a manager, although in many cases it leads to quite ridiculous and harmful consequences. It is obvious that all functions necessary for supplying a product to the customer are equally important; the stress on what is called 'direct labour' is an anachronism in highly mechanized industry. It becomes utter nonsense in the conditions of full automation, because then there is no direct labour at all in the conventional sense of the word. The ideological consequences of automation will reach far beyond the mere change in administrative outlook or in accounting techniques. With the automata performing the majority of physical and lower metal tasks, the myth of work as a value in itself, the idea of almost every kind of work being intrinsically good, will be destroyed. A human being was, so to speak, 'made' for a reasonably high level of activity, but this is not synonymous with being born for work. In fact, relative to the time the human race has existed, work is rather a recent innovation, peculiar to a civilized way of living. It is certainly not a part of human nature, although in the civilized state it is the predominant form of activity available to men.

When automata take over almost all routine tasks, physical

or mental, the efficiency of a worker in terms of his output per unit of time will become meaningless. The technical skill in dealing with occasional faults in automata, the ability to co-ordinate and to keep in synchronism various automatic processes, to make quick decisions and so on will become more important than sheer hard nervous and low grade mental efforts in operating the non-automatic machines, or processing by pen and ink endless masses of data in the office, as at present. In fact, the operator and the office worker will both turn into technicians or managers. Their performance will be no longer easily measurable by a stop-watch and by the number of units of work executed. They will be in a position to make decisions, sometimes quite important, and therefore, although the technical knowledge will be at a premium, loyalty to the organisation may become more valued. Each employee will be an important, often indispensable member of the staff with great responsibilities upon his shoulders. These highly trained men, experienced in the working of the process peculiar to the given enterprise will be not easily replaceable. For their skill and loyalty they will have to be rewarded accordingly, not only in the sense of high wages, but also in terms of long-term prospects. As the worker-technician of tomorrow will not be paid for the amount of direct work he does, and as his performance will not be expressable in terms of easily measurable quantities, his progress will depend presumably on the length of service, on his professional qualifications, and on esteem earned in the eyes of his superiors. Thus his position will be that of a professional man of today. The planned career and bureaucratization of the worker means that there will be no longer a gap between the working population and the supervisory and professional middle class. This boundary is already very much blurred today and will completely disappear when automation achieves maturity. The worker will, in effect, be raised into the present middle class and will presumably acquire its ideology and way of living, since the character and conditions of the occupation have a strong influence on the whole mentality. The beginnings of this process are visible already, and its social consequences will be very large. Although I doubt whether it will lead to the dissolution of trade unions, as present experience teaches that even the most professional of all professional men, the doctors, can be induced by circumstances to form an organization which has many features of a union, this powerful social movement will undergo deep changes with the disappearance of the old idea of a working class.

The generally more exacting demands of technical knowledge, due to automation, will require a mighty effort on a national scale for their satisfaction. The automatic factories and offices will need highly-qualified men to run them. The worker, in the present sense of the word, will gradually disappear, to be replaced by a technician, perhaps of degree standard. Increasing complexity in the mesh of mutually interdependent manufacturing and data processing units coalescing into integrated systems, the need for long-term planning and the growing necessity for interpretation of technological advances in terms of their sociological effects, will lead to the arrival of a new type of administrator, capable of blending several scientific disciplines with intuition and leadership. The value of knowledge will keep growing gradually and will become more important in relation to sheer ability for harding working over long hours. In the end, a man without a high degree of knowledge will be unable to do any useful work at all. Almost all physical and simple mental tasks will be performed by the machines, more cheaply, faster, and more efficiently than any human being could ever hope. Man will be able to make contribution only on a higher level of thought, where creative abilities, intuition, superior judgement and other advanced mental factors of the human brain come into play. If he is incapable of reaching this advanced level, he will be more or less useless from the community's point of view. Knowledge has always been a most precious thing, but in the era of automation it will become the most important part of the capital investment of any enterprise; a true basic capital.

All this will necessitate the allocation of a greater part of the national income to education than at present. But not only to the education of young people. The massive transfers from one sort of occupation to another, due to the introduction of automata, must be matched by an equally massive educational programme for adults, not only purely occupational. The fast pace of technical progress results in continuous changes and adjustments in all sectors of social life. We are experiencing already what is probably the highest rate of change ever witnessed by any society in history and this rate is on the increase. In such conditions it is not enough to give a child the fixed packet of knowledge which is supposed to be sufficient for a lifetime. With changing circumstances we must continue to add to the basic mental capital, if the individual is not to feel lost in a strange world on reaching middle age. The expectations of longer life and the ageing structure of the population makes this problem even more important. The mind, accustomed to certain views and ways is suspicious of major changes. It seems to feel almost instinctively threatened by them, and it tends to oppose them.

If all obstacles are to be successfully surmounted, a gradual change of the whole mental outlook is required. This task cannot be left to the press and to television. The true potentialities of automatic control and of data processing can be fully exploited for the benefit of mankind only if the general level of education is vastly increased. And, most emphatically, not only technical education. To counterbalance the effects of growing mechanization on men and women a good measure of what are known as the humanities must be included in any syllabus. Stress must be placed on the development of mental qualities which are considered most characteristic of the human being. A type of personality truly intellectually balanced must be made predominant, otherwise the indirect consequences of the machines which we invented to ease the labours of man threaten to turn us into half-conscious beings living in the conditions of a technically advanced ant-heap.

To sum up: it can be said that the manufacture of anything involves three basic elements. Firstly, there must be the materials, including so-called raw materials and the tools to transform them. Secondly, there must be a supply of power to activate the tools. Thirdly, there must exist a controlling intelligence to direct the application of this power. Pre-industrial societies developed highly complex tools but they did not know how to exploit the power resources present in nature. Hence the main supply of manufacturing power was that of the human body and this power starvation imposed definite limits on the standard of living of pre-industrial man. The first industrial revolution created an abundance of mechanical power and thus liberated man from almost all heavy physical tasks and increased enormously the productivity per head, but the vast majority of controlling functions still had to be performed by human beings. The almost exclusive supply of controlling intelligence was the human brain. However, the controlling ability does exist, so to speak, outside human skulls. There are of course no deposits of intelligence in nature which to dig up like coal and metals, but machines endowed with controlling abilities can be built. With the advent of these the whole manufacturing process can be performed without direct human contribution. Pre-industrial man was a beast of burden; industrial man up to the second industrial revolution, although he did not have to earn his daily bread by unrelenting toil, was nevertheless chained to the machine as its controller; but the man of the automatic era will be free from both physical toil and routine controlling tasks. He will be not only much richer but also he will be able to use his tremendous energies as he pleases. It will be his choice whether he reaches new heights of thought and expands towards the stars, or whether he sinks into leisure and inactivity and to degeneration of body and mind.

PART TWO

CHAPTER 5

Philosophy, Life and Machine

THE superior intelligence of man, as compared with any other living creature, permitted him to gain a measure of independence from the forces of nature, and in the last few centuries to obtain even a limited mastery over them. This process was very slow at first, hesitating and uncertain, as if the emerging human mind were groping in the dark for the path to choose.

This mind was something new to the planet, there was never anything like it before. During the two thousand million years of evolution the earth witnessed the rise and fall of almost all imaginable forms of life. Living creatures progressively conquered the oceans, the lands and the air, producing an incredible variety of bodily shapes and sizes, means of locomotion, organs of sensorial perception, habits of feeding and breeding and ways of co-habiting and co-operating. From the sub-microscopic viruses to the huge beasts treading the hills and the plains of the earth, from the plankton filling the oceans to the ichthyosaurus and the whale, from bacterial spores carried on the wind to the eagle sailing majestically in the sky, from fungi to roses, there seemed to be no limits to what life could create. Yet none of these billions of species could be credited with a truly rational mind. Hence the emergence of the latter during, perhaps, the last few hundreds of thousands of years—only a minute or two on the geological-scale was something very new. At first it was almost unnoticeable. The small human population, scattered in tiny groups over the vast continents, armed only with fire and primitive stone tools, could hardly claim the mastery of the world. And yet these creatures of animal appearances, conferring in gutteral sounds, concentrating almost exclusively on food gathering, sex and survival, were already the potential lords of the earth, destined to split the atom and land on the other planets. The process of gaining independence from the brute forces of nature accelerated greatly with the first human civilisations, and erupted in cataclysmic fashion with the advent of scientific method. In a couple of centuries, a mere twinkling of an eye as compared with the eons elapsed since the creation of the first organic molecules, man has come to command powers capable of the total destruction of life on this planet. But the new master of the earth wears a look of amazement and wonder on his face.

Every man, whether he wants it or not, must have certain basic views on the world, a fundamental set of opinions and notions which regulate his attitudes and reactions. He may never think about those basic axioms, he may even scorn their very notion, but they form in his mind all the same. During the process of maturing they become so dominant as to appear to the given individual as the obvious and unquestionable and as much a part of himself as his hand or leg.

All the philosophic systems and world-views can be basically divided into two groups: those which maintain that man possesses a certain extra-material element, and those which hold him to be nothing but a very complex physico-chemical system. The variety of philosophical systems is bewildering, almost as many as there are species of animals. All sorts of approaches to the basic questions confronting the thinking human being have been made and a great variety of answers has been offered. Yet one feels that the whole of man's philosophical effort can be reduced basically to one fundamental division according to their answers to the question: are we something more than machines or are we only just that? For nearly everything else depends on the attitude to this problem. If we believe that a human being possesses a certain extra-material element we can discuss immortality, the problems of good and evil, free will, the purpose of life, individually or as a race, ethics and morals. We can talk of intrinsic human dignity and of unique human mental qualities, never to be equalled by any automaton, and we are permitted to consider man as the measure of all things. If, on the other hand, we start with the assumption that man has no extra-material element, then it follows logically that he is only an extremely complex physical system. Hence he must be completely subject to the same general laws that govern the behaviour of all matter and energy in the universe and all his activities, mental or physical, without exception, must be explainable in terms of those laws. In consequence religious beliefs of any kind are inadmissible and the problem of good and evil is meaningless. A machine cannot commit virtuous or sinful acts. All ideas generally considered noble, beautiful or inspired, are brought to the level of impulse patterns in the brain and as such do deserve no more respect than a light-switch. The difference between man, dog, bacteria and aim-seeking electronic gadgets appears only to be the degree of complexity in the internal organization. As a gadget manifestly does not possess a free will, neither can a man belonging basically to the same category .

The behaviour of any physical system, however complex, is entirely governed by the internal structure of this system, the properties of the environment and the general natural laws. This is equally valid in the deterministic and the indeterministic frame of reference. If we assume the rigidly deterministic view of the universe then the future behaviour of any physical system acting in the given environment is, in principle, strictly pre-dictable. There is no room even for the semblance of free will. If we subscribe to the probabilistic world-view then we say that the system can pass from state A to either state B or state C, and we associate certain probabilities with either of two trans-itions. But this still does not imply that the system has any wilful choice in the matter. Either transition is the result of a chance happening, like the toss of a coin, only more compli-cated. Nobody would attribute to a penny the capacity of freely choosing on which side to show up. Hence it is logically in-admissible to allow the capacity of free will to any other purely physical system, because the latter is subjected to the same laws, of deterministic or probabilistic character, as the penny. Without free will, all ethics become senseless. Any human being simply cannot help doing what he is actually doing and it would be no less silly to blame him for anything at all than to reprove a car for breaking down.

If we are nothing but matter, then we must be governed by general laws in everything we do, which puts us immediately on the level of the machine. It is nonsense to tell people that they are nothing but a complex arrangement of atoms and then appeal to their supposedly nobler side. This is what, for example, the Communists are doing. Their official ideology professes a rigid deterministic materialism (although they had to use the theory of probability to make the atomic bomb). At the same time the Party requires a high moral standard from its members, involving great sacrifices, even of life itself. Now why should anyone make these sacrifices? Presumably for the safety and happiness of other human beings. But if one adopts materialistic principles, then machine, virus, and man, all belong to the same category, the difference being only in the level of complexity. Then why should a man sacrifice as much as his little finger even if the life of the whole nation depend on it? And if he does sacrifice his life why call him a hero? A man who injects himself with dangerous bacteria to enable them to grow and multiply in his body would be as heroic. Even if we assume that to inflict pain on systems capable of feeling should be avoided it still remains that the destruction of millions of people in Nazi concentration camps would be from the German point of view no more deplorable than, from a farmer's angle, the eradication of the Colorado beetle. For that matter the destruction of all life by atomic weapons would be, on moral grounds, no worse than scrapping Dr Walter's batch of light-seeking mechanical tortoises. It would be exactly the same kind of thing, differing only in magnitude.

Lest I give the impression of being a confirmed follower of idealistic philosophy I hasten to say that this is not so. On the contrary, it seems to me that advances in science lend progressively more supoort to the materialistic brand of philosophy. The world of primitive men was inhabited by demons of all sorts. As no natural explanation was known for the majority of observable phenomena the intervention of extra-natural forces had to be assumed. But with the growth of knowledge more and more phenomena could be perfectly well explained without reference to spiritual entities. The further science progresses the smaller becomes the area from which the ghost cannot yet be exorcised. Assuming that this process will not meet some insurmountable barrier, which cannot be yet excluded, it seems that finally everything will be explainable in terms of natural laws. This would prove materialism right and all the idealogical consequences presented above would in-invariably follow. The very possibility is frightening, but it must be faced. There is no good in supporting fully-fledged materialism on the one hand and to talk about human dignity, honour, charity, compassion, etc., on the other. Even if one admitted both materialism and the conduct of life based on humanistic ideology on pragmatic grounds, this would simply be self-deception. The necessity of a given ideology is not a logically sufficient condition to make this ideology true. The latter cannot be even admitted as a hypothesis if it contradicts some other theories which one is not willing to discard, and, in my opinion, full-blown materialism contradicts almost all human values as I know them. Our very language is full of words stating or implying the moral judgement of other people and we are continually referring to other men and women as capable of making free choice. We approve or disapprove of their actions, their feelings and views, not in the way we speak of useful or faulty machinery but on ethical grounds. The most ardent materialist cannot avoid doing it or he would be no longer speaking the language of humanity as we know it now. But he has really no right to do so.

The controversy between the vitalistic and the mechanistic world-view, the dichotomy of mind and matter and the question whether we are intrinsically different from any other physical system or not must be honestly faced. It is becoming imperative to form a certain mental attitude to these problems at a time when science is developing the techniques for the construction of machines which can perceive the environment, seek the aim, learn and modify their behaviour purposefully and is on the threshold of creating life artificially. It is not possible to discuss the further reaching consequences of automation and automatic data processing without forming certain opinions about the problems mentioned above. Hence, in this part of the book we concern ourselves with various topics related to the human mind, consciousness and ways of thinking, and compare them whenever possible with their mechanized counterparts. As could be expected, no final answer to our basic question 'are we only machines or something more' is reached; nevertheless certain suggestions about the path on which the solution may be found are made.

Mediaeval man in Western Europe considered himself the most important creature in the universe. In fact he thought that the latter was created mainly, if not exclusively for the purpose of serving man as his habitat. It followed naturally that man's home proper, the earth, was the centre of the universe, with the sun to keep it warm, the moon to give the traveller a pale light at night and the fiery stars to guide ships on distant seas. Galileo's telescope, the heliocentric planetary system of Copernicus, the laws of Kepler and Newton, the relatively recent studies of our galaxy and the discoveries of immense galactic systems, revealed earth as a tiny speck of dust in the immensity of the universe. Our point of reference has been transferred from earth into far-distant cosmic space in the sense that we now consider our planet and everything that happens on it from the viewpoint of universal law, applicable to the whole cosmos. But these astronomical discoveries did not necessarily by themselves destroy man's faith in his uniqueness in the universe and his own importance and intrinsic superiority over other creatures. The people who really pulled man from his exalted pedestal were Darwin, Marx and Freud.

The theory of evolution demonstrated the development of man from the lower forms of life through successive stages. Although Darwin's original theory, supplemented by the modern additions of the laws of heredity and the law of random mutations, is now generally accepted, it must be said that the factual evidence is still incomplete. The question of the link between the truly human forms and the animal types immediately preceding them is not yet settled. Also, although the experimentally varified laws suffice undoubtedly to account for the evolution of the species, the problem of differentiation into the more diverse forms of life, the question of the creation of new classes, is not quite so easily explainable. Nevertheless, knowledge continuously accumulates and fills up the gaps slowly. The recent work by Remsch contributes much to the clarification of the question of why the findings of transitory fossil forms are much rarer than the fossils of more stabilized types. It also gives strong support to the view that the laws of evolution are sufficient to explain the development of any form of life, without the necessity of recourse to some new, usually mystical factors.

In conclusion, although the theory of evolution has not yet been proved in the same sense as, e.g. the universal validity of the law of conservation of energy (at least in so far as the latter is referred to anything on earth) the evidence in favour of the former is overwhelming and sufficient for its acceptance beyond any reasonable doubt. One cannot help feeling that the doubts and views contrary to the theory of evolution bear the stigma of the fanatical rejection of ideologically unpalatable truth in spite of all the physical facts.

The acceptance of the theory of evolution brings a tremendous ideological upheaval. Although much has been written in a desperate attempt to reconcile the former with accepted religious views, all this sounds not really convincing. The conclusion still remains that if man developed from the lower forms of life then his uniqueness is immediately challenged. Far from being in a class of his own he appears simply as the last link, so far, in the long chain of successive types of animals. This chain links man through mammals, reptiles and fishes with amoeba, and to attribute to him any qualities intrinsically different from those possessed by the animal therefore appears to be very difficult on rational grounds. At which stage were these qualities injected into the evolutionary stream? Where did they come from? Further, apart from the creation of the first living matter, which is another problem, the continuous intervention of the Creator is made unnecessary. Evolution proceeds according to natural selection, the survival of the fittest, the genetic laws of inheritance and random mutations. It constitutes a process which is extremely complex, to be sure, but still subjected to the universal laws similar to any other physical process.

The randomness of the mutations is particularly harmful to human pride. According to the modern theory of evolution, the properties and features of the given species are transmitted from generation to generation by genes carried by the chromosomes of parental reproductive cells. The genes determine all the hereditary traits of the organism which are thus fixed for every species. Sometimes however, a gene changes at random under the influence of radiation, chemical reactions, etc., giving rise to a new feature of the organism called a mutation. The majority of mutations are harmful, which is what one would expect, because they occur at random in the conditions of delicate and complicated balance between organism and environment. The undesirable mutations are eliminated through competitive struggle and the survival of the fittest, but by the same token the few useful mutations have a better chance of survival than the orthodox forms and, being hereditary, increase in pro-

portion with each generation resulting in a gradual change of
the whole species. This leads to the inescapable conclusion that
man is the product of a random process, which is continuously
being 'weeded' by the environment. What a step-down for a
creature who believed himself to be God-like!

The theory of evolution of the human form found its counterpart on the social plane in the works of Karl Marx. Man usually
considered the societies which he has built as the product of his
conscious efforts. Although the influence of environmental
factors was obviously admitted, the structure of the society was
regarded as the result of man's rational thoughts and conscious
actions, as something which can be changed within limits as
man wishes and which is under man's control and supervision.
Even now, history is still thought of in terms of kings and
emperors, victories and defeats, clearly implying that man's
conscious efforts were the directing of historical forces. Marx
put forward the theory according to which the social and
political structure of the community is mainly the function of
the technological level in the given period, or in other words
depends on means of production. Although it has been said that
his theories were not entirely original—as if any theory could
ever really claim that—the fact remains that he stated the above
thesis much more clearly than anyone had done before. The
rejection en bloc of all Marxist ideas, customary now in
Western literature for political reasons, is a pity, because
Marx's great contribution to human thought cannot be denied
and his intellectual honesty cannot be seriously doubted. Although his hypotheses have been proved theoretically and
practically incorrect on several scores, this does not mean that
they did not add substantially to the development of social
science. Also the frightful human sufferings resulting from the
practical applications of his theories do not constitute a
rationally sufficient case for the invalidation of the latter.

Seen through Marxist spectacles, human society grows like
a tree, passing through successive stages of development,
almost independent of the activities of any particular man or
group of men. The kings and princes, the leaders and the
victories all resolve into insignificance. Under the pressure of
inexorable laws, similar in their nature to the physical laws,
society proceeds from one level to another and nobody can
do anything about it. The most which a group conscious of this
historical process can do is to work in sympathy with it, thus

assisting the transitions to pass more efficiently and with a reduced total amount of human discomfort. It is difficult to resist the impression that the historians and sociologists of the last hundred years, even those who most vehemently deny Marx, follow in fact his basic trend of thought. In their studies many factors other than economic ones are introduced and quite rightly so, but the idea of societies developing under the influence of powerful impersonal forces is very evident. We see in their works the empires and civilizations growing and crumbling to dust and new social structures appearing and giving way in their turn to still other forms of human organization. Although not everybody subscribes to the idea of the existence of certain historical laws and although some people insist that, if history teaches anything at all, it is the fact that it never repeats itself and is essentially random and unpredictable, these views form a minority of opinions.

But the worst is still to follow. Even after man's earth was found to be only an insignificant satellite of an insignificant star, belonging to a galaxy consisting of billions of similar stars, this galaxy itself being only one of billions of galaxies; even after he was told that his ancestor was an ape and that his communal way of living is more the product of natural laws than of his conscious effort, man could still maintain his pride by pointing out that he is the only creature which is predominantly rational. The idea of perfect rationality of man has been very strongly embedded in religious and philosophical views, in fact in almost any domain of human thought. Witness the relics of it appearing in modern economy. According to it, man's behaviour is not pre-determined by his inborn instincts and desires and by his environment, but he is capable, within large limits, of conscious choice and he makes this choice mainly on rational grounds. This is putting it in a nutshell and many variants of the above idea can be found; but the central theme of man's rationality and capability of making a free choice was generally accepted. The Viennese psychiatrist Freud put forward other revolutionary views on the subject. Cutting his argument to the bone, it can be said that according to Freud all human mental life can be divided into three parts, id, superego and ego. 'Id' works below the level of consciousness and compromises all elementary instincts, desires, and urges; it is brutish, selfish and animal-like. Superego consists of all rules which condition and

F

restrict human social behaviour; hence it is learned and acquired during life. 'Ego', consisting of conscious mental processes, is a sort of mediator between the exacting demands of superego and the elementary urges of 'id'. Hence the role of rational thinking is severely limited. The whole of human behaviour is seen as stemming from complex subconscious processes which proceed not only without the control of conscious volition but without the awareness of the individual concerned. Only the results of these subconscious processes are delivered, so to speak, to consciousness in the form of emotional urges. The other factors conditioning man's activity is the straight-jacket of rules and taboos imposed by his social environment through various kinds of teaching. The role of conscious mental effort is seen mainly in keeping the balance between the other two parts which generally oppose each other. Incidentally, the subconscious processes become sometimes distorted, entangled and contradictory to such an extent that the resulting tension disrupts, in a lesser or a larger degree, the whole mental life of the unlucky individual. The role of the psychiatrist in treating mental illness is, according to Freudian psycho-analytical therapy, to bring the tangled knot of subconscious urges into the field of consciousness and help the rational ego to sort them out.

It is easy to see the ideological implications of these doctrines. The rationality of man appears only as a thin crust upon the vast bulk of subconscious processes. Far from being master of itself, the rational mind of man is seen as a servant of sub-conscious urges and emotions battling among themselves in the dark abysses of the brain over which of them is to dictate the final aims of the given individual. The rational mind does not even know anything about these decisive struggles, only the final orders are delivered to it to be followed. The rationality of man becomes a mere tool for achieving the aims dictated by the emotions and instincts. Although Freud's original theories have been either partly abandoned or greatly modified by modern psychology, their core still remains infused in the modern basic ideas about human mental life. The whole world view of our epoch has been greatly influenced by them. Among the out-standing examples are the exaggerated pre-occupation with sex in all forms (Freud's primordial motive-power) and the partial abandonment of the concept of personal responsibility. The word 'sin' became an anachronism and there are few people, apart from dwindling numbers in religious circles, who would dare to use it without an apologetic smile. Today we prefer to explain human misbehaviour in terms of complexes, neuroses, maladjustments etc., implying the absence of personal guilt in a moral sense. If somebody hits you on the head, this is because he was not loved enough when he was a child. If a young thug steals your car for a joy-ride and wrecks it in the process, it is because he had to compensate for his inferiority complex stemming from maladjustment to his environment. It is anyway your fault for leaving the car to tempt the child (six-foot tall and 180 lb. in weight).

Man, believing once that he was created in the likeness of God himself, that the whole world was made for his convenience, travelled a long way down. Inhabiting a tiny speck in the immense universe, child of an ape and grandchild of bacteria, living in communities developing according to all-powerful, impersonal forces, even his own mind is not under his control. What is still left for him? Yet recourse to a dogmatic ideology exalting the so-called human values will not save the day if we want to be honest with ourselves, and without intellectual honesty how can we keep our self-respect?

We will now consider very briefly the basic features of living beings and see how they compare with those of modern machines. Perhaps the most distinct characteristics of any living creature are its ability to feed, to grow, to breed, to react to its environment, to perceive it, and to behave purposefully. The last two features are particularly evident in the case of animals and are only exhibited in an elementary fashion, by comparison, by the plants. Feeding means the intake of organic or inorganic matter from the environment, together with its assimilation, meaning the conversion of it into the body of the feeding creature, or most generally, into the structure of the feeding system. This matter is used partly for chemical reactions supplying the energy of the system, partly for the replacement of the worn-out parts and sometimes also for building of additional new parts leading thus to the growth of the system. It is characteristic for living beings to preserve their forms while exchanging matter and energy with the environment. Breeding means the capacity of the creature to produce other creatures of the same kind, sometimes in co-operation with a partner (sexual reproduction). All living beings react to their environment, exhibiting the property of homeostasis. This means that when the internal equilibrium of the organism is disturbed by the environment, the former has the capacity to re-establish this equilibrium within certain limits. The ability to sense or perceive the environment is particularly prominent among animals. Their whole behaviour is definitely purposeful in the sense that they strive to achieve certain aims. However, only the highest animals show the very elementary capacity of rational thinking, apart, of course, from men. All the others react to external stimuli more or less automatically, similarly to servo-mechanisms, but in a much more complex manner. In fact, the lower the animal stands on the evolutionary tree the more striking this comparison becomes.

All living beings are either unicellular or consist of many cells. Hence the cell can be considered as the basic complete unit of life. The cell comprises several component parts, more or less well defined. Each of these consists of many extremely complex organic molecules belonging to the types characteristic for living matter. Some of the organic molecules consist of many thousands of atoms arranged into very complex patterns. At any time there are literally hundreds of highly complicated chemical reactions proceeding in any living cell. Hence it is an extremely intricate physical-chemical system in a state of dynamic equilibrium and it is more complex than any machine that man ever created so far. Any cell exhibits all features of life, like feeding, growth, reproduction and reaction to environment. The organ directing all processes in the cell, including the reproduction, is the cell's nucleus, consisting of substances known as nucleic acids. These are the chains of certain types of groups of atoms. They are spiral atomic structures capable of reproducing themselves and somehow of controlling the living processes and development of the cell, and with it the whole multi-cellular organism. Whether all these are only a matter of chemical reactions, or whether some other force, of a different nature, is involved, is still an open question, although almost any biologist would be in favour of the former alternative.

Many types of organic molecules can be synthesized from purely inorganic compounds but nobody has yet managed to produce in this manner a substance which would exhibit all the properties of true living matter. So *omnia viva ex vivo* and the vitalists' supposition that all living matter is driven by the *vis viva*, a mysterious force of life proper only to living beings, cannot yet be categorically invalidated. Nevertheless, vitalism is becoming progressively less probable, particularly in view of the spectacular advances in biology in the last decade. If it is ever possible to synthesize all basic living substances from the inorganic or dead constituents and if the processes of life are fully understood, and in particular the directive action of nucleic acids, it should be possible to create living beings artificially. Of course, not in the sense of putting them together cell by cell as we assemble machines from component parts. One would rather imagine this being done by synthesizing first the appropriate spiral atomic structure of nucleic acids from inorganic substances and then placing them in a mixture of basic organic constituents, also synthesized from inorganic matter.

Due to the directing action of the nucleic acid the desired organism would be grown in a similar fashion as it does in nature when developing from the fertilized ovum in the womb. It is well known that the fertilized ovum contains all the information needed for the full growth of the organism, its master plan and the directing force. Fertilization itself is the combining of chromosomes and genes of both parents. As the former are built of nucleic acids, fertilization is essentially the formation of a new specimen of nucleic acids characteristic for the given individual and resulting from the union of those acids of the parents. But fertilization completed, the main function of the body of the mother is to supply food to the new organism. How those organic substances, derived from the mother, are arranged into the tissues of the new body is governed finally by the nucleic acid of the fertilized ovum. Needless to say, if the artificial creation of living creatures becomes possible, even if only of a very simple kind at first, the vitalists' position would be rendered, *eo ipso*, completely untenable and one of the biggest mysteries of nature would dissolve, like many others have done before, under the impact of scientific investigation. Even then it would probably be possible to assert that the artificial creature, although indistinguishable in all features from its natural counterpart, is only a machine whereas the latter is truly alive. But this would be merely an ideological fanaticism. According to informed opinion the artificial creation of elementary living substances is quite likely to be achieved before the end of this century, and maybe even within the next one or two decades. Consequently, we may not have much time to prepare ourselves for the tremendous ideological shock which this discovery, if realized, is bound to have.

Going down the scale of life below the level of the cell, we see that the boundary between living and non-living matter becomes progressively blurred. There exists for example certain beings too small to be seen by any optical microscope, which are responsible for many diseases and which are known as viruses. They consist essentially of nucleic acids covered with a layer of proteins, and although they are incapable of independent existence, except in a living cell acting as host they exhibit the capacity to penetrate the outer membranes of some cells and take over, so to speak, the reproductive properties of the cell's nucleus. Hence, instead of reproducing its own kind, the infected cell produces the given sort of virus and disintegrates during the process. Thus viruses are capable only of parasitic existence. Some viruses can be crystallized and in that state behave like other crystals, the latter being traditionally considered non-living matter. But virus crystals can be brought back to life in suitable conditions. The difference between, for instance, a dog and a stone is immense and seemingly unbridgeable. But is the crystallized virus dead or alive?

It appears that on an elementary level the passage from inorganic to organic matter is continuous and the boundary is a question of an arbitrary definition. Nature does not exhibit sharp divisions between the various types of its creations, which merge smoothly one into another through intermediate forms. It is the human mind which puts distinctive boundaries between groups of physical objects, because this is the human brain's natural way of perceiving and describing the environment. To complete the picture, a few words must be said about the possible creation of life in nature. The famous experiments of Pasteur did not really prove that spontaneous creation of life from dead matter is impossible. All they demonstrated is that life has not been generated in the particular conditions of his sterilized and sealed vessels, but this does not rule out the possibility of the creation of life from billions of possible kinds of chemical mixtures in an almost unlimited variety of combinations of temperature, pressure, electrical discharges, electro-magnetic radiation, radioactive processes and so on. The scientific theories of the creation of life in nature are many, but the majority of them can be essentially reduced to the following hypothesis: In the conditions of primeval earth first the various kinds of inorganic components came into being. Then some of these inorganic molecules combined themselves into long chains capable of growth and reproduction, thus forming the first organic or living matter.

The exact nature of the extremely complicated processes that led to the creation of the first living molecules is still a matter of conjecture. Some biologists think it happened in the primeval seas, others prefer to see clammy clays serving as the master moulds. Whether it happened only once or many times and in many places is again still in the speculative state. Some think that the creation of life was an event of an almost incredibly low probability of occurrence, others hold contrary views. The fact remains that the structures of nucleic acids, present in all known forms of life from the lowest to the highest, exhibit convincingly certain common features proving that we all belong to the same family. But this does not exclude the possibility that several different and competitive living structures arose thousands of millions of years ago. Perhaps the ancient oceans were the battle-ground between billions of sub-living molecules belonging to several diverse types. It has been argued that even if spontaneous generation of life still occurs from time to time somewhere on earth at present, the relatively feeble newborn molecules would be an easy prey for omni-present modern species of bacteria, hardened through aeons of competitive struggle. It also has been pointed out that the primeval atmos-phere did not contain oxygen, which is the product of the biological activity of plants. The exclusion of the possibility of oxidization may be the essential condition for the formation of the first living molecules.

At this point it will be useful for further discussion to des-cribe certain features of the human brain.

The human nervous system consists of a great number of cells called neurons, capable of generating and propagating impulses. These impulses, which can be considered as short-time disturbances on a molecular scale of a combined electrical, chemical and mechanical character, constitute the elementary signals in the nervous system. All modes of functioning of our brain, from the most elementary to the most complex, are, in principle, expressible by extremely involved series of elementary impulses, although the actual correspondence between the psychological and the physiological states is at present unknown. The most interesting feature of the human brain is the fact that its operation is mainly, although probably not exclusively, digital in character. Hence in this respect the brain is similar to digital computers. This means that any number or logical concept involved, is, as a rule, not represented by a corresponding value of a certain physical quantity (analogue representation) but is expressed as some combination of elementary pulses. The number of basic cells contained in the human brain is about ten thousand millions, a staggering amount, considering the limited volume of the human skull. It is several orders higher than the number of active elements contained in the present largest digital computer. It is also plausible that because of certain complexities in the stimulation of neurons, the equivalent number of active elements of the brain is still higher by one or two orders. Also, certain operations of an analogous character may be taking place in the brain. Although the nerve cells are about ten thousand times slower in their operation than electronic valves, they are so much smaller that, considering the number of operations per unit of time performed by a unit volume comprised of nerve cells, or of electronic valves, the natural elements are thousands of times superior. Concerning the matter of data storage, or memory, in the human brain, very little is known. We do not know what is the actual character of the physical process, by means of which information is stored in the brain, or even where this memory is located. The possibility of the memory consisting of active regenerative processes has been suggested. One thing is certain: considering the known receptive capacity of our sense organs, combined with the strong possibility that anything experienced during a lifetime is never completely forgotten, the human memory must be enormous—presumably many millions of times greater than that of the largest digital machines. More detailed considerations of the working mode of the data processing elements in the human brain leads to the conclusion that they operate with low precision but the system as a whole has inherently high reliability. The low precision suggests that, in order to get any meaningful results at all, the operation must be parallel, meaning the simultaneous processing of many data in parallel, thus keeping the logical depth to a minimum and consequently reducing cumulative errors. This kind of operation places additional requirements on the size of memory storage. The logic of the elementary brain operations is not known but in all likelihood it is very different from the logic of our language or of mathematics.

A comparison of the gross features of a human brain and a present-day computer shows the former to be immensely superior. A human brain has enormous powers of selective perception, self-organization, learning and adaptability. Starting from almost a complete blank at birth it can arrange an immense amount of impinging sense stimuli into patterns, producing thus a mental model of the environment on which an activity, useful to survival, is based. It can form from these elementary patterns structures of increasing complexity, expressing more general concepts about the environment. In time it can learn to reject automatically the sense stimuli of low interest for the organism and admit to consciousness only those which are important.

It can learn by trial and error and organize itself into a progressively complex system. It can distinguish meaningful sequences of causes and effects in extremely complex situations and when faced continuously in everyday life with the necessity of making decisions of a probabilistic character on the basis of insufficient information, it can make excellent statistical estimates involving many interacting factors. It possesses a mysterious property of self-awareness which so far has eluded any explanation. Although the most advanced experimental computers can perceive, learn and form judgements in an elementary fashion, the computers commercially available are, by comparison with the human brain, almost complete morons. All they can offer, principally, is enormously superior speed and a relatively high reliability of operation. Hence they are more efficient than human beings only for the execution of rigidly specified data processing tasks. However, one should not draw too definite conclusions from this comparison. The science of cybernetics and the technology of data processing machines is only in its infancy and there seems to be no basic theoretical obstacles to the artificial creation of systems equal or superior to human beings in the specific fields of mental endeavour.

The gradual disappearance of a distinctive dividing line between living and dead matter on the microscopic level has its analogy in the similarity of the gross features exhibited by multicellular animals and certain types of cybernetic machines. As pointed out previously, the open-loop machines take into account neither their own inaccuracies nor the effects of environment. Thus the difference in performance between them and animals is very apparent. The open-loop machine seems, by comparison, to act like a blind, senseless force, which in fact it is. The introduction of feedback controls changes the situation. The closed-loop machines can measure their errors due either to their own imperfection or to disturbing influences of environment, and correct their performance accordingly. Such a machine reacts to the environment in a purposeful manner and as a result is strikingly similar in behaviour to the lower types of animals. In fact, almost anybody who has seen Dr Walter's mechanical tortoises in action cannot avoid the impression that their performance is animal-like. Yet these electro-mechanical devices comprise only two basic feedback loops. By employing digital computers much more highly organized machines can be made. Because these advanced systems possess memories they cannot only store a large number of instructions and act accordingly to them, but they can learn by trial and error to select the most effective path leading towards a certain goal. In addition to the normal use of error as a correcting signal these machines can modify their internal parameters in accordance with changes in environment. Hence the very characteristics of the system, and the mode of its whole behaviour can be adjusted to certain aims in variable external conditions. Machines have been built which can sense the environment and build from the stimuli sensed the patterns in their memories, which model certain features of the world external to the machine.

Hence, the capacity of animals to perceive the environment, to distinguish meaningful patterns in it, to learn by trial and error and to adapt themselves to the external world can all be stimulated by the machines, although admittedly still in a very elementary fashion. The most powerful digital computer today would not surpass the intelligence of an earthworm. As pointed out previously the basic elements from which these machines are built are still far too bulky and expensive. Also theoretical knowledge about the planning of their internal structures (the logical design of these machines) is still in the early stages of development. But both fields, engineering techniques and logical design, advance by leaps and bounds and there is little doubt that in a couple of decades it should be possible to construct machines comparable in intelligence and versatility of performance to lower types of animals at least.

Concerning reproduction, the other basic feature of living beings, the following can be said: Firstly, there is no reason why the machine should not be able to attend to its maintenance. This would be analogous to the regenerative and healing properties of living bodies. When combined with the intake of fuel or any other form of energy it would constitute an analogy, at least in the gross aspects, to exchanging the energy and matter with the environment while preserving the characteristic structure of the given system. Secondly, it is theoretically possible to make a machine which, on the basis of information stored in its memory, could make other machines, either different or similar, from available stocks of component parts. This is what reproduction essentially means. The fact that the machine would start with pieces previously manufactured does not invalidate the analogy in any way. There is no reason why the initial materials should not be natural stuffs and anyway animals feed and breed only by the intake of an organic matter, which is of much more complicated structure than any component part is likely to be. The fact that the processes in living bodies during assimilation and reproduction are of an entirely different character than the assembly techniques employed by our hypothetical reproductive machine has no bearing on the similarity of the final results. Finally, it can be proved in theory that a machine could be built capable of constructing others more complex and superior in some respects to itself. The fact that we are still technically far from the creation of such machines does not matter at this stage of the discussion. We are concerned at the moment with the comparison of basic features of living and non-living systems and thus for our purpose a mathematical proof, if sufficiently rigorous, is just as good as an experimental result.

One often hears the saying that a machine can only do what the maker built into it. If this means that the designer planned and foresaw everything that the machine will do, the statement is simply not true. It may be correct for open-loop machines, but even the relatively simple feedback-controlled mechanical tortoises have exhibited on one occasion a behaviour pattern which surprised their maker, although when once observed, it could easily be explained. It is quite inconceivable that the designer of a really complex cybernetic machine could predict everything that it will do in any environment. But, one may object, it is still possible to do so in principle. Yes, if the environment is known and the machine is of a deterministic type. But it is possible to build a machine whose internal workings would depend on a random choice at several nodal points; in fact it has been done. The behaviour of such a machine would be predictable only in a statistical sense, so the designer could never be quite sure what it would do. Furthermore, such a probabilistic machine could have inbuilt the capacity to remember and to learn by trial and error. After a long period of interacting with a complex environment and modifying its constants and behaviour accordingly, and always including the random choices in the whole process, its final mode of behaviour would in fact be unpredictable.

If somebody still insists that it would be statistically predictable or that it would be practically possible to establish the limits within which the behaviour would be contained, one can then say the living animals are no different. Bearing in mind the properties of the fertilized ovum, which is entirely a product of the action of the parents, it can be said that an animal is nothing but what its parents made it and what its environment taught it. Although the genes do not determine how the individual will act in a certain situation, nevertheless, they establish the set of all possible reactions. One would have to prove the existence of *vis viva* peculiar only to living creatures, to be able to demonstrate that they are, therefore, different in their reactions to any conceivable machines. But the vitalist's position, although not finally disproved, appears progressively less tenable. For that matter, if we do not assume that human beings contain an extra-material element it can be said that none of them is anything else but what his parents and environment made him. In concluding this paragraph it can be said that there is lack of a definite sharp boundary between the basic features of the living creatures and of cybernetic machines. The theoretical possibility of the evolution of machines, analogous to the evolution of living beings, not only cannot be rigorously rejected but on the contrary can be mathematically supported. The fact that it may never happen in practice does not concern us here.

CHAPTER 6

The Fundamental
Modes of Thinking

IN the previous chapter we have discussed among other things the basic features of living and non-living matter on the microscopic and macroscopic levels and we concluded that in both cases it is not possible to observe a sharp dividing line. In the present chapter we will review some fundamental modes of human brain processes and try to consider whether these can be paralelled by the machine processes. For the purpose of this discussion we can divide all mental processes, which belong to the broad class known as rational thinking, into two groups: deductive and inductive reasoning. The discussion which follows does not pretend to conform with the orthodox theory of logic and serves merely as an illustration of the problems involved.

Deductive thinking starts with certain axioms or basic statements which are assumed to be true. These fundamental propositions are either the results of previous logical activity—that is they have been logically deduced from other more fundamental axioms—or they have been demonstrated experimentally or are a matter of choice or belief. To the second category belong all statements serving as the basis for predictions of the outcomes of physical processes. Such statements are usually referred to as natural laws. Although the latter are only the hypotheses, nevertheless, in a given scientific or technological argument they assume the role of axioms. Among the examples of the third category are the dogmas of revealed religions and the statements which we take as obviously true, for instance, the axioms of Euclidean geometry. Certain principles of thinking or logical rules are then assumed and, by operating through them systematically on the basic axioms, conclusions are reached. The first obvious weakness of any deductive system, and in particular of the system intended to be the description of certain features of the physical world, lies in the choice of the axioms. The first category of axioms are really not axioms at all as they depend on the statements from which they have been deduced. The physical laws filling the second category cannot be taken as being absolutely true, not only because there exists always the possibility of their modification by future experimental discoveries but also because of a more fundamental reason, namely that the whole scientific method is based on one axiom, which although very likely to be true, is in the final analysis a matter of faith. To this we return later. Within the third category, religious dogmas are a matter of belief and here the divergence of opinions is certainly possible. The axioms which seem obviously true, for example, that only one straight line can pass through two points, can unfortunately also be challenged. It has been maintained in philosophy for thousands of years that certain statements or categories of thinking are obviously true and do not require proof. They were thought of as given *a priori*, as the basic truths in any kind of thinking. Although there was plenty of disagreement as to which statements were to be considered as belonging to the above class, their existence was generally explicitly assumed or at least implied in all theories. For example, the concepts of space and time seem to be intuitively obvious. The human mind perceives space as something which 'is there' even if no material objects are present in it. Similarly time is a quantity immediately given and everybody understands it in a similar way. It seems obvious that time must be the same here or there, or on a distant star; not, of course, in the sense of identical readings on the clocks but in the basic meaning of the term. There are many other concepts of a similar nature. As said before, axioms of Euclidean geometry are among them.

Alas, modern philosophy and science have indicated that all these apparently obvious axioms and categories of thinking are in fact far from being so. On the contrary they are only assumptions convenient for certain purposes. Perfectly consistent systems of geometry have been built on the basis of sets of axioms different from Euclidean. Space and time in the theory of relativity have very different meanings from those commonly accepted. Thus it is possible that times are different for observers situated in the systems moving relatively to each other with a velocity which is a significant fraction of the velocity of light. These times are not different in the sense that the clocks went haywire but in the fundamental sense. The average human mind recoils from such ideas and is quite unable to picture them, but their truth, or shall we say their usefulness, is confirmed by experiment. It is apparent now that even the most fundamental and obvious concepts which we employ in our thinking cannot be accepted as unquestionably true. On the contrary, it appears that the mind creates them only as efficient tools enabling the description of the mental modelling of the environment. They are true in the sense that if the world is described in their terms, consciously or subconsciously, the actions based on this description are useful, in the broadest sense, for the individual. Hence, the axioms are true in the pragmatic sense and are arrived at through attempts of the mind to establish the patterns from sensorial stimuli, or in other words, to build a mental model of the external world. As we all live in a basically similar environment and our brains function in essentially similar fashion, it is not surprising that we form fundamentally similar categories of thinking. For example, apart from modern scientific experiments, we never encounter velocities which are significant as compared with the velocity of light. Hence our intuitive concepts of space and time are such as to be perfectly valid for all practical purposes in the conditions of these relatively low velocities, but they break down when applied to the velocities comparable with that of light. Therefore we probably cannot claim an absolute, universal validity for anything which seems even most true and obvious. The alteration of basic concepts is usually the consequence of their application in describing new experimental or mental discoveries. Then they lead to inconsistencies which suggest that they can be abolished only by giving new meanings to the old terms. Of course, the formulation of new basic concepts demands tremendous intellectual courage and a capacity for breaking with the customary mental categories, usually the mark of a true genius.

We cannot go here into the discussion of the desperate efforts of many brilliant minds to find unshakeable foundations for their philosophical systems. Perhaps the best known among them is Descartes. However, all attempts failed in that it was impossible to find a statement or a concept which would be universally accepted as true. What appears obviously correct to one man may seem dubious to another. As the concepts in question are basic it is extremely difficult to discuss them, because the very discussion must be conducted in terms which are often based implicitly on the fundamental ideas discussed.

In conclusion, we can say that the axioms used in any kind of deductive reasoning, and serving as cornerstones of any system of thought, are in the last analysis a matter of opinion or belief.

The second basic weakness of deductive thinking is the fact that what we have said about the axioms applies also to the rules of rational operations performed on them, or to logic. Our very basic logical categories are arrived at in the same way, by testing the results of our mental processes against the happenings of nature. If the correspondence is found satisfactory for all practical purposes, our mind accepts the basic rule as true. By repeated use of the latter it becomes an integral part of our thinking and we cannot think otherwise than by using it on the appropriate occasion. This does not, however, make our logic necessarily universally true or unique. In fact, the logical systems devised so far are imperfect in a very profound sense. The validity of axioms underlying any philosophical system is always open to doubt if these axioms truly represent the reality. The methods of operating on the axioms are open to similar doubts. In addition, even the purely abstract logical systems, laying no claims to mirroring reality, are not free from imperfections. One of the most difficult problems in designing any system of thought is the definition of a consistent set of axioms and methods of operating on them. Apparently, no logical system can be free from paradoxes. By a paradox we mean that, starting from the same statement and following two different paths, both strictly according to the rules of a given logic, two different and contradictory results are obtained. Some famous paradoxes survived thousands of years and defied the most strenuous efforts of the best thinkers to solve them. Further, it has been demonstrated that in certain logical systems it is possible to construct theories which, while belonging to the system, are unprovable by the rules of the latter. Hence such a system either remains incomplete (if the offending theorems are excluded) or contains unresolvable propositions if completed. In other words the consistency of the system cannot be proved by the rules of this system. It is

G

rather shattering to learn that our arithmetic is one such system and that it can be proved that no general method of solving all arithmetical problems is obtainable. This seems to suggest that there exists some fundamental and, perhaps, inherent weakness in human logic.

However, even if we assume that the axioms and the logical rules of operation in a given system are consistent, and therefore that the conclusions reached by deductive reasoning are perfectly valid, the question still arises. But do they add something really new to knowledge? The answer seems to be no. All possible conclusions that can be deduced from the axioms by means of logical rules are already there and do not bring anything essentially new. For example, given all the axioms of Euclidean geometry and the rules of logic, all geometrical theories possible within this system are given and would be immediately obvious to a being with the IQ of say, one thousand. Hence all deductive sciences, as for instance mathematics are really a tautology. A very useful tautology but no more than that. These remarks are not made to insult the mathematicians, for whom I have the greatest personal respect, but to show that once the axioms and the rules are given the rest is a matter of systematic, rigidly determined mental processes or, in other words, of perfectly definable data processing. But this is something which even the present day digital computers can do within quite considerable limits. There is no reason why the machines of the future should not be able to perform any kind of deductive thinking, including the formulation of the concepts of progressively more general meaning, the creation of new mathematical systems and the establishment of new logical schemes. In fact, considering the tremendous speed and accuracy of computers, they should eventually achieve a great superiority over the human mind in the deductive modes of thinking. It is quite feasible that they will be able to work the systems of mathematics, which, although very useful for modelling phenomena in nature, will be completely baffling to the human mind, because of the complexity and novelty of the basic axioms and of the rules of their use.

The unifying effect of deduction, consisting of pulling several theories together into one major rule, can be seen in modern science. Science aims clearly at establishing a deductive system of knowledge so that finally any process in the universe, however complex and involved, and of any nature whatever, will be explainable in terms of the few basic and preferably simple rules. In formulating this system, and especially in using the rules established for the prediction of future phenomena, the computers will be indispensable tools.

Perhaps the most impressive demonstration of the deductive powers of digital computers is their ability to find inconsistencies in relatively simple logical schemes. Let us consider what happens if we try to put some well established clerical system on the computer. Such a system also rests on certain basic rules or procedures which, so far as the former is concerned, can be regarded as its basic axioms. When this clerical system has been translated into the computer's language or when the computer's programme has been written the first obvious thing to do is to test it for consistency. Such a test, as a rule, reveals that certain inconsistencies exist which nobody ever suspected. This means that although the given clerical system operated satisfactorily over many years, it does break down in certain unusual situations. That this was not discovered before means that fortunately those rare occasions never arose in the actual experience of the organization. The computer could pin-point these inconsistencies because, due to its tremendous speed, it was able to go through a great number of possible operational variants of the system, which would be impractical or quite impossible for any group of clerks. Similar findings are an everyday experience during computerization of mathematical problems. Various analytical methods break down unexpectedly when applied to certain unusual tasks. This leads either to the modification of the method, making it more generally applicable, or to the definition of additional constraints, removing the inconsistencies. We are not asserting by this that any major inconsistencies in basic mathematical theory have been discovered by the use of computers. Computers have so far proved themselves only as a powerful means of searching for the inconsistencies at a much more modest level. But there is every reason to hope that the much more powerful computers of the future will be profitably employed on logical research at more advanced levels.

Turning now to the inductive way of thinking, we shall here limit ourselves to the ampliative or incomplete induction as used in natural sciences. The basis of this kind of argument is an observable experiment. For example, we immerse an object in a liquid and measure its apparent loss of weight. By repeating the experiment and employing many different objects and using many different liquids we obtain results from which we draw the general conclusion that the apparent loss of weight of the immersed body is equal to the weight of the volume of liquid displaced by this body. Hence, we follow the path described in Chapter 1. We observe a group of certain phenomena, we describe them in terms of measurable quantities, and we suggest the relationship existing between the latter. This relationship is then our theory, permitting the prediction of the outcome of other similar experiments. The establishment of the law is an inductive process, while prediction on the basis of this law is of a deductive character. The theory can be invalidated if only some experiments to which the theory is supposedly applicable are found to contradict it. So far everything seems perfectly obvious. But, as stated previously, obvious things are always to be suspected. What is the very basis of our confidence in prediction based on previous experiments? Of course, we assume that the instruments and implements used were of the required standard, that we were not dreaming the whole thing up, that no physically unknown and influential factors were contributing, etc. We then trust our prediction because we believe that if the experiment is repeated in an identical manner the outcome must also be indentical. For example, if anybody jumps from a ten-storey building, assuming the absence of a hurricane, hidden anti-gravitational machines etc., there is no doubt at all in his mind that he will fall down and not up. Anything else would be considered ridiculous. Hence the very basis of our trust in experiment lies in the belief in the uniformity of nature. Everything being identical, things happen the same way. If we find that one event invariably follows the other then we say that the latter is the cause of the former.

For example, if I strike a gong a sound will be emitted. Hence, I say that my stroke is the cause of the sound. We say that everything being equal, the same cause always brings the same effect. How else could it be? The principle of causality and the underlying belief in uniformity is the very basis of our outlook and it is hard to imagine that things could be otherwise. Whether people belonging to any historically known civilization or living in prehistoric times had the same views on causality is debatable (actually the belief in various demons and spirits causing things to happen is still an essentially causalistic view). Nevertheless, they certainly always acted upon such views. All living things, from the humblest worm to man, learn by trial. But to learn by trial one must accept, consciously or subconsciously, if only on the dimmest instinctive level, that nature is uniform, that things always happen in the same way. If things happened completely at random, then it would be obviously of no avail to base expectations on one's past experience.

However, because it is useful to believe in the uniformity of nature, because a penny tossed up always came down, this does not constitute in itself an absolutely compelling reason to assume causality as an obvious axiom. An identical and simple experiment has been repeated millions of times and always yielded the same results. For instance, regarding the penny, why do we think, why are we absolutely certain, that if we toss up another it too will come down? Because we believe in the uniformity of nature, but this in the last analysis is only a belief.

Lest somebody should think that to doubt causality and to admit even the faintest possibility that the penny may remain suspended in mid-air is ridiculous, let us point out that the consequences of rigid determinism are less palatable. If we believe that in the absence of any other significant factors the same cause will always bring the same result in any elementary experiment, as in the case of a tossed penny, then we are bound to admit the following. Let us set aside the possibility of extra-material elements or beings, to whom this law may not apply, and let us assume that all things in the universe belong to the categories of matter and energy. Then we can certainly say that any process in the universe, however complex and involved, can be thought of as entirely composed of a great multitude of elementary processes. If it is apparently so obvious that each of the latter is strictly governed by the laws of cause and effect and hence completely predetermined, then the course of the whole universe, star, amoeba and man is also entirely foreseeable to the smallest detail. Hence, if we only knew exactly the state of this immense system, at any moment of time, the whole future could be completely definable. That this is practically impossible is here beside the point, but the theoretical possibility gives immediate support not only to all the rather nasty thoughts expressed at the beginning of Chapter 5, but would leave no room for a truly chance happening. This state of affairs seems intuitively almost as unacceptable as the penny floating in the air. Hence it was perhaps not entirely a waste of time to have pondered for a whole over the basic problems of determinism and induction.

In conclusion, the principles of uniformity in nature and the validity of inductive reasoning are questions of belief. Although many attempts have been made to prove induction unshakably valid, none of them is really convincing. Some of them try to prove induction by some kind of inductive reasoning which is, of course, a vicious circle. Others can be reduced to the statement that induction does not need any proof because it is true in its own right. But the question still remains, is it really? No system of thought can avoid the introduction of axioms based, *in fin dei conti*, on a belief, and science is no exception. It is true that scientific method works, that its applications, both purely scientific and technological, are immensely successful, but to deduce from the latter the validity of scientific law is in itself an inductive process, so we are again where we started.

Returning now to our main question let us ask 'Can a machine perform the equivalent of an inductive mental process?' The answer is certainly 'Yes'. A machine can be equipped with units which will sense its environment or in other words register the data of a character that is visual, audible, tactile etc., coming from the world external to the machine. From this data the machine can build patterns mirroring certain features of the environment and store them in its memory. The machine can have an aim initially inbuilt. It will now purposefully activate its motor-parts in accordance with its aims and with the patterns arrived at previously. It will then sense the results or the reactions of the environment and, if necessary, modify accordingly the patterns modelling the latter. Acting in this manner it will arrive at a certain final pattern representing the behaviour of its environment. This pattern will be, as far as the machine is concerned, a law of nature. Confronted in future with a similar situation, the machine will try to realise its aim, acting on the basis of the above pattern. Hence, it will act by predicting deductively the outcome of future happenings on the basis of a law previously established by an inductive process of learning. The fact that the present-day computers can perform this process only in a very elementary fashion should not disturb us here. The very possibility that it can be performed at all by mechanical means lends support to the view that the computers of the future will be able to execute very advanced inductive processes and act purposefully on that basis.

While discussing the subject of inductive and deductive knowledge we were thus far firmly on the grounds of determinism, in that we followed classical physics. This assumed, as an act of faith, the validity of induction, at least so far as applied to physical phenomena, and believed in the strictly determinable causal chain of happenings in nature. True, the idea of chance had crept into classical physics, nevertheless, the employment of the former was considered as imposed by the shortcomings of the investigation, but not to be an essential feature of nature.

For instance, it was well realized that no measurement could be absolutely free from error. The exact causes of error (apart from so-called systematic errors) were, by definition, unknown, in the given experiment. Otherwise they could be avoided or at least mathematically eliminated from the final results. But as in practice there were always certain inaccuracies in experimental techniques, which could not be entirely accounted for, it was convenient to assume that these errors happened at random. This, however, did not mean that anybody admitted a truly random behaviour of the system under investigation. It was assumed, in principle, that everything was strictly deterministic and that by refining our techniques we could approach in every case the true values as closely as we liked, although we never actually attained them. Hence, our knowledge was believed to be of an asymptotic character with respect to the absolute truth. Similarly, when applying the statistical theories of classical physics to the study of enormous aggregates of molecules e.g. to the volumes of gases, nobody really suggested that the particles of gases behave randomly. On the contrary, it was realised that the motion of each molecule is strictly determined by its momentum and position at a given time and by successive collisions with all other molecules. Hence, if we only knew the momentum and the velocities of all particles inside the container at one instant of time, we could, in principle, predict the future behaviour of the system without recourse to the notion of probability. As this was impossible on practical grounds, we had to assume that the system behaved *as if* every particle moved in a random fashion, because only in this way could we manage the problem mathematically. In modern physics quantum mechanics made a break with the principles of determinism honoured through centuries. It was found that when describing the phenomena on the level of sub-atomic particles the idea of chance must become an inherent feature of the system. The reason for this revolutionary view can be put in the following grossly over-simplified form.

The description of sub-atomic phenomena in terms of the usual variables of classical physics, like position, momentum, energy etc., leads to operator equations which do not admit the simultaneous solutions for any pair of such variables. No experiment can be devised permitting the simultaneous, accurate measurement of two such variables as the measurement of one variable necessarily disturbs the value of the other in an unpredictable manner. In fact, the more accurately we measure one variable the more uncertain the value of the other becomes. The subsequent measurement of this other variable has the same kind of effect on the first variable and the product of uncertainties in both measurements is a constant. These apparently odd conclusions are, very broadly speaking, the consequences of certain hypotheses which are essential for explanation of some observable facts. For instance, to achieve a satisfactory description of certain phenomena of radiation of heat, it had to be assumed that the energy of radiation, and by implication any other kind of energy, is not continuous or indefinitely divisible, but that there exist certain minimum packets of energy called quanta, which cannot be split any further. Now when observing by any means whatever a sub-atomic particle, for example an electron, we must act on it with some energy since, an observation involves the idea of contact. Even the least disturbing of all, the visual kind of observation, still involves the exchange of energy contained in rays of light or in any other kind of radiation. In no case can this be avoided, because energy cannot exist in infinitely small quantities and the exchange of one quantum of energy is the smallest disturbing effect that can ever be achieved. However, it happens that even this small energy is quite enough to disturb substantially the motion of an electron. The effect of this disturbance cannot be accurately calculated for both the variables describing the state of the moving electron, and hence we never know what the simultaneous values for the true position and the true momentum of an electron were before the observation. Therefore, the position or the momentum can be only described in terms of probabilities and from this the probable results of the next measurement can be estimated.

Several conclusions shattering to our common sense can be deduced from the above facts. First of all, as said before, probability becomes an essential feature of the system. Someone may say that the phenomena are in fact of a deterministic nature but on a level more fundamental than the one we can observe. This may be so, but we will never know, not only for practical reasons, but because of the essential features of nature. Not even theoretically can we expect to exchange anything less than one quantum of energy during any observation. Hence the controversy between the deterministic and indeterministic view is transferred from the field of science to that of philosophy or religion. A scientist cannot debate something which cannot be proved or disproved by an experiment, not even in principle. And what he can measure imposes the probabilistic approach. Secondly, the subject is introduced back into the experiment. It has been a proud boast of science that it investigates the phenomena objectively and that this gives its laws universal validity, independent of the scientist himself. But, as seen, the measurement itself cannot fail to influence the behaviour of the system, and when very small particles are concerned this influence is by no means negligible. Thus complete separation of the subject and object is impossible. Thirdly, as the measurements are discontinuous we cannot say, strictly speaking, what happens to the system in between the measurements. This is bewildering to our customary ways of thinking and we are bound to exclaim 'Well, the electron must be still there moving in such and such a manner'. But this is unjustifiable, because as we cannot know experimentally what happens between two consecutive measurements, not even in principle, we simply cannot say anything about it. Any other interpretation lead in quantum theory apparently to hopeless theoretical contradictions.

It must be emphasized at this point that although the quantum theory forces us to abandon full-blooded determinism, it does not really abandon the principle of causality. The consecutively succeeding phenomena are still causalistically connected but the bounds are no longer uniquely determinable. Instead of saying that the system must pass from the given initial state to some other state, completely predictable, we say that the system may pass from its initial state into several other states and we associate certain measures of probability with every transition. Hence, a given cause has a choice, so to speak, in bringing about several different effects, each of which is characterized by a certain chance occurrence. This, of course, is very different from complete indeterminism, from abolishing the cause entirely and believing in the complete randomness of the universe. Moreover, the believer in determinism has another fact to comfort him. Although the behaviour of a sub-atomic particle is essentially of a probabilistic nature, according to the quantum theory, the behaviour of a large aggregate of such particles is almost completely predictable in its gross features. This is the so-called 'law of great numbers' and its validity can be observed even in everyday life. For instance, the prediction of the length of life of Mr Brown necessarily involves a relatively large chance of error, even if his state of health, occupation, living conditions etc., are well known. But the prediction of an average life-span of a million men belonging to Mr Brown's category is much more reliable. In fact, the predictions referring to the average outcome of large numbers of similar cases are so reliable that insurance companies, operating on relatively narrow safety margins, can accept profitably risks relating to death, accident, fire, etc. Thus, as the majority of the phenomena commonly met in life obviously involve enormous aggregates of molecules, the causality in the strictly deterministic sense is almost completely valid for nearly all everyday purposes. However, even here there are some exceptions, as for example, the fact that genetic mutations, having decisive bearings on the laws of inheritance, are believed to be of a significantly probabilistic character.

We see then that classical mechanics is on the one hand the limiting case of relativistic mechanics, when the velocities are small as compared with the velocity of light, and on the other hand it is the limiting case of quantum physics when quantum numbers of the system are large. Also, one must not forget that any scientific theory is, after all, only a hypothesis. Among the physicists themselves, there is not yet complete agreement on the matters discussed above and even assuming that such agreement will be reached some day, there is still no reason why some future discoveries would not be able to upset it again and to introduce some new ideas. We will return to these matters again when discussing sensory perception and introspection.

As mentioned above, as far as the majority of physical phenomena in everyday life is concerned, it matters little whether one subscribes to rigid determinism or to partial indeterminism. The results of throwing a stone are for all practical purposes identical, which ever line of thought we follow. What makes us use the idea of chance continually is the fact that as a rule we have to act in a situation where many important factors are unknown to us. In other words, we have to decide on the basis of incomplete evidence. For instance, if I am about to go on a long car journey, even if we exclude for the sake of argument the chance of an accident, I have to take into account the possibility of the car's breakdown. Now, if prior to the journey, my car is examined in every conceivable detail by a large team of specialists, and if all faults found are repaired, it should be possible to say with certainty for all practical purposes, that the car will not break down. In the absence of this knowledge, I have to take the possibility of breakdown into my planning and my best guess will be based presumably on the record of the car's past performance. We are doing this sort of thing all the time, mostly subconsciously. Our mind can be called a great gambler which continually makes estimates about chances of future happenings. We know little about the rules of the calculus of probability going on in our subconscious mind, but we are not completely in the dark. Although our minds can make mistakes, the very fact that we manage to survive in an extremely complex environment means that the human mind is a supremely adaptable and efficient statistician. Hence we see that our learning, at least so far as the business of living in a given environment is concerned, is always inductive and predominantly of a probabilistic nature.

Again, we can say that it is possible to build a machine which on the basis of repeated trials could estimate the chances of future happenings. In other words, such a machine would build up in its memory a pattern of the external world not in a deterministic fashion, but would include the probabilities of various things which can happen in its environment. It would act then on the basis of this statistical pattern according to the rules of probabilistic logic and strive to achieve its aim.

Very elementary machines of this sort have been built already.

Having thus arrived at the conclusion that the equivalents of the straightforward mental processes of the human mind can be performed by machines, at least in theory, the problem of the more complicated, supposedly typically human ways of thinking, known under the names of intuition, imagination, creativeness, naturally suggests itself. Here no definite conclusion can be reached. It may be that there is something in these higher modes of mental activity which will for ever remain out of the reach of any kind of machine. After all, we know that so far the artificial creation of even the humblest living cell has not yet been achieved, so it is conceivable, although it is becoming progressively less likely, that living matter contains even in its lowest forms some element or force which will for ever elude us. And even if the artificial creation of elementary forms of life were a fact, that would still not preclude the existence in the human mind of forces and capabilities of such a nature as to make them impossible to an artefact.

The majority of people accept this view; nevertheless, the other view is also possible. We can imagine that even the most lofty mental processes are composed of millions of elementary patterns of inductive and deductive character built into an enormously complex structure by various subconscious and conscious processes. The patterns would be built from elements of perception of the external and internal world and joined together, very broadly speaking, by the processes discussed previously. When the information received in every second of our waking life is expressed in binary notation we begin to realise its tremendous amount (estimated as 14×10^{10} bits per second from all external receptors). This continues through every moment of our lives; hence the quantity of information stored in our brains is truly fantastic. It is easy to see that patterns of almost any complexity can be built from this amount of stuff. These patterns are continuously being rearranged, regrouped, and modified under the influence of new experiences, reshuffled by thousands of mental processes proceeding day and night in our brains throughout life, then stored in the memory again and used subsequently for the building of even more complex structures. Is it entirely impossible to imagine that the results of this incredibly versatile and complex process may be the creation of a symphony, of a picture, or a successful national leader?

And if we admit this possibility, then there seems to be no definite reason why a sufficiently complex and versatile machine could not be constructed capable of performing all these things on an even higher level than any human being could ever hope to reach.

To fix our ideas, let us consider the case of imagination. It is fairly obvious that this consists essentially, at least on a lower level, of the ability to build purposefully from known elements a mental structure representing the possible trend of physical events. If I want to decide on the course of action to take, I consider various possibilities from which to choose. In doing this I am building several hypothetical models, each picturing an alternative train of events in my environment. This ability to experiment with mental models of the environment gives us a tremendous superiority over animals, which in all probability do not possess such facilities, except perhaps on a very elementary level. We can foresee 'what would happen, if' by forming long, hypothetical deductive chains starting from the basis of our previous experience. Thus we can choose the best course for the realization of our aims. It is plausible to extend this interpretation of imagination to its more subtle levels.

It has been maintained by many thinkers that it is impossible to create an image of anything which does not consist of patterns or elements experienced sensorily before. Even the greatest painter cannot imagine a colour which lies entirely beyond the range of the spectrum perceived by the human visual system. He may be able to imagine any colour which is a mixture of basic colours, but he cannot form in his mind the imaginary visual sensation of ultra-violet or infra-red radiation. And what is the sound of a pitch beyond the range of any human ear? Nobody can imagine that. When dreaming of a most fantastic Martian monster we can only do so in terms of elements which, in the last analysis, belong to our familiar world. Speaking now of intuition, it is quite feasible that it consists of complex mental processes and of features not entirely dissimilar to those discussed above. But in this case only the final result is delivered to the consciousness. Also the logic of subconscious intuitive process may be very different from that used during our conscious commonsense thinking. The former may be more appropriate than orthodox logic in certain situations, and this would explain the striking success of the intuitive approach in some cases.

The capacity known as intelligence depends on the ability of perception, on the volume, permanence and quick accessibility of the memory, on versatility in association of ideas and on some other features. Among all of them the ability to associate various ideas is very important and this makes the concept of intelligence partly overlapping in its meaning with that of imagination. In fact, some people think that the ability to construct quickly several mental patterns of possible courses of events and choose the best is perhaps the most distinctive mark of intelligence.

Here the possibility of a mechanical aid is obvious. Let us consider the following problem (which is actually well known to any production engineer): We have four manufacturing machines and we have to make four items, each of which must be processed on each machine. The sequence of operations is fixed for technical reasons for each item. But we have a choice of which item to begin with on the first machine, which is the next one, and so on for each machine. We want now to know what is the best complete sequence, from the viewpoint of total manufacturing time, utilization of particular machines, etc. Elementary combinational analysis shows that even in this extremely simplified case the total number of all possible sequences is well over three hundred thousand. Anybody experienced in the permutations on a football pool coupon can easily verify that. Now it is not a practical proposition for a man to go through all these sequences in order to find the best. But a computer could do it in this elementary case. Actually in the case of a shop equipped with hundreds of machines and processing many jobs, the above task becomes prohibitive even for the biggest present day computer.

Speaking now in more general terms, we see that in cases where a choice has to be made from the enormous number of possible patterns and where it is not possible to do otherwise than by constructing every alternative in turn, a computer can choose on the basis of instructions stated by a human being. Hence a computer can work as an intelligence amplifier in this limited sense, because of its vastly superior speed of operation. It would amplify, as far as this sort of task is concerned, the powers of the human brain in a fashion similar to a huge steam engine amplifying the relatively puny strength of its operator. Of course, in certain cases it is possible to arrive at the optimum sequence without the necessity of slogging through all the possible alternatives, although even in such cases the volume of actual calculations makes them often more suitable for a computer than for a human being. This sort of problem is considered by a branch of mathematics known as linear programming or, when multi-stage processes are concerned, as dynamic programming.

While considering these matters one factor must be firmly kept in mind at all times. Although present day computers, including both the models commercially available and the research machines, can perform the equivalents of the lower mental functions with tremendous speed and accuracy and can imitate the rudiments of more advanced ways of thinking, they are so enormously inferior to the human brain that one must be very cautious in drawing any rush conclusions. Nothing would be more erroneous than to imagine that we are just on the threshold of creating machines comparable with the human brain. In all advanced fields of mental endeavour the human mind reigns supreme and it is still a matter of conjecture whether any machine will be able ever to give a comparable performance. However, the considerations of this chapter and the tremendous advances in computer engineering and logical design achieved during the last two decades suggests strongly that even if a machine never achieves the all-round performance of the human brain, nevertheless, in the centuries or millenniums to come, computers will be built superior to human beings from the point of a given task within quite wide limits.

CHAPTER 7

The Brain
and the Mind

IN the previous chapters, wherever we compared the performance of machines with that of the human brain we were always careful to say that the former can only imitate the mental processes or perform their equivalents. At all times we were very much aware that no machine can, so far, perform even the simplest mental processes in the same way as the human brain does. This is to say that, although the end results may be identical, the mechanism of the process is certainly very different in either case. We know how our machines work because we built them, but we have only a very rudimentary knowledge of the detailed working of the brain. What exactly happens in one's brain when one adds two and two nobody really knows. To our summary account of the working of the human brain from Chapter 5, we can now add that although many mental processes cannot be, so far, localised to distinct parts of the brain, nevertheless we know that some areas of the brain are connected with certain functions e.g. with visual perception, audible perception, speech, tactile perception in various parts of the body, etc. In fact, we can induce the perception of unspecified imaginary pictures or sounds by direct electrical simulation of the corresponding parts of the brain. Although this is a great jump forward, it still represents only the first few steps on the long road towards understanding the working of the brain. The knowledge of the correlation between the electrical excitation of many millions of cells and the resulting mental experiences is comparable with the statement of a technician that a given part of the computer, consisting of a great number of elements propagating electronic impulses, is concerned e.g. with reading input documents. Although such knowledge is better than nothing, it is a far cry from understanding the functions of a computer.

Of the physiological processes exactly corresponding to our seeing, hearing, speaking, imagining, learning, associating ideas etc., we know practically nothing as compared with the undoubtedly tremendous amount that there is to be known. What is the pattern of the connections between all these billions of cells constituting our brains? If a man develops a complex, a neurosis, or any kind of mental illness, what actually goes wrong physically in the brain? Nobody can offer more than the vaguest suggestions in reply, to questions of that nature. The techniques of measuring the processes in our brains have yet a long way to go to make physiology of the brain a truly quantitative science. If a man falls asleep, certain electrical signals produced by his brain and measurable by means of electrodes placed on his skull, change their frequency. This is instructive compared with the knowledge of fifty years ago, but it says little more about the workings of the brain than a flicker on a T.V. screen tells us about the internal construction of this receiver.

In the case of the brain, our ignorance about the correlation between the psychological and physiological phenomena, that is between our minds and our brains, is even deeper, because they appear to belong to essentially different categories. Let us consider for instance what happens when we perceive a certain object visually. As is well known, the electro-magnetic waves generated by a certain source of light are reflected by this object, which thereby modifies their pattern, frequency and intensity. The reflected waves reach our eyes, are focused by the lenses and produce certain chemical reactions in the light-sensitive retina. As a result, a train of electrical impulses is generated and conducted through the optical nerve to the brain. There the impulses are presumably processed into the patterns corresponding to the shape of the object, its colour, its position with respect to the observer, etc., although we know next to nothing about what these patterns are like and what is the correlation between the characteristic features of the patterns and those of the object. Nevertheless, we may assume that in principle this correlation could be established. However, here our understanding, even in principle, ends. We see the world not in terms of electro-magnetic radiation of a certain frequency

H

but in terms of shapes and colours. How a certain kind of radiation is transformed in our brains into the perception of greenness or redness as comprehended by the mind, we do not know at all. The three-dimensional resolution of our visual perceptions, the fact that a square is recognized as such even when we see it tilted so that the actual picture on the retina must be far from a square, the highly accurate estimates of velocities of moving bodies, and other similar abilities of the brain are amazing enough, but they can be, at least in principle, explained and may be simulated in an elementary fashion by existing computers. But the comprehension of electro-magnetic radiation of a certain intensity and frequency as a colour is a complete mystery. We perceive in terms of colours, sounds, tastes, smells and we think in terms of good, evil, bad, anger, love etc. All these perceptions and categories of our thinking are completely inexpressible in terms of any physical quantities. We can accurately describe the vibration of the air corresponding to given sounds in terms of the basic physical units of measurement, but the impression of this sound as perceived in our minds is entirely indescribable in physical terminology. Yet it is very real, as far as the hearer is concerned.

The almost complete inaccessibility of mental phenomena by any sort of physical instrument, so far, and the impossibility of expressing them in the usual physical terms, made some scientists attempt to ignore them completely and to base their whole psychology on these aspects of human beings which can be measured, that is on their external behaviour. Behaviourism seems consistent with the general scientific approach in the sense that we cannot discuss scientifically anything which cannot be measured and observed even in principle. And it certainly seems that although patterns of impulses in our brains may be measured, we have not the faintest idea how we could directly observe the mental creations of our minds. On the other hand the latter are so real to our consciousness that a psychology which rejects them seems to be no psychology at all. Our behaviour seems only a faithful shadow of our mental life. How can we make sense of the working of this shadow if we exclude the forces behind it?

One answer to this would be that what constitutes our real thinking are the trains of impulses in the brain, and the outcome of those purely physical processes in our nervous system activates our behaviour. The mental images and concepts of the mind, of which we are conscious, are only sorts of pictures accompanying the patterns of pulses, but the former have no influences on the latter. Hence, all our mental life, as we perceive it by introspection, would be just a series of images. We delude ourselves that we operate on the latter, because in fact they are given to us as determined by the outcomes of information-processing which takes place on a physical, neural level. It is obvious that the acceptance of either view is a matter of belief, and here we come to a very important and difficult point.

It has been said before that the whole scientific method can be challenged at its very foundations because it is based on an induction which can never be definitely verified. Now we will go even further. How do we know that our senses inform us about the true state of the world, in fact, how can we be certain that the latter exists at all? All that we receive are the trains of sense-data which we interpret in a manner peculiar to our minds. This interpretation may be correct or incorrect, but there is no compelling reason to assume either. Our senses can be obviously deceived by mirages, clever arrangements of sensory stimuli, etc. But, one objects, these are only tricks of nature or of man, and barring these, everything we experience through our senses is unquestionably true. Well, why should it necessarily be so? We could, after all, be dreaming the whole thing up. The sense data lead to consistent inferences, but dreams can sometimes be pretty consistent too, and they seem very real while they last. This sort of doubt has been expressed by philosophers hundreds of years ago, before anybody ever thought about the wave theory of matter or about electrical impulses in our nervous system. Today we can add a little to the subject.

We know with near certainty that all stimuli received by our sense organs from the environment are transmitted in the form of electro-chemical impulses along the nerves into the brain, which then perceives them in terms of the usual categories of colours, shapes, sounds, pain, pleasure etc. Now, if we only knew the exact pattern of impulses transmitted along the optical nerve, when for instance a man sees a beautiful woman, we could, by placing the suitable electrodes in the nerve, generate this pattern by some electrical means and send it straight to the brain. Then, as far as this man was concerned, the perception in his brain would be identical in both cases, so long as he restrained himself from trying to embrace the lady. He would be sorely disappointed in the simulated case, unless we injected another appropriate train of impulses into his nerves, transmitting the tactile sense-data, as soon as his arm reaches the position corresponding with the visual perception based on the first kind of simulation. An elementary (and clumsy) means of evoking the simulated sensorial perceptions by exciting the corresponding areas of the brain electrically has already been mentioned.

Hence our senses can be cheated, at least in principle, and with a refinement in techniques it might be difficult for the individual concerned to say which is the true sensory perception and which is not. The artificial excitation of various senses could be organized in a coherent pattern and coupled retro-actively with the reactions of the subject, via, for instance, a powerful computer. This could give a feeling of consistent reality, at least in certain simple situations. One can only speculate whether entertainment in the far distant future will be of this nature.

Lest somebody finds these speculations fanciful, at the elementary level of present day techniques, let us say a few words about how far we can trust our senses even when nobody is trying purposefully to deceive us. We know from the discoveries of modern physics that the real world is very different from what our senses tell us. To recall Eddington, the table on which I am writing is far from being a solid object, instead it is really a void, sparsely filled with protons, neutrons, electrons and other elementary particles; but because of fields of forces existing among them my hand does not go through. Nor is there anything static about this table, since the electrons contained in it encircle the nuclei of their atoms millions of times per second. And anyway, in the last analysis, the whole seemingly solid thing is only a complex pattern of probability waves. Can anybody imagine that? Of course, the whole account of my table is not really fair, because it all depends on how we define words like 'solid', 'static', 'hard', etc. We have no right to use these words in their everyday meaning when we are describing phenomena on a sub-atomic level. One thing is certain: whether our senses inform us correctly about the real nature of things in the world or whether they are deceiving us depends on the definition of the term 'the real nature of things'. Whole libraries have been written on the above problem and various philosophical schools offer different views. But sometimes I doubt whether the above term can possibly have any meaning at all. Maybe, it is just one of those categories of human thinking which can be used meaningfully up to certain limits of applicability and become meaningless beyond them.

Be that as it may, it is fairly obvious that there is no absolutely compelling argument to prove our senses trustworthy, and in order to believe them a certain minimum of good faith is necessary. Again, we confirm our previous conclusion that at the basis of any kind of world-view there are some axioms which are a matter of belief.

There exist some other kinds of perception which we shall call the extra-sensorial or inner perception. For example, no special sense organs are responsible for detecting the feeling of happiness or anger. When I am angry I am as sure about the reality of this angry feeling as I am about the existence of a tree when I see it. Somebody may say that inner feelings depend on a level of certain hormones in the blood produced by my endocrine glands. It might well be so, nevertheless, when under the fire of heavy artillery during the last war, I do not remember ever feeling the adrenalin in my veins, but I recall the feeling of fear and anger. In any case, the exact correlation between some more subtle feelings and the composition of chemical substances working in our brains is not known. So far there is fairly general agreement that the emotional states are knowable by means of inner perception only. The divergence of opinions starts when some people claim the possibility of obtaining knowledge through the inner or extra-sensory perception, not only about themselves but also about the external world. A mystic in an exalted state of mind knows, for instance, about the existence of God, and this feeling of God's presence is so strong, as far as a holy man is concerned, that it is more real than the very earth under his feet.

It is very easy to dismiss this sort of experience as hallucination, but do we have the right to do so? Why am I quite sure that I had a meal some time ago? Because I remember it. Now, assuming that I am trusting only in the reality of things revealed to me by my senses, a meal while it lasted was a sensory experience and therefore real. But the memory of it is un-doubtedly an experience through the inner perception. Some-body may object that I could verify my recollection of having a meal by perhaps certain crumbs left on the table, and hence by means of the actual sensory experience, or by asking the opinion of somebody else and seeing how it correlates with my memory. Even if I were now flying on a rocket to a distant star, never to return and quite incapable of further communication with the earth, I would still be completely sure about this meal in the past. Hence I would entirely trust my memory, or my inner perception. It is obvious that if we believed only in the reality of our immediate sensory experience in the strict sense of these words, and rejected everything else, then any kind of thinking would become impossible. We have to use our memories even in the most elementary discourse. How do I know that it is I who have written the previous sentence? Because I remember it. But any memory is not given through our senses, although it is plausible to assume that it consists of sense-data suitably processed and stored. And as far as consistency is concerned, how can we prove that the inner perception of the existence of God is inconsistent with anything?

Let us now consider how we know what other people think. All that we experience sensorially are certain vibrations of the air, caused by the motion of our interlocutor's vocal chords, which we perceive as sounds. By observing the correlation between certain objects or happenings and sounds, we form in our minds early ideas about the meaning of elementary words. By continuing this process for many years, and by defining the meanings of other words in terms of the words previously learned, we arrive at an extensive collection of sounds to which we attach certain meanings. The more often we employ them and notice how other people use them, the more precise the meanings of the words become to us, but we can never be really sure that anybody else understands a given word in the same way as we do.

Some words are easy to define operationally. For example, if I say 'close that window' and the other person obeys my command, I can be sure that the meaning of it is the same, or very nearly the same, for both of us. But how do I know the meaning of red? How do I know that what I am perceiving as red all the rest of the human race does not see as green and vice-versa? There is no way of finding out, since my reactions would be consistent with those of the others in either case. Of course, as we are all human beings it seems sensible to assume that we perceive fundamentally in a similar manner. But this is reasoning by analogy and hence involves an act of faith. By the same token, an intelligent being equipped with a different set of sense organs, capable of receiving quite different kinds of physical signals from the environment from those which the human senses can register, would perceive this world of ours in an entirely different way. Whose version of reality would now be true, his or ours? Presumably both, one for him, the other for us.

All perceptions are the creations of our minds and there is no obvious reason for rejecting these experiences obtained without the sensory apparatus. We are entitled, of course, to believe that everything that enters our minds must go first through the usual channels; sense-organs and nerves. But by doing so, we are assuming implicitly that our bodies can act only as machines. Nothing can enter the brain directly and no extra-sensory perception is possible. Theologians are often accused of anthropomorphism in their ideas of God. However, the view expressed above is a machinomorphism and is just as dogmatic. We have the right to assume it, provided we clearly realise that it is only an assumption. The mystic is as sure about the reality of his inner perceptions as we are about the reality of objects which we see, hear, or touch. The mystical state of mind may be dismissed as a kind of temporary mental illness, induced by severe physical privations; but there is not sufficient evidence for doing so.

Our discussion would be incomplete if we did not mention phenomena like telepathy, clairvoyance, telekinesis and the like. Serious scientific research is now proceeding in these fields, but the results are inconclusive. Experimental results are of a statistical nature and their interpretation leaves plenty of room for argument. We must be open-minded on these matters and should not reject them as entirely impossible. The progress of science uncovered more than one field of force—magnetic, gravitational, electrostatic, and the still imperfectly understood forces holding together the atomic nucleus, and it would be most surprising if we have discovered by now all the basic kinds of forces existing in nature. Our brains may command certain powers, not necessarily of an extra-material nature, about which we yet know nothing. When one thinks of the innumerable magical or mystical practices, which are probably as old as the human race itself, one cannot help wondering whether all of them are really bunk. The majority undoubtedly are, but maybe there is among them some residual core of sense. Of course, magic and mystic rituals can be dismissed as the attempt of pre-scientific man to give an interpretation to physical phenomena, and to endeavour to manipulate his environment accordingly. They can also be accounted for, at least partly, by the confusion arising in the primitive mind between the words themselves and the real objects which they denote. But it is also possible that our civilization, concentrating through the ages on direct physical experiment and on rational conscious thinking, has lost the techniques to manipulate some of the other powers which the human mind may command.

Perhaps the least explainable feature of the human mind is its self-awareness. If there is anything in the world of which I am quite sure it is the fact of my own existence, in the sense that I am conscious of my own being. When regaining consciousness after an accident I might doubt for a while my being alive, but I would be still unshakeably certain in perceiving myself as a being, for if I ever doubted that, then everything else would immediately cease to have any sense whatever. Excluding for the moment sub-conscious phenomena, whose existence we have no reason to doubt, we can say that everything else in our mental life, as we are aware of it, is given to us through our consciousness. This sounds like tautology, but what we want to say here is that even the ideas of behaviourism, which attempt to disregard creations of the mind and to reduce the whole of mental life to its external behaviouristic manifestations, have arisen in the consciousness of the originators of this school of psychology. All rational thinking operates consciously on mental concepts, or at least we think so.

If we assume then that our real thinking takes place on a physiological level, we obviously delude ourselves that we can influence it by operating on the level of mental concepts, because in this case they are only a moving picture of the real processes and we could not influence the former at all. It is again our old story that if we are nothing else but matter and energy, then we cannot help what we are doing, we simply have no say at all. But even then the question still remains—'What are those concepts or mental images and what is this "I" which can perceive them?'

Various theorems of how the human consciousness might have come into being have been proposed and we will now examine some of them.

It is well known that any action which one performs repeatedly requires a progressively decreasing amount of conscious control. Thus walking, which demands quite complicated co-ordination of muscles, is largely sub-conscious. During long marches it is not uncommon for a marcher to fall asleep and yet still keep on walking in step with the others. In many industrial establishments one can observe workers repeatedly performing complicated operations without paying much attention to them, chatting among themselves and obviously being only marginally conscious of their work. This seems to be a sort of mental economy. Our conscious thinking is believed to constitute the highest level of our mental life. When we have learned by conscious effort to perform certain actions, the centres of the brain which are somehow correlated to consciousness gradually delegate the control of this action to the sub-conscious layers. In this way the consciousness frees itself for new tasks. It is an old truth that we can concentrate on only one thing at a time. Whether it is literally true or not, it is obvious that the illuminating spotlight of our consciousness can cover only a very limited area. If a condition of performing any action were the fully conscious perception of it, we could do very little. Our consciousness is only like a top grade controller, checking here and there and leaving the bulk of the work to the sub-conscious centres. Some processes like digestion, heart-beating and many reflexes are entirely outside conscious control, although it is apparently possible to gain control of some of them by means of special exercises. Facts of this kind led some people to believe that consciousness and self-consciousness are phenomena of the zone of evolution and are the products of the latter. We are conscious mainly of new things, of new kinds of actions which we perform, hence we are conscious of our adaptation to an environment while it is actually taking place. Once we achieve this adaptation, presumably by trial and error, the finally chosen response becomes routine and sinks slowly into sub-consciousness. On the higher plane, we can say that due to evolution (we mean here mainly the cultural evolution of the human race) the type of human personality predominant in a given community gradually alters. These changes are usually originated by a few exceptional individuals, who break the 'cake of custom'. It is well known that such people seem to possess an intensified consciousness of their doings and they are very aware, often in a painful manner, of the battle in their minds raging between the old and new ideology. Hence their self-consciousness is more acute. Extending this argument we can say that our feeling of self-consciousness is due to the change taking place in one's personality.

Others consider consciousness as a product of the coalescence of many nervous processes into one central nervous system. Hence consciousness would be a result of the integration of our mental life. In a similar manner, the distinction existing in a person's mind between his body and everything else could be explained by the saying that the body continuously generates kinesthetical sensory data like pain, touch, position of the limbs, etc. The resulting perceptions are often of great intensity and connected with a high emotional content. Some of them are always present and this continuity and repetivity distinguish the perceptions due to the body from those due to the environment. The latter are much more differentiated and non-permanent. Hence the idea of one's own body as being something essentially different from everything else develops from infancy. Characteristic confirmation of this sort of argument are the psychological effects of the long use of an artificial aid, for instance, false teeth. After a time one tends to associate them, at least while they are actually in the mouth, with the perception of one's own body.

Still another theory suggests that consciousness is of a social origin. Through years of observation of other human beings and through continuous interacting with them, we form in our minds the concepts of what other people are like. In consequence, we also develop the idea of how others see us. This process starts in the early days of our life and by continuous thinking on these lines, largely sub-consciously one would add, we finally develop the idea of ourselves. Hence, according to this theory our consciousness would be a self-portrait as others see us. It would be most interesting to investigate whether a child who grew up exclusively with animals is still self-conscious, and if so, how it used to perceive itself before the first contacts with the human beings were established. Such children have been found on a few occasions, as mentioned at the very beginning of this book, but I do not know whether any competent psychological investigations have been conducted on them.

The concept of consciousness occupies the central position in the teachings of many mystics, in particular those of Eastern origin. According to them, there are several levels of consciousness, broadly speaking, the highest only rarely achievable by means of prolonged and strenuous physico-mental exercises. This looks like an agreeable argument. We all know that our consciousness of ourselves and of the environment depends on state of health, emotional excitement, particular happenings around us and many other factors. It seems plausible that by appropriate exercises one can heighten one's feeling of consciousness. The controversy starts when some people claim to reach awareness of the existence of God or to obtain understanding of the universe in the highest state of consciousness. According to them, this is the only way towards true knowledge, the latter being quite inaccessible by any kind of rational thinking. Hence, from this point of view our Western science is really a waste of time.

Clearly, inner perception cannot be dismissed lightly. The fact that a mystic's utterances about his experiences in an exalted state of mind are usually imprecise and incoherent is also easily explainable. These states are extremely rare and little wonder that there are no words in everyday language to express them. The meaning of words depends on the correspondence of the mental images of speaker and hearer; we will have something more to say on this subject later. Here we can merely state that as people never normally experience the mystic states in their lives, they simply cannot have in their minds the corresponding concepts or images, which any words could evoke. In fact, if a mystic could describe clearly his experiences in everyday language, in such a fashion that anybody could get a fairly good idea about them, he would be suspect, because such mystic experiences would be, by the argument above, nothing special. It is striking how the accounts of the mystics, living at different ages and belonging to different civilizations and creeds, give an impression of similarity, although we can only guess what they are really trying to express. One cannot help the feeling that if these unusual people could only meet, they would very well understand each other's experiences. The modern psychiatrist would probably say that due to similar kinds of mental and physical mortifications, similar kinds of mental disturbances develop leading to the same kind of hallucinations and delusions, and he may be right. He could also add that the mystic apparently can do little with his supposedly superior knowledge, as far as the manipulation of the environment is concerned. Although this is in the main true, it must not be forgotten that some parts of our scientific knowledge also cannot be easily used in the manipulative sense. We might know, for instance, a great deal about some peculiar mountain range on the moon through astronomical observations, but unless we get there, we could not possibly affect these mountains by virtue of our knowledge of them. It may be that the mystic's understanding of the universe is on a level which intrinsically could not be useful in any physical manipulations of our environment.

Lastly, we have to examine the views which deny the existence of any single self-conscious centre in the human person altogether. This is very evident in Indian thought, which maintains that the concepts of one's distinctive 'I' is an illusion, leading to all the miseries of life like greed, emotional involvement, etc. The eradication of this illusion and the acceptance of the conclusion that any supposedly distinct self-conscious being is only a part of a greater whole, is the chief aim of life-long exercises. Carried to a logical conclusion it should lead to the dissolution of personality and the merging with the eternal Nirvana or the greater Mind or Self of the World. This ideology is based partly on the evident inconsistency in human behaviour, the succession of various moods to which we are all subject, the obvious battles in our minds between contradictory feelings and emotions, and so on. All these suggest the lack of a single directing organ in the human mind, and make it plausible to assume that the latter consists of a number of semi-independent centres fighting among themselves for control of the whole human behaviour. Hence the behaviour of a given person appears different, depending on which centre gains control at the given period. Similarly, what we consider normally as volition may be seen as the result of the intensity of various mental associations of the moment.

In certain cases of mental disease loss of consciousness and the dissolution of personality are apparent. Some of these unlucky people become conscious of being somebody or something other than their normal selves. Some of them exhibit drastic changes of mood, as if to confirm the complete lack of any central organ controlling, or at least moderating, the activities of all parts of the mind. In the bad cases 'the split personality', as it is commonly called, may become complete. Such a person acts as if several different personalities inhabited the same body and were taking control of it alternatively, sometimes even without being aware of each other's existence.

In conclusion, we see again that what is obvious to some may be uncertain to others. One can be perhaps easily open-minded about various theories explaining the origin of consciousness because they do not dispute the fundamental fact of the existence of the latter. But the views denying it altogether are much harder to accept and one wonders whether the extinction of the feeling of self-consciousness can be thoroughly achieved. And if so, is it because of the merging with the superior Self, embracing 'I' and 'you', or is it a hard won mental illness. As in cases of all fundamental concepts, it is a matter of belief which view one accepts.

Whether a machine exhibiting self-consciousness will ever be constructed we can only guess. In any case it is very difficult to imagine how we could possibly check the self-consciousness of a machine. It certainly would not be enough for a computer to print the message 'I am aware of my existence', since any of the present-day machines could easily be programmed to do that. If the computer of the future could react rationally, in a manner indistinguishable from the human being for all practical purposes, then the conclusion would probably be obvious. But a machine could exhibit the feeling of self-consciousness in a manner very different from man, making the whole problem extremely involved.

As seen from the foregoing, the gap between the brain and the mind seems unbridgeable. The former operates on a physical level (whether we follow mechanistic or vitalistic philosophy) although the processes involved are unimaginably complex. The latter works with concepts which are inexpressible in terms

of any physical quantities, as we understand them. It is easy to
see that in this situation the idea of a soul, an entity essentially
different from anything material, 'inhabiting' the brain, becomes
very suggestive. However, the concept of an extra-material soul,
operating through the brain and the body as its tools, creates
immediate difficulties. If a soul is fundamentally non-matter or
non-energy how then can it make contact with the latter?
How can it direct them? And again, how does the soul originate
and where does it come from? The development of any material
system is continuous and it is easy to see, in principle, how the
body and brain originate by the union of the parental cells and
how they grow, absorbing matter and energy from the environment. But the mind or soul, what could possibly be its origin?
There is something here which completely baffles human understanding. Many philosophers, pondering on the above problems,
were forced in the end to assume the existence of God, an
omnipotent Being, Who creates the minds or of Whom the
latter are parts. God could also co-ordinate the activities of mind
and brain, either in the sense of synchronizing the two parallel
but essentially non-interacting processes, or by his continuous
intervention enabling the spiritual mind to control the material
body. The fundamentals of any religious view are a matter of
belief and as such cannot be disputed. Here we can only remark
that such views offer little help in our investigations of the
problems of mind and brain, so long as we remain on rational
ground, because they simply substitute one mystery for another,
even greater.

Mind cannot be directly observed, not even in principle, at
the present stage of our knowledge. We infer its existence from
our own innermost experiences, as discussed in previous para-
graphs of this chapter, and by an analogy we attribute conscious
minds to other people. Consequently we consider some physically
observable actions performed by these people, as the manifestations of the activity of their minds. Whether we believe
in the immortality of mind or soul is again a religious matter,
but as far as the observable, supposed manifestations of mind's
activity are concerned, they come to an abrupt end with the
person's death. Hence, for all we can infer from observations,
mind is born and it dies. This suggests strongly that the mind is
somehow intimately connected with the brain and is not a
separate entity. During deep sleep the outward manifestations

of mind's activity cease, together with the inner perception of the self-consciousness (we ignore dreams which are not always present during sleep). If the mind were a separate entity how could this happen? It is easy to say that, because the layers of brain corresponding to the conscious phenomena become inactive during sleep, the mind cannot operate, because its tools are temporarily out of use. But this is not how we feel. We do not have a feeling during sleep that consciousness has been made temporarily impotent in its outward manifestations because the brain is 'switched off'. If one of our limbs is temporarily paralysed, we are perfectly conscious of this fact and aware at the same time of our unaltered 'selves'. Although we want to move the paralysed limb, it does not respond. We do not experience anything like that during sleep, as we simply lose consciousness altogether. Hence the soul or mind cannot even be aware of itself without the active brain. What can it do, then, on its own? If the answer is 'nothing', then what need or right have we to assume the mind as a separate entity? This sort of argument can be used to disprove the existence of a spiritual 'self'. A true self of spiritual nature would have to be at least capable of self-consciousness without the help of any-thing or anybody else. It would also be permanent and im-mutable as comprehended by itself and all changes in the character of its activities would be due to alterations in the physical apparatus, which is under the command of the 'self'. Some may also add that a true 'self' could not be born and could not die, because this would mean that its existence is the out-come of other phenomena or causes lying outside the 'self'. Do we ever experience anything like that?

Our minds obviously can be affected by various drugs, by the secretions of our glands, by the state of our bodies, by innumerable happenings in the environment, by the kind of food we eat (e.g. lack of certain vitamins can produce profound changes in the personality) and in every case we have no feeling of the tools of the mind going out of action and of our inner selves remaining unaltered. On the contrary, in all these examples it is 'we' who change, if only temporarily, in our very deepest self-conscious 'selves'. It seems, then, that we have no right to separate the soul or the mind from the brain. On the other hand there appears to be no way of connecting them conceptually either. Mind occupies no space, and it cannot be located anywhere in it, unless by an act of faith, when we say that the mind is in the brain. But what does the word 'is' mean anyway, when referred to an entity which cannot be described in terms of the usual physical categories? Mind is not a form of energy, although minds do communicate among themselves by the energy-systems consisting of nervous-networks, vocal chords, vibrations of air and organs of audible perception. So in the words of Sherrington, 'mind goes more ghostly than a ghost'.

Mind cannot be divided into component parts like any other system. This non-granular nature of mind, its wholeness and the integration of its activities, which incidentally are also the characteristics of even the simplest living organism, lead some people to doubt whether we shall ever be able to comprehend the nature of mind and of life, even if the latter are purely physico-chemical phenomena. This objection is raised on the grounds that the investigating techniques of human beings, and in particular of the scientists, are of an analytical nature. When confronted with complex phenomena we dissect it into simpler processes which we then consider in turn. Our description of almost any object consists of the enumeration of several characteristic features of the latter. Hence we split the concept of the whole into separate simpler concepts. The analytical way of thinking seems to be a characteristic feature of the conscious mind, because our very language is predominantly suitable for this kind of description. One does not forget here that an idea like 'a tree' is of a synthetic nature because it refers to all trees and not only to a particular specimen. But we always seem to start with an analysis, for instance, by saying that a tree is something with such and such properties, and we build a more general and synthetic concept from the latter. The above method undoubtedly works, as our mastery of nature clearly demonstrates. But there may be a limit to the applicability of this scheme of thinking. Certain things may exist which cannot be split into parts, not even conceptually, and can only be comprehended as a single indivisible whole or not at all. It has been suggested that life may belong to this category. Somewhat analogous ideas have been put forward in the field of psychology by the Gestalt school, which maintains that we always perceive first the whole pattern and then split it into its constituents in our mind instead of perceiving the elements first and building the pattern from them subsequently.

It may also be that we will never find out what life is, because the very observation of the essential life-phenomena would disintegrate it or kill it, somewhat as the observation of an electron cannot fail to affect its motion. I doubt whether the situation regarding the research of life-processes is so pessimistic. Life seems after all to be a phenomenon on a molecular or atomic scale and not a sub-atomic level. There seems to be no compelling reason why the observing system has to disturb the functioning of the living body under observation, or disturb the integration of its activities. But it may well be that life will elude us until we develop synthetic methods of investigation, perhaps, as opposed to the present analytical method. Emphasis on the wholeness of the performance of the system and on the synthesis of all processes within a complex whole is already very evident in modern cybernetics.

Examination of the evolutionary development of the brain through the successive stages of living beings towards the higher levels of complexity throws some light on the main tendency of this process. First of all, it can be seen that a powerful brain is a distinctive advantage to an animal. The huge reptiles of the past had brains the size of a nut and with all their strength had lost the day to the generally much smaller but more highly organized mammals (the blue-whale, the largest animal which has ever lived on this planet, is an exception so far as body-size is concerned). Hence the evidence available strongly suggests that the complexity of the internal organization and its integration, corresponding to a more versatile and intelligent behaviour, is at a heavy premium in nature. Body-building alone, unaccompanied by the corresponding mental development, is of little use, as the fate of the dinosaurus can show us.

Higher forms of brain developed from preceding lower forms not by evolving into something entirely new but, broadly speaking, by adding a new part to the previous construction. Hence we see new layers of the brain added to the old, the former corresponding to the higher mental functions. The higher the animals stand on the evolutionary tree, the larger and better developed are the layers corresponding to these higher functions, as compared with the parts of the brain performing more simple operations. It also appears that these higher centres exercise

I

relatively more of the control in higher types of living beings. Of course, one can object that the size and structure of the brain determines in no small way where we put the animal on the ladder, so maybe the more brainy animals are higher only according to our definition. Nevertheless, these more intelligent animals are more successful in the sense that they command a wider range of environments. We must not however forget that many animals of a relatively primitive organization survived hundreds of millions of years substantially unchanged. This would indicate that such species achieved nearly perfect adaptation to their environmental niche, and thus became stabilized and arrested in their evolutionary development. Generally speaking, however, these species can exist only in a very restricted range of environmental conditions.

The procession of brains culminates with the human brain, exhibiting not only a very large size relative to that of the human body (although some not-so-high animals exceed us in the brain/body weight-ratio), but also possessing enormous cortical parts. The brain/body weight-ratio is not quite a fair comparison, because the brain must provide the end points for all nerves spread on the surface of the body. As the body's weight increases with the cube of the animal's dimensions but the skin's area only with the square, the part of the brain corresponding to the surface-area nerves would be relatively smaller for a larger animal. But the significance of an enormous human cortex is unmistakable. Cortex represents the most highly developed and organized part of the brain, and as such is usually associated with the highest mental functions.

Here an interesting observation can be made. If the mind is inseparably connected with the brain, then by an anology we should attribute minds to all other animals possessing brains, however primitive. Naturally, we could only guess what these minds are like. But perhaps the mind is only, or at least predominantly, connected with the most complex cortical parts. This would connect causally the unique development of the human cortex, compared with that of any other animal, with the uniqueness of human mind. Judging by the outward manifestations of mental powers, only the species homo is 'sapiens'. Although animals, at least the higher ones, do exhibit some kind of activity which could plausibly correspond to certain mental processes, nevertheless even in the case of the higher apes we seem to be dealing with a very different and much lower level of mental phenomena.

The development of cortex areas in man, supposedly connected with higher mental processes as exemplified by rational thinking, points the way towards future developments. The bulk of human mental activity can still proceed on the sub-conscious level, but even if our conscious processes are only a thin crust, this is the best part of our mental life. The very idea that we can heal the sub-conscious mind by bringing its entanglements into the light of consciousness implies the superiority of the latter in dealing with complex situations. In his later years Freud, 'the father of sub-consciousness', paid increasing attention to the domination of the 'Ego', the conscious part of the mind. In connection with this, one cannot help feeling that all the so called 'life philosophers' are fundamentally mistaken. Here is our emerging mind, a rational faculty trying to arrange the mass of sense-data into meaningful patterns, trying to make some sense of a seemingly bewildering variety of phenomena in nature. Then somebody comes along, be it Lao-Tze, Rousseau, Nietsche or Bergson and says 'You had better stop trying, because you are barking up the wrong tree. Not only will you never make any real progress on the rational path but the straight-jacket of your rational thinking severely limits the activities of your emotions, feelings and instincts. And only these can get you somewhere. Go back to the ancient way of living and rely on the uncomprehendable Tao (Lao-Tze), get rid of the perverting influence of civilization and go back to nature (Rousseau), put your will-power before your reason (Nietsche), rely on your intuition and *élan vitale* (Bergson)'. Where is all this supposed to lead us? Agreed, rational faculties are still relatively weak, imperfect, often mistaken and unable to comprehend at all many things. But is this the reason for their condemnation and rejection? The whole development of human civilization and knowledge, from paleolithic times, testifies to the progressive growth of the faculty of rational thinking. Bright patches of rational thought, existing here and there in separate fields, grow and coalesce covering increasingly large areas.

To defy rationality is to condemn in the end the whole effort of human civilization. This is, of course, admissible if one is inclined this way. Maybe rational thinking and the development of civilized life is one of those blind alleys of evolution which lead nowhere, an experiment of Nature which is unsatisfactory and has to be scrapped. Maybe the instinctive way of living is the only possible way in the long run and any sort of rational thinking leads inevitably from the stone-axe to the hydrogen bomb and complete annihilation. If so, then after the apocalyptic catastrophe occurs, Nature may be, figuratively speaking, very sorry for having tried the human experiment at all, as in the flashes of thermonuclear bombs men may well perish together with all the higher forms of life, developed through hundreds of millions of years of evolution. Possibly so, but personally I believe that life, which after two billions years becomes self-conscious for the first time in the human form, endowed with rational thinking, will successfully overcome the difficulties and develop towards an even more rational level, most probably through the better use of the powerful instrument already in existence, the human brain.

We have said before that rationality seems to be only an instrument for satisfying the aims of emotional urges and desires. Although emotions and urges can be in turn modified and altered by intensive rational thinking, some people would say that this interaction takes place only on the superficial level but basic urges cannot be affected. Whether this is true or not is debatable, because modern psychology shows the tendency to consider a new born baby as almost a complete blank, a self-organizing system which under the influence of environment can develop into almost anything. But even assuming that the fundamental, unalterable instincts do exist and cannot be substantially affected by rational effort, there is still no reason for surrendering for ever our future to them. Admittedly, we cannot imagine at the moment how anything else but emotions could be at the basis of our mental life. Even if we prefer rational processes, this preference itself is a desire, hence an emotion. Nevertheless our rationality, in the fully developed form, is a way of thinking completely incomprehensible to any animal. Is it too fanciful to admit the possibility, that future developments on the path of rational processes will bring us to a level of mental life, which would be, at the moment, so incomprehensible to us as differential calculus is to a dog?

CHAPTER 8

The Synthesis

IN the present chapter we will summarize what has been said previously about life, brain, mind and machines. We will suggest how the reconciliation of materialism with human freedom might be achieved. We will also try to establish the correlation between the two apparently essentially distinct groups of phenomena—those of a neurological and those of a psychological character. While discussing these extremely involved problems two things must be borne in mind. The first is that human knowledge in these fields is at a very rudimentary level. Secondly, the human language, in terms of which the problems of life and mind must necessarily be discussed, is an inadequate tool for that purpose. Let us consider the implications of this second statement.

Remembering what we have said about how the meaning attached to certain sounds forms gradually in our minds, it is clear that the semantic content of any word is only imperfectly known. Although some words are nearly perfectly definable, operationally, the meaning of the majority of them can be stated formally only by the employment of other words. Since the latter must be, in their turn, similarly determined, we deal here with an endless series of definitions, which in view of the limited number of words in any language, must be necessarily a vicious circle. However precise we may be in our definitions and however good is our logic, the meaning of any word depends on the mental image attached to a given sound, and the former can never be perfectly described. How can we possibly explain the meaning of a colour to a blind person? If the mental image of a colour is completely absent in the mind there is no way of creating it by means of words. How can we define the meaning of being, of time or space, if not by using some other words expressing similar ideas? Few words have exactly identical meanings, hence to express semantic content of any word by means of its substitutes is nearly always imprecise. We can learn the meaning of a word really only by observing how it is being used in relation to objects and actions and in conjunction with other words. Hence, rejecting the possibility of the presence of a priori ideas in our minds, the only conclusion is that we associate certain groups of perceptive experiences, suitably processed in our minds, with the sound representing the given word.

It is reasonable, then, that two people will rarely arrive at exactly the same meaning for any word. When two men look at a typical table they both call it by a proper name. But if we confronted them with a series of objects passing very gradually in appearance from a typical table to a typical chair it is a fair guess that each of these two men would select different objects in the series which will be to him no longer a table but more like a chair. This is because the mind of any man produces the idea of a table from the common features of a certain group of objects. The set of these features results from his perceptive processes and ability to discriminate and generalise, both of which depend on innate capabilities and on learning, hence they are most unlikely to be identical in two individuals. One continually hears arguments based on the fact that a given thing appears to one person like this and to another person like something else. This is true even in the case of simple concepts, but what happens when we come to more advanced ideas? Obviously the meaning attached to the latter must be even more vague and imprecise. And the definition of involved notions by means of simpler ones, although helpful, can never attain perfection.

Vagueness in the meaning of words does not matter in the common use of language, as a high precision of expression is not required. The trouble starts when we begin to employ our language, which, after all, has been developed through the millenia for the purpose of everyday use, in the discussions of abstract philosophical problems. As the concepts of classical physics do not apply in the subatomic world or under relativistic conditions, so our language, grown in the conditions of common life, is not really suitable for use at much more advanced levels. As these heights words are being employed beyond the limits of their applicability, leading to endless argument and confusion. Does this support certain derogatory views about metaphysics and philosophy as useless intellectual activities?

Definitely not. The brave attempts of thinkers wrestling with the most difficult problems have led to the formulation of abstract ideas of a progressively higher order. This is perhaps the essence of the intellectual progress of the race. Any world view, which every thinking human being must possess as a set of basic reactions to his environment, belongs essentially to the field of metaphysics. However, the more difficult the ideas discussed are, the more effort should be shown in the manner of their expression.

This is not to deny that there are certain ideas extremely difficult to communicate. In view of what we have said about the meaning of words, one could expect that at any stage of the development of an intellectually progressing civilization, there are bound to be certain concepts, only dimly outlined in the minds of the intellectual leaders, which cannot therefore be generally comprehended and communicated, as perhaps the corresponding words have not yet been created. Perhaps certain ideas cannot be communicated directly at all, but only by means of certain types of long meditations, which bring the mind to a desired state.

Let us now summarise briefly some of our findings of the previous three chapters.

We have stated that although the phenomena of life are still only very incompletely understood, the field of our ignorance in these matters is rapidly contracting and there are strong reasons for supposing that life is essentially an extremely complex physio-chemical process, all aspects of which are explainable in terms of natural laws, without recourse to any mysterious forces. Further, although the mechanism of processes on a molecular level in the living cell is not yet known, nevertheless the microscopic or gross features of living beings, like homeostasis, perception of environment and reaction to it, purposeful behaviour, feeding, growth, breeding, and even the creation of the form of increasing complexity, can either be directly simulated by experimental machines or at least are theoretically possible. Also, the artificial creation of living matter is likely to take place in the foreseeable future.

On the other hand, the correlation between the physiological processes in the brain and psychological processes of the mind is very little understood and largely unknown. The mind is not a form of energy and its working cannot be described in terms of physical concepts. The mind possesses the capacity of consciousness of its own existence and of that of the environment. Although various theories explaining the phenomena of consciousness have been suggested, none really appears convincing and the former remains still a mystery. Whether mental processes take place on a level of the mind or whether the latter is only a pale reflection of the neural processes of the brain, we do not know, but our consciousness of the mental life or inner perception tells us that we function, at least partially, at mind's level. And, unless we feel inclined towards the mechanomorphism, there is no reason to trust more the outer than the inner perception. In fact, all perceptions of the environment of which we are conscious we receive finally at the mind's level, similarly to the perceptions of our inner mental life. However, we do not disregard here the fact that our conscious life represents only a relatively small portion of the total mental activity, the bulk of which occurs at the subconscious level. Also, although we believe that rational thinking is the highest form of the mind's workings, we are nevertheless aware that this mode of thinking is, at the present stage of man's evolutionary development rather a tool of the subconscious urges and desires than their master. In addition, we keep an open mind with regard to the super-natural phenomena like clairvoyance, telekinesis, etc.

Finally, we observe that science not only explains a progressively greater number of the phenomena of life in terms of natural laws but also discovers certain laws applicable to our thinking, to our emotional life, to our perception of our environment or to our modes of reacting to it. It cannot be denied that many observable regularities exist in human mental life, and that the behaviour of an individual or of a group is predictable to a considerable extent. But human behaviour does not appear to be entirely predictable. This may be either solely because we have not yet discovered all the laws in that field or because the human being possesses a certain essential freedom of choice, however limited. Our consciousness tells us that we are free, that we can choose.

Now, if one accepts that we are nothing but extremely complex physio-chemical systems, whether of deterministic or probablistic character, one is bound to admit the validity of all the appalling consequences of unbridled materialism, which lead finally to the contradiction of all our accepted values, beliefs, and even of the concepts of everyday language. Any purely physical system, in the conventional meaning of the word, cannot help doing what it is actually doing, it has no choice, no say in the matter. Its actions depend entirely on its internal state and on that of the environment and no amount of sophistication in systems structure, the inclusion of feedback and of random parameters, can change this fact. Hence, on the basis of pure materialism everything at the end becomes senseless, since even the man who is discussing the problem cannot help saying what he is actually saying.

It is obvious that what is needed is not the continuation of the dichotomy between the mind or spirit and the body, between the vitalistic and mechanistic theories, or between materialism and the belief in free will. Each of the above theories or concepts expresses the truth, but only a part of the truth and thus none expresses the whole truth. This seems to be the basic reason of endless controversies, ranging through millennia, about these fundamental problems. The supporters of either side managed to produce many plausible arguments, but neither view was entirely acceptable; each covered only a part of reality and is not applicable to the whole of it. There is something in these basic questions which seems to elude the human mind and the concepts of our language appear to be inadequate for the task. This may be fundamental and unavoidable. After all, if we are a part of the universe, how can we hope ever really to understand it? The whole cannot be contained in its part so there will always be some problems hidden from our knowledge. And the questions of mind or of free will in the physical universe may be some of these. However, we hope that the situation is not quite so pessimistic; at least, we can try to make some progress. What is most required is not more new facts but rather the discovery of a new way of looking at the latter, or in other words, the creation of new ideas of a synthetic nature embracing both life and the inorganic world, mind and body, materialism and free will. Such tendencies appear vaguely in the writings of certain contemporary thinkers and in the next section we attempt to study them a little further.

This is our thesis. We postulate that mind and matter are not two separate things but two different aspects of a single, more general entity. The aspect of mind manifests itself in extremely complex and closely integrated systems; it is not produced by them but is an essential feature of them. Matter, in the conventional meaning, does not create the mind any more than mind creates matter, but the entity embracing both concepts can manifest itself in two ways. It may be admissible that the mind is a theshold phenomenon and it is apparent only if the complexity and integration of the system exceeds a certain level. Alternatively, perhaps the rudimentary traces of the mind are connected with any arrangement of matter. The complexity of the system is not sufficient in itself to exhibit the mind aspect clearly, but the internal relationships in the system must be of a certain character for this to happen. What kind of relationships exhibit mind we will not even try to guess, but close integration of the system seems to be among the essential conditions. The mind-matter entity, of which the whole universe consists, has the tendency to organize itself into progressivly complex arrangements leading to greater manifestations of the mind aspect.

This thesis may at first sight appear far-fetched, but after a little close consideration it becomes perhaps more plausible. We start by pointing out that matter and energy were treated through the centuries as two completely distinct entities. Both were considered indestructible; everybody familiar with elementary classical physics remembers the law of conservation of mass and the law of conservation of energy. The changing of matter into energy, or vice versa, seems preposterous to our common-sense thinking. We cannot imagine how something solid can disappear, cease to exist at all as matter and appear as pure energy. Even less can we imagine how a particle of matter can be created from pure energy. Yet modern physics has demonstrated both theoretically and experimentally that matter and energy are transmutable. The conceptual step which must be taken in passing from the complete separation of matter and energy to the admission of their transmutability is not necessarily smaller or easier to take then the fusion of mind and matter into a single, more general entity. Whether this kind of ideology can be called an extended materialism or not is a matter of definition, and there seems to be little point in discussing it at this stage. One thing is certain; matter connected intimately with the mind, tending towards the formation of extremely complex systems and exhibiting manifestly the mind aspect, is very different from the spiritless matter of conventional materialism.

If the above views are admitted our whole outlook on the universe has to change completely. Although very strange initially to our customary ways of comprehension, this new world view seems to remove many of the old contradictions and in this lie its greatest merits.

The second law of thermodynamics, which ranks among the most fundamental physical laws and claims universal validity, states that in any closed system (completely separated from the rest of the universe), undergoing the irreversible change of state (the latter term applies to almost all natural processes), the entropy increases. In other words the system passes from the more to the less organized states. Considering now this general tendency towards chaos and uniformity on a cosmic scale, the logical conclusion is that the universe, once created, must as a whole, be moving to the progressively less differentiated states. Hence, although the process may take more than thousands of millions of years, perfect uniformity over the whole cosmic space must finally be achieved or maximum entropy reached, when nothing further will ever happen. This is often referred to as the heat-death of the universe. These pessimistic conclusions are avoided if we assume, according to our views previously exposed, that in fact there are two universal and opposing tendencies in action: one towards chaos and the other towards order and their interplay is responsible for all the phenomena in nature. Additionally, the hypothesis gives the universe an intellectually satisfying symmetry. It could also be said that it revives the old Freudian concepts of the will to live (sex instincts) and the will to destroy and die (apparent in many normal and psychotic states respectively).

The apparent freedom of the human being is not now in contradiction with the natural laws but it becomes one of them. The mind manifests itself in extremely complex systems and freedom of choice seems to be an essential attribute of the mind. As the creation of complex systems is assumed to be the essential feature of the matter-energy-mind entity, the capacity for producing conditions where the laws, which are valid elsewhere, do not fully apply, becomes also the feature of this general entity and as such is a law of nature. Hence, all the appalling consequences of materialism can be avoided without recourse to mysterious super-natural entities. The dignity of the human being is restored by pointing out that he is the most complex system known, so far, in the universe. Therefore, far from being just lumps of matter and not really different from the dirt under our feet, we are the supreme expression of a tendency towards organization, and if we assume that the latter has an upper hand in the cosmos, we are the very spearhead of the universal advance. Although each of us has to die and return to dust, we are while we live, the highest beings which nature has produced. In this sense, all the evolution of inorganic and organic matter has, up to the present stage, been so to speak for our benefit, and the whole of nature has been working for us for thousands of millions of years. This is surely as good as to dwell on a planet around which the whole universe rotates. The essential freedom of extremely complex systems, of which the human being is a supreme example, permits us to discuss meaningfully morality and ethics, maintain our customary values, and talk in terms of purpose or good and evil. We can now praise or condemn a person for his or her actions, although while we are doing so we must always keep in mind that human freedom of choice is in all probability more limited that it now appears to be as many more regularities in human behaviour will undoubtedly be discovered in the future. The development of an individual and of society ceases to be governed, in our new world view, entirely by impersonal laws and the conscious and wilful contributions of free mind also play an important role. Effort and heroism do not appear useless, as they do in the framework of conventional materialism.

The infliction of pain or the wanton killing of a human being acquires the stigma of the supreme evil. Far from bringing man down, the new world view enables the development of full-blooded humanism. We may be made of the same matter and energy as the rest of the world but these two aspects of reality are not the only ones. There exists another: the mind, expression of the relationships between things. This organization or relationship between various material objects is just as real and essential as matter or energy themselves. One may say it is superior to them. We are the supreme example of organization and mind, and thus the true lords of the earth.

The subconscious no longer appears baffling, or threatening us with its dictatorship. At the highest conscious level freedom of mind is most evident, but it gradually disappears at the lower mental levels, where the aspect of mind interacts and merges with the aspect of matter, the latter manifesting itself through the neural processes. Hence although the subsconciousness has an enormous influence, and is probably predominant at the present stage of evolutionary development, it is not entirely dictatorial. Our mind is very young on the geological scale, in fact, just emerging from nature. No wonder then that it is still weak, confused and highly imperfect. It is just becoming aware of its tremendous power and flexing its muscles for action in the ages to come. But to help it means to develop our conscious and rational faculties and not to attempt to 'return to nature' under one guise or another.

The creation of life is no longer baffling but it becomes a natural consequence of the properties of the universe and it is very likely to appear in many places in the cosmos, probably under different forms and based on different chemical processses, again in agreement with modern tendencies in biological thought. The appearance of mindful creatures on the evolutionary ladder ceases to be mysterious, but becomes again something to be expected during the process of the development of progressively more complex forms.

The duality of mind and body and all the difficulties connected with the interaction of the two essentially dissimilar entities disappear. The interaction of mind and body in health and sickness, the phycho-somatic illnesses, the effect of hormones and drugs on the mind, the effects of injuries to the brain, the birth and death of the mind, the phenomena of sleep, are no longer puzzling but something to be expected. It would now be strange if the two aspects of the same entity were mutually independent. Consciousness is a characteristic feature of the mind, and as the latter can reach various stages of development, so can also the former. The higher stages of consciousness claimed by the mystics not only do not appear impossible; on the contrary they strengthen the feasibility of our hypothesis. Perhaps at the present biological stage of the development of the brain, these higher states can only be attained through years of exacting exercises, but in future they may be quite common among the superior beings into which homo sapiens might evolve. It is quite feasible that like many features which appear in developed forms in the human brain, but only exist in rudimentary traces in the brains of animals, so the so-called super-mental phenomena of telepathy and others may manifest themselves only marginally in the human brain, but be the ordinary powers of the systems of a still higher degree of complexity.

The concept of the Mind of the World is compatible with our theory, not in the sense that the cosmos as a whole feels and thinks, but that the mind, being one of the aspects of a general entity of which the universe is built, is spread across the latter, if only potentially, and capable of manifesting itself in the complex systems. Also the possible lack of a single directing centre in the human personality is plausible on the grounds of our thesis as there is no reason to expect that integration of the system must be perfect.

The fact that the mind, although quite real, is not a form of energy does not surprise us any longer, as the former is another essential aspect of a more general entity. Whether the mind is transmutable into matter or energy and vice versa we will not discuss here. That such transmutations have not been observed so far should not surprise, because the coefficient of proportionality may be very large, as in the case of matter-energy transmutation. (Remember here that a minute mass gives rise to an enormous amount of energy, and until we could perform refined experiments such changes were too small to be detected.)

The lack of a sharp boundary between organic and inorganic matter is quite obvious on the basis of our hypothesis. The existence of such a boundary would immediately invalidate it. Also, the ability of machines to imitate processes of the more involved, gross phenomena of life appears quite natural. Life is probably only one kind of process by means of which the extremely complex systems can be created. Very likely there exist some other processes leading to similar results. Hence the creation of a mindful machine, self-conscious and endowed with feeling would not be surprising. Its mind and feelings could be very different from those of human beings, but just as real. By a similar argument the artificial creation of life is quite feasible. The fact that the brain and mind work in terms of entirely different categories is quite plausible on the grounds of our hypothesis, but the close correlation between two trains of phenomena is to be expected. The mind does not rule the brain but neither is it the pale reflection of the working of the latter, an epiphenomenon. Both processes are equally valid and interacting, being the dual aspect of the more general processes. The physics of tomorrow will have to establish the units in which the performance of the mind could be expressed, and create the instruments by means of which the latter could be measured.

The possibility that further stages of the process aiming at the creation of the systems of increasing complexity and integration will belong to machines cannot be excluded. Perhaps man is the highest stage life could produce, or perhaps, although the latter is able to create a more mentally advanced species than homo sapiens, progress will be quicker through the evolution of machines. Maybe the two evolutionary branches, that of living beings and that of machines, will develop in parallel. It is not entirely impossible that in some distant future, when cybernetic brains higher than their human equivalents have been constructed, humanity will have to decide whether it is really after the progress of intelligence in the universe or whether it prefers to foster its own ends of domination.

This discussion does not lay any claims to logical rigour. It is only too well understood that the concepts are vaguely outlined and are not entirely free of contradictions. The intention here is more to suggest a new line of approach to the problem than to state a formal thesis. If real progress is to be made in the studies of life and mind on the fundamental level, then the whole of our mental attitude must be changed. The old, customary ways of thinking lead only to hopeless contradictions in this field and therefore are perhaps the greatest barrier to further advances. This is becoming even more imperative in view of the progressive intrusion of machines into our everyday life. In the field of automatic data processing, with which the present writer is familiar by virtue of his professional activities, it is becoming increasingly clear that the technical excellence of the computers is of secondary importance to the problem of the integration of men and machines into one smoothly operating system. This is likely to become of supreme importance in future decades, when vastly more powerful computers will be available. Hence the necessity of finding a common denominator for both men and machines. But in our present ideological climate this would lead to the degradation of men by bringing them down to the level of still relatively simple machines. It seems that the only way to avoid it, and at the same time to satisfy the requirements for the co-ordination of men and machines, is to admit that the latter have the potential possibilities of the former. Then, although men and machines will be viewed as essentially not dissimilar, the mental capacities of the former will be clearly seen as superior and the whole system will be designed from the human angle. The human mind, if freed from the deadly mental drudgery of repetitive work has nothing to fear from the computer for centuries to come. It can only gain in status; one appreciates the true potentialities of the human mind as one comes to learn how nearly moronic is the performance of multi-million pound machinery. It then becomes acutely apparent what a waste it is to employ men on tasks that a machine can perform. When present machines are assessed not only in terms of speed and accuracy, but those which are most characteristic of human performance, like imagination and creativity, the immense inferiority of machines stands out a mile.

It is by treating machines and men as essentially different entities and by measuring their performance in different terms, or in terms which do not really apply to human beings, e.g. in purely economic categories, that the true distinction disappears and men become the slaves of machines.

PART THREE

PART THREE

CHAPTER 9

The Birth of
a New Epoch

MANY scholars studying various social and political facets of Western civilization have expressed the view that the year 1914 marked the end of the historical epoch known as 'modern times'. The idea that the First World War brought to an end the development of the world-view originating from the times of the Renaissance is progressively gaining acceptance. It is not being suggested that the war itself brought this stupendous change. The war and the developments which have followed it up to the present day were themselves the outburst of powerful undercurrents which could no longer be constrained. We feel dimly new forces arising around us, although we can only vaguely perceive their true nature. Perhaps the scholastics of the late middle ages had the same feeling, of an unknown threat creeping into their cherished intellectual world, when they were confronted with the first stirrings of modern thought.

No doubt to the Communist the answer would be simple: we are witnessing the death-agonies of the capitalist system and of everything for which the latter stands, and we are about to enter the new millennium of Communism. Whether his hopes are justifiable or not we will not discuss here, mainly for the reason that we feel the changes now taking place in the world are deeper than the mere question of an economico-political ideology. We will see that both communism and the political systems opposing it share certain common traits, which are developing and becoming perhaps more important from the long-term point of view than the struggle itself.

The ideological change from scholasticism to modernity in its day affected only one corner of the planet. The change from modernity to the post-modern ideology, although also a typical product of Western civilization, will inevitably affect the whole world. This is because all races and nations are now rapidly learning the science and technology of the white man, seeing in them the best means of enrichment and power. And while learning these, they cannot but assimilate the white man's culture. It is becoming abundantly clear that the pulsations of Western technology are much more than the hum of endless rows of machines. The latter, even if the knowledge of their design is included, are worthless by themselves alone. They can only be gainfully employed within a certain very intricate social structure, which must inevitably be based to a large degree on the Western world-view. One can say that this proves the Marxist's theory that the means of production condition everything else. Alternatively, one can say that the mental attitude which results in designing and operating modern machines develops also a world-view essentially similar to the Western. Whatever the preference, one thing remains fairly clear: any major change or crisis of Western thought is a world-wide ideological event. If a true world-culture ever develops, civilizations other than the Western will undoubtedly make their contributions, but, if only because of its sheer tremendous technical superiority, Western culture will play the dominant role, at least during the opening centuries. For these reasons, we can speak about changes in the ideological climate of Western culture in the first half of the twentieth century as about the change in global culture.

The world of the modern man was that of increasing order and rationality, of growing recognition and respect for the rights of any human being (at least of white skin-colour) however humble, and of the progressive extension of humanitarian practices into all fields of life. There were wars and revolutions, ups and downs in the progress towards the shining ideals, but the trend was unmistakable. Under the pressure of world-opinion even the worst despot had to pay increasing attention to the legitimacy of his actions and to the human rights of his subjects. Man might be a miserable sinner but nevertheless he was thought of as a predominantly rational being. Differences of opinion could have been settled by force of arms and many atrocities were committed during the wars, but this was considered, at least in principle, regrettable. Social institutions might have been highly inperfect and unjust, but belief in the possibility of vast improvements was widespread. Mass-persecutions, torture, extermination, and the shameless appeal to the lowest human passions were again, at least in principle, unthinkable in the Western Europe of the early twenthieth century. Scientific determinism triumphed and it was sincerely hoped that in due course the whole world would become a place where fundamental human rights would be respected, full of tolerance in the national, religious and economic sense, where all men would be educated and would go rationally about their business. The firm belief in freedom and the rights of the individual, the cult of personality and the idea of human rationality were perhaps the most distinctive features of the modern age.

Ideological theories contrary to the above views were widely known and discussed in leading intellectual circles, but they did not make any profound impact there and were almost totally disregarded by the vasts masses. It is one thing to discuss the simian origin of the human race or the possibility of man being only a plaything of subconscious urges, a sort of machine; it is another thing to base one's attitude to one's fellow men on such beliefs. This orderly, humanitarian and rational world came to an abrupt end with the Great War. Millions of cultured men, of the type who would be deeply shocked at seeing a dog kicked, were transformed in a few weeks into barbarians tearing out each others guts with bayonets on the battlefields of Europe. Atrocity followed atrocity, human rights dwindled to nothing as the most fundamental right—to live—was disregarded in senseless slaughter on the fields of northern France. With an enormous shock it had been realized how very thin the crust of civilization was. Beneath the mask of a city gentleman the savage, cruel beast reigned supreme, killing, raping, torturing just like any other animal, only with more ingenuity. With the war over an attempt has been made to restore the previous order. But it failed.

The reckless industrialization of the nineteenth century, with the profit-motive as its new-found God, destroyed the ideological back-bone of our civilization. Science undermined the old values but did not create the new, at least not such values which would appeal to the simple minds of the common men. The generations of exploited workers turned their backs on religion. So did the narrowly specialized technologists, who in addition, had no time for any ideology at all as he was too busy with his slide-rule. The business men thought about profit by day and dreamt about it by night. The artist, disgusted with the lack of appreciation in the utilitarian society and with the growing ugliness of the industrial world, turned towards an abstract, symbolic art and cut himself off from his fellow beings. The rapid and unplanned transformation of society under the impact of machines destroyed old customs and ways of living and no-one thought about creating new ways suitable for an industrial society.

All the effects of headless, blind, mass-introduction of the machine, discussed previously, have sapped the ideological strength of our civilization, which was made into an empty shell. And this shell had to cope with tremendous changes in every aspect of human life, absolutely inevitable in the presence of rapidly advancing mechanization. Man with no real ideological back-bone, apart from greed for material goods, had to cope with physical forces under his control millions of times greater than at any other time in history. How could he possibly do this? In the second half of the nineteenth century, when we were still apparently progressing along the old lines, the whole structure was already really moving under its own inertia. It was becoming empty inside and the great war burst it open. The old order collapsed and from its ruins the new order is now growing. Let us see, as far as we can, what features does it show in the dim light of its birth.

With the rise of Fascism and Stalinism the underground man of Dostoievski and Nietsche became very much evident. The primordial urges of the human animal gained the upper hand over laboriously built structures of humanistic ideology. The Stalinists have shown complete disregard for the basic human rights of both the masses and their leaders and have killed, starved, and otherwise destroyed millions of human beings and exploited mercilessly hundreds of millions, but at least they claimed they were doing it for the sake of a better life for future generations. How a happy life can be born out of murder, slavery and degradation is not always easy to see. But perhaps one could point out that the ideals of the French Revolution, which are now generally applauded, were also born in rivers of blood. Such were the histories of many social movements. But as far as the Nazis were concerned even such a feeble apology is not possible. This was not a case of atrocities being committed and regretted, even if falsely, or excused for the sake of some future aims. Here the basic urges of our animal past were plainly and openly made into the guiding ideology. Almost all the values accepted over thousands of years of civilized life, if only in theory, were reversed. The extermination of tens of millions of human beings solely because of their racial difference (often imaginary), the enslavement of whole nations in the name of the insane ideology of the master-race, murder, pillage, robbery on a national scale were openly hailed as the highest aims. Millions of young people were purposefully indoctrinated with cruelty, brutality and sadism. The evil genius of Hitler found a new way of appeal and persuasion. He did not rely on the rational method, the basis of education in the modern age, but instead he developed together with his clique the masterly, although still rather amateurish, means to get directly to the subconscious minds of his followers. Nazi propaganda and their rallies were provoking and moulding for their own purposes the sub-conscious urges and desires of men. They appealed to the beast in man—hence their dislike for the intellectuals, whose rational armour was more difficult to pierce. The fact that Nazi propaganda was in general so successful only proves the sad truth of how thin and feeble is the structure of human culture and civilization, and gives some justification to the Nazi's contempt for them. In a few years a magnificent nation, one of the leaders through centuries in philosophy, science, music, poetry, etc., boasting proudly of its high cultural level, succumbed almost completely to the ideology of insane bestiality. And still more sad is this: although one could find in the typical German mentality of past ages certain traits which served as weak gates to let the Nazis in, and although the humiliating political and economic position of Germany after the first world war was undoubtedly favourable for extreme solutions, it is not true that Nazism would not have arisen in other societies. Given a favourable set of circumstances it could have happened anywhere.

Fascism was defeated after a long and bloody world war that cost tens of millions of casualties and the expenditure of hundreds of billions of dollars. The world-wide political supremacy of Europe was destroyed and the cradle of Western Civilization is today politically merely one of the areas of conflict between powerful forces of the West and East. In 1939 the possibility of a Russian attack on united Europe would be something to laugh at. Today Eastern Europe is almost totally under Russian domination, and the politically divided nations of Western Europe can maintain their precarious independence only under the protective umbrella of American air power. The brutality of totalitarian régimes destroyed part of our cultural heritage. Human life and basic human rights lost some of their sanctity. We are nowadays less shocked by the abuse of power, gross violation of law, political imprisonment and mass murder. We, in the West, still live within the framework of old legal institutions, but their spirit seems partly to have gone. Some people attribute even the increase in crimes of violence, especially among the younger generation, and the continuous slaughter on the roads, to the generally lower values associated with human life.

As mentioned before, the modern age put great stress on the individual, on the distinctiveness and uniqueness of every single human being. While the influences of the social environment have never been denied, it was thought that the creative powers of the individual are the most important single factor in the development of society. This ideology reached its peak with the romanticists, whose hero was a type of solitary genius harbouring feelings and emotions unattainable to average people. Nations were thought to follow the courses laid down by their greatest sons. The men of genius were to lead, the masses to follow. An individual was thought of as the source of spontaneous creativeness, only partly conditioned by the environment. It was believed that it is largely up to the individual what he did with himself, how he developed his mind and personality and what course his life would take. Consequently he was held fully responsible for his actions and could be praised or blamed accordingly. Today, the individual is falling into the background of the social philosophy and the mass and environment are coming to the fore. Whoever one is and whatever one does is considered to be the result of an infinite number of forces outside one's control. Any particular human being is thought of as a nodal point of an extremely complex dynamic network of forces, which almost completely determine his behaviour. It comes again to our old question: 'Are we only machines or something more?' However, even on a purely intellectual plane the answer to the above is far from being obvious, as we have seen already and there are strong indications that there is something in us, or perhaps in every extremely complex closely integrated system, which cannot be comprehended in terms of the present physical concepts. Hence the twilight of the individual is unlikely to be caused solely by a mechanistic outlook on life. And when one adds our Christian heritage with its ideas of salvation depending largely on individual effort (in addition to the essential grace of God), if one thinks about centuries of modern philosophy supporting the predominant position of the individual, and above all if one has not forgotten that every human being feels himself free to choose, it becomes obvious that some other than purely intellectual forces must be at work to bring about the downfall of the individual.

These forces are not difficult to discern in view of everything we have already said in Chapters 1 and 4. They are mainly due to the rapid introduction of the machine with a purely economic aim in view, disregarding everything else. The extreme specialization, simplicity and deadly monotony of the majority of work available in present highly industrialized societies stunt the mental development of man. The purely utilitarian, mass-produced goods kill his feeling for beauty and standardize his tastes and desires. These effects are strengthened by incessant high-pressure advertising. The over-growth of the industrial metropolis, again the consequence of the neglect of everything but the economic aspect, gives the average man little choice in the kind of life he may lead. The extremeness of the division of labour, the penetrating means of communication, standardized goods, standardized entertainment, the rigidly scheduled transportation network, etc., give him the feeling of being caught into a web of forces outside his control and filling every aspect of his life.

These seemingly impersonal forces make the individual feel tiny and helpless, a mere speck of dust carried on the wind. In his work he is a mere cog in a huge machine, replaceable, an automaton to perform certain, usually simple, actions. He gets his orders and follows them without knowing, or caring, what final aim his efforts serve. Nobody really cares about his feelings and ambitions; even if the social relations officer of one kind or another makes a routine contact with him, both of them know very well that this is being done, ultimately, solely for the reason of greater efficiency of some huge organization. Man cannot fulfil himself by some silly hobby or by a civic evening. He needs conditions where he can exercise his powers to the fullest, he needs real freedom of choice in matters which are important to him, not a sham freedom of an apparently benevolent, but all-pervading large organization, with all the decisions made for him. And what about the men at the top; are they any more free? Perhaps a little more than their subordinates, but they too are in the grip of an advancing system which they are supposed to control. Due to the extreme complexity of modern large-scale industrial units and the presently very inadequate methods of data processing and techniques of control, the 'bosses' rule mostly by more or less inspired guess-work. Chosen mainly for their loyalty to the organization, for a quality known as 'executive drive', because of social connections, pleasant manners, the ability 'to sell themselves' or simply by sheer luck, they frequently lack the mental ability to grasp a complex situation or to look far into the future.

But the machines are so powerful, their efficiency and output so great that even with every kind of monumental blunder we cannot help getting richer. So everything seems fine and the whole gigantic structure advances half-blind, until some violent eruption now and again uncovers the other, less admirable aspects of glitter on the surface of industrial societies.

Present industrial society produces the standardized and colourless type of man, who goes through his life nearly automatically, has a standard job, a standard house, standard car and clothes, enjoys standard entertainments and remains in standard relations with all other people. An ideal material for a strong-willed despot or for a social scientist with ambitions for personal power. The life of such a standard man is ruled by powerful social organizations, the most important of which is perhaps the one for which he works. Consequently his relations with other human beings are based more on functions which these people assume in the organization than on a truly personal basis. As some put it, the individual is alienated from himself, he sees himself much as others see him, he does so many things because others tell him to, directly or indirectly, that in the end he loses faith in his own personality and gives ear to the theories telling him that he is completely conditioned by external forces. That ideology, apart from suggesting itself indirectly through nearly every aspect of life in an industrial centre, is also the most convenient to accept. In one step it makes all personal effort unnecessary and absolves a man from his trespasses. All he has to do in order to stay happy is to conform with whatever society approves. Then the cosy and prosperous life is assured.

In Western societies the twilight of the individual is mainly the consequence of the various factors already mentioned, but it is not so far part of official ideology, which is still based, broadly speaking, on Christianity. But under totalitarian régimes, which now govern one third of the human race, the glorification of the mass and the insignificance of the individual is a very important part of official doctrine. Mass is the only thing which matters, at least in theory. Whereas the historians of the modern age interpreted the past in terms of kings and leaders whose actions were supposed to make the history of the nations, the Marxists see the latter entirely as the outcome of mass movements. The leaders are seen simply as the most typical representatives of the social currents of their times, but, being entirely themselves the products of their environments, their personal contributions are regarded as comparatively negligible.

As in all other matters the human mind tends invariably to take the extreme solution. Hence general opinion in almost every important matter that cannot definitely be proved fluctuates through the ages between two opposites. Regarding the question at hand it seems most reasonable to say that while the tremendous significance of the cultural environment in the development of the individual is undeniable, it is also obvious that some people, living in similar conditions to the majority of their contemporaries, have managed to make contributions to the development of the society out of all proportion to the average, and in this sense they do assume historical importance. Even Communist ideology makes an exception to the rule of exclusive historical importance of the mass for the benefit of party leaders, who are omniscient (while in power) and are supposedly making enormous historical contributions.

Totalitarian Communist régimes are ready at any time to sacrifice the individual for the benefit of the mass. This is part of their accepted ideology and for the sake of argument we may disregard the fact that such sacrifices are even more often made for the personal benefit of the ruling clique. In cold-blooded calculations aiming at maximization of total happiness it seems plausible that in certain situations an individual, or even a sizable group of individuals, could be profitably sacrificed for the benefit of the millions. However, one thing must be remembered. The mass does not feel; the mass consists of individual men and women, who each have the capacity to rejoice and to suffer. Hence if all fundamental rights are taken away from the individual in order to benefit the mass, the result is that everybody lives constantly in fear and uncertainty lest he may be the next sacrifice. Thus life becomes a nightmare for everybody. This is the situation in totalitarian states, and in fact the higher one's position there the more dangerous one's life becomes. Therefore, whatever one thinks about the relative significance of the mass and of the environment on one hand, and of the individual on the other, respect for the basic rights of the latter must be an essential feature of any social system intended to promote a happy life.

The gradual decay of the cult of individuality, the conformism of masses, the powerful impersonal forces attempting to control every aspect of life, the rise of fanatical and mystical ideologies like Fascism, and, to a certain extent, Communism, led some thinkers long before the second world war, to describe our new epoch as the 'second middle ages'. The myth of 'the common man', supposedly the very salt of the earth, was created in the past as an antidote to the theories about the divine rights of kings and the rule of titled aristocracy. Today, when aristocracy and kings no longer have any power, this might lead to the worst tyranny of all, the tyranny of the masses. This is not to say that masses do rule, in fact, or that they ever will, because in any political system the directing power can only be exercized effectively by a small group. But the standardized masses produced by industrialized societies strongly impose their norms on everybody who lives in their midst. Their intolerance is more opressive than that of any despotic king, because they reach into almost every aspect of life by the sheer pressure of social opinion.

Yet at a closer look one easily discovers that public opinion rests on little more than the sheer strength of the group; it represents the sum of the opinions of a vast number of individuals, mediocre and average by definition, and usually ill-informed about the particular problem of the individual in question. Public opinion is conditioned by tradition and other sets of beliefs, often of little value. It can easily be moulded by various means appealing to the human subconscious. What is most important, it varies from group to group, from society to society, often being diametrically opposite on the same issue. How many times in history has this general opinion been completely wrong! How many times was it the cause of persecutions, cruelty and unimaginable stupidity! Although everybody must obey certain basic rules, because only in this way can an organized group function, an individual must have the courage of his own convictions and must make his own decisions on personal matters, because he knows best all the factors involved. He must act as he thinks fit, apart from gross violation of existing laws, even if everybody else condemns his actions.

Modern social psychology places enormous weight on the adaptability of the individual to his environment. The ability to co-operate perfectly with the group, to accept the prevailing way of life and the standards of behaviour, to work in a team, are the rules of our day. Conflicts with the group must be avoided at all costs, because those lead, so they tell us, to most destructive complexes, are the root of all crimes and miseries. There is apparently nothing worse in the world than an unadjusted individual. The recipe for a perfect life is the cheerful adaptation to every social group through which man passes from infancy up to death, presumably under the guidance of a guardian angel with a Ph. D. in social sciences who will always manage to 'fit' his protégé into a suitable group. While agreeing that a good deal of co-operation on behalf of every member of the group is *sine qua non* for the group's operation, nevertheless to make adaptation the chief virtue is typical of our epoch. Although perfect adaptation is perhaps not synonymous with absolute conformity, nevertheless it is dangerously close. All progress is made by people who do not accept entirely the ways and opinions of their contemporaries, and the more they disagree with them the more chance they have for creating original thoughts and progress.

It is well known that creative achievements are usually born in response to a challenge presented by the physical or human environment. Some historians see in the challenge of the environment one of the most important factors in the development of civilization. A perfectly adjusted man, living in a scientifically developed and economically rich society, could well go right through his life without meeting any obstacles. Hence the incentive for creative actions would be entirely missing. As with whole civilizations, so with a single individual the challenge must be contained within certain limits. If it is too severe it breaks instead of makes. Hence the conflict of the individual with the group should not be too acute, and in this sense one can speak about the range of creative maladjustment. It is characteristic that the leaders of commercial organizations often fail in the psychological tests, designed to check applicants for employment, in qualities of co-operation and working in a team. In the last analysis all this can be reduced to a question. Are we aiming at providing conditions favourable to the development of man's creative powers or are we attempting, through the glorification of adaptability, to produce a race of human robots, perhaps happy ones, but still only robots?

Some psychologists tend to think that the growing number of mild mental and nervous disorders is actually the sign of the vigorous basic mental health of the race. The standardized life in the industrial ant-hills is unnatural for human beings in the sense that it does not give an outlet for the vast energies and potentialities with which the average specimen is endowed. It forces him to act within very narrow limits and creates unbearable stresses. The stress is most felt by the mentally vigorous and healthy individual and he is therefore more likely to develop symptoms of nervous disorder as a sign of rebellion against the way of living forced upon him. In an abnormal society the really healthy people are abnormal, by prevailing standards. Their nervous symptoms are an expression of deep-seated, mainly subconscious, dissatisfaction with conditions they cannot accept but have no power to alter. By the same token, a person cheerfully accepting an abnormal way of living and apparently well-adjusted to it is really sick. While this interpretation of the increasing mental disorder is perhaps controversial, the very fact that mental illness is on the increase, while rising prosperity and protective measures remove the sources of obvious stresses, furnishes strong evidence that something is basically wrong with our civilization.

One of the symptoms of revolt against standardized life in

industrial society was the rapid spread of existentialist philosophy in Western Europe after the second world war. This philosophy was born of a reaction against the mechanistic determinism of the second half of the nineteenth century, but it became a powerful ideological force only in the last few decades. The movement is complex and divided into several factions and a proper account of it is outside the scope of this book. We limit ourselves to stating that existentialism puts the individual and his freedom of action above everything else. It believes, accordingly, that man is free to choose his actions and can achieve fulfilment only if he rejects all ideological constraint, customs and rules imposed on him by society. This does not necessarily mean anti-social behaviour, but the idea is to try at all costs to act as one feels right, not as others tell one to do, directly or indirectly through accepted ethics. 'Express yourself, make your true self felt in all you are doing, be free in your mind, even if you cannot be completely free physically'. These are the slogans of existentialism.

Belief in the essential freedom of the individual leads existentialists to regard their freedom as the most precious factor, a starting point in their thinking. They openily base their systems on purely subjective feelings, usually those of disgust with the world around them. They attack systematically almost all accepted fundamental values of our culture, and in their plays and novels, show how much the bases of our social life and ethics are a matter of convention, and cannot therefore be unquestioningly accepted. They have little time for scientific methods of inquiry, apart from their purely utilitarian technical value, because they reject the objectivity of truth, maintaining that it's highly subjective for every intelligent being. Their philosophy, written often in highly specialized logical jargon, concentrates on the question of being and often reaches pessimistic conclusions about life, the position of man in the universe and other related topics.

As a counterbalance to the mechanistic world view, to the standardized life based on mass-production, and to mass adulation, existentialism is a healthy movement.

On the other hand, although existentialism debunks in a masterly fashion many values that rest on nothing but ancient convention, it seems to offer little as substitute. And how is one supposed to build a socially useful ethic on the basis of complete subjectivity? This would mean that an individual could do anything he liked, and surely no group could function continuously on such foundations. How do we construct a purely subjective logic? It is not surprising that existentialism is branded by Marxists as the swan-song of a dying bourgeois culture, although one suspects that the spread of disruptive tendencies and influences by existentialists ideology in Western societies is welcomed in the top echelons of Communist parties.

Some men are so full of energy that even the aimlessness of our present civilization does not discourage them from prodigious effort. For this type of person and for many others the only possible way of living consists in being continuously occupied with something, even if the final aim of all these activities is not defined. In fact, they never bother to think about this. Thoughtful contemplation is for them an unusual occupation. Their idea is that activity is an aim in itself. We are becoming a community of jobbers and this is little surprising in view of our previous observations. When the mind is shallow and the energy great, the only way to discharge the latter lies in performing a few simple tasks incessantly.

Lest one should think that the author has ascetic tendencies, let him be assured that nothing could be further from that. He has, in fact, a normal standard of living, including the possession of a fast car and a large T.V. set, which he switches on occasionally. He would certainly not refuse a gift of a million pounds, but he would be most unwilling to spend all his life-energies, or even a major part of them, on acquiring that sum, even if it were within his reach. The accumulation of material goods is sensible, provided it has some definite purpose. It is senseless when it becomes an end in itself, or when it results only in a relatively small increase of the simple types of enjoyment at the expense of sacrificing all energies to the aim of enrichment, with unavoidable mental impoverishment or, at best, the very incomplete development of the capacities for more sophisticated kinds of pleasure. A man who can afford the best seat at an opera, but has little appreciation of music, will enjoy the performance far less than the student in the gallery. Hence the expensive ticket will make a smaller contribution to the happiness of the former, than the small entrance fee to the latter. It is the richness of internal life and the capacity of perception which is most important for the happiness of the individual. It is more enjoyable to travel abroad on a motorbike and sleep by the roadside, if one has the mental ability to comprehend new things and relationships in a foreign country, than to cover the same route in a chauffeur-driven Rolls Royce, staying in five-star hotels, when one's mind is dull and unreceptive. Other things being equal, material wealth offers increased possibilities of enjoyment. But if one concentrates exclusively on gaining that wealth, other things never are equal, because there is bound to be the lack of energy and desire to develop the mind in any other direction.

The meaninglessness and emptiness of a predominantly utilitarian and economic civilization mirrors itself in the problem of teenagers; juvenile delinquency is only a small aspect of the plight of the younger generation. These well-fed and physically splendidly developed youngsters are bubbling over with energy and unable to find an aim in an aimless society, attempt to discharge their vitality in less laudable ways. Faced with a stereotyped life, with the dreary monotony of the majority of available work, with the absence of ideals capable of firing their imaginations and no need to struggle for survival, they wander aimlessly around, living for 'kicks'. What else could be expected? When all his essential needs, like food and clothes and shelter, are easily satisfied, man requires something to keep him in trim, to provide a real outlet for his energies. Youth clubs, hobbies, etc., are only the palliatives and the stop-gaps to prevent the worst consequences of ideological emptiness. The real need is for great aims. But where are those ideals to come from, if the adult part of the population is without them too?

Through hundreds of thousands of years, life was for man a hard struggle for survival. In the civilized pre-industrial societies life was easy only for the privileged small minority: the rest had to work hard just to satisfy their needs. Only in the last few decades have the most economically advanced Western societies reached the level where the satisfaction of fundamental needs, and often more than that, is easy for every normal individual. The problem of over-abundance in the past faced only a few exceptional individuals, and as such had no social importance. Its opposite, mass poverty, was the main pre-

L

occupation of all sociologists. Today the question of an excessive supply of goods and especially of leisure time seems to be facing whole nations. It is not only the United States, with the highest standard of living in the world, which are affected by superabundance. The nations of Western Europe are also well on the way towards the same dilemma with the Soviet Union perhaps only one decade behind. If the reckless growth of world population is successfully controlled and if the underdeveloped countries recieve vigorous help from the more advanced nations, the problems of an 'affluent society' will become those of the whole human race. It is therefore absolutely imperative to find aims to absorb the tremendous energies of billions of healthy people, to enable them to develop all their potentials and to lead full and truly human lives.

The modern age and our post-modern epoch both show a belief in progress. We are all so strongly conditioned to the idea of continuous innovation that we can hardly imagine life in a static society. We are trying continuously to make everything better, whether it is our industrial wares, our standard of living or our social institutions. Continouus progress is taken for granted as something obvious and natural. And yet the dynamic world view is not the only one possible. There have been many civilizations, which, after reaching a certain point of development, were quite happy merely to preserve the status quo. None of them, of course, succeeded. Change seems to be a fundamental law of nature and human societies are not immune to it. The hidden and only dimly understood social forces inevitably break the 'cake of custom' sooner or later. Civilization in a static state loses its vitality and ossifies into a rigid structure, which breaks down finally under the pressure of new forces which it tries to suppress. The dynamic civilization can adjust itself accordingly to internal and external pressures and thus preserves the continuity of development. Perhaps the best hope for the much threatened survival of our own civilization is the fact that its capacity for change is not yet exhausted.

In fact the rate of change is definitely increasing. But here comes the snag. We are certainly progressing scientifically and technically, and nobody in his right senses could deny it. But is this the right kind of progress? Our social and political institutions, our ideologies and our fundamental world-view seem to be thousands of years behind our technological progress.

The cave-man tribe-mentality, based on continuous warfare over hunting grounds, because 'it is either we or they who starve', is idiotic in a world of potential plenty. Greed for material goods, again a legacy from our hungry past, prevents people from concentrating on culturel developments leading to the enjoyment of better things. Unrestricted breeding, necessary in times of tribal warfare and the very high mortality due to diseases, threatens in times of great medical advances to flood the world with billions of human beings which this planet will be unable to support. The extremely dangerous position into which we managed to manoeuvre ourselves by the development of atomic weapons, and from which we seem unable to extricate ourselves, makes the whole human race look like a baby playing with a glittering razor blade. These are only a few of the many obvious anachronisms brought from the caves into a world of atomic energy and interplanetary flight.

The glaring disregard for real human needs during the development of our industrial civilization makes some people ask: 'Are we really progressing?' Even if we manage to avoid blowing ourselves to pieces with nuclear weapons, which is rather doubtful to say the least, a sober look at hundreds of millions of human beings doing repetitive jobs, doped with slogans of one kind or another, going aimlessly through their lives in an aimless world, physically admirably healthy but with an increasing number of mental disorders, forces one to ask: 'Is this what we want?'

Perhaps we are not progressing at all, perhaps all our rockets to the stars, our superbly designed machines, the conquest of distance and of physical illness are only a glitter on a structure which is rotting inside. The uneasy feeling of doom, of imminent catastrophe, is widespread, in spite of an unprecedently high standard of living. Our incessant struggle for greater efficiency, for higher productivity, for a higher standard of living, for more of this and for more of that almost, poses the questions: 'What are we really trying to achieve?' And no-one seems to be able to offer a convincing answer.

One of the fundamental issues the new epoch will have to face is that of individual freedom versus subservience to the community. The modern age learned the bitter lesson that reason and freedom are not synonymous. The ignorant masses have obviously not been free, but it does not follow that freedom would flourish in an educated and scientifically advanced community, especially if education means predominantly narrow specialization, as it does today. An educated man will naturally be a less gullible prey for any crooked ideology and will tend more to assert himself, but with the development of scientific means of communication and persuasion, and with the increasing complexity of the social structure, the power of rulers to impose their wishes also increases.

To this we shall return later. Here we say only that the fundamental question is that of a general aim. Are we after the maximum progress of the human race or only after the simple happiness of all its members? Because these two aims, unfortunately, do not seem to be synonymous. The former demands the creation of conditions where every individual could develop to the fullest, hence a good deal of freedom in thinking and acting seems indispensable. Experience teaches that although competent work is possible in an atmosphere of slavery, the highest flights of the human mind are not likely to take place there. Even the Communists had to remove the commissars from their fighting units during the second world war, and to give more freedom to their scientists.

One could speculate on the possibility of vast numbers of specialists, each entirely conditioned to his limited field, with a group of 'bright boys' at the top running the whole show in an atmosphere of relative freedom. But it is almost certain that such an arrangement would not be the best in the long run. Any sort of heavy conditioning means narrow specialization and the latter is deadly for fundamental progress. It may lead to improvement in techniques but it is unlikely to create something really new. If, however, the second objective is chosen, that of a happy and safe life, then a very high degree of conditioning does not seem objectionable. To the majority of us, brought up in the ideology of the modern age, with its heavy stress on the freedom of the individual, human dignity, etc., human conditioning appears horrifying and distasteful. However it cannot be denied that a completely conditioned human being could still be happy. In fact, the only means of permanently eliminating all social stresses and strifes would be a thorough planning of the whole of social life and perfect conditioning of each member for playing his part. To insist that such people would not be really happy seems rather beside the point. Perhaps we highly individualistic remnants of the modern age could not be happy in such circumstances, but there is no compelling reason why other generations, brought up in an entirely different atmosphere, could not. A happy robot-man is not entirely a character from science fiction. Nevertheless, there is another argument which makes such a perfectly planned community unlikely to survive over a long period. Such a way of living would mean the extreme specialization of the social structure, and evolution teaches in unmistakable terms that excessive specialization is the surest way to extinction. This is one of the reasons why we said earlier that the current tendency towards social conformity and unquestioning adaptation to the prevailing way of life are dangerous from the long-term point of view. Hence, on the right choice between individual freedom or the strife-free community of perfectly conditioned individuals the whole future of the human race may well depend.

The creation of a basic ideology for a large community poses an extremely difficult problem, because there seems to be a fundamental and perhaps insoluble contradiction at its very basis. If a sincere and widespread belief in a certain set of fundamental truths exists among members of a given community, and if the latter are of such a nature that they can serve as a useful basis for the erection of a civilization, then there is no problem at all. But supposing that such a faith is not present, what then? Historical evidence strongly suggests that a society can develop only on the foundations of an all pervading ideology, stating clearly the ultimate values. The latter determine the behaviour of each individual, and they must be widely shared if the group is to exhibit the necessary degree of cohesion. In particular, when men's immediate needs are satisfied, it is essential for them to share certain ideals leading to a concerted action towards the common end. Otherwise disintegration is bound to result. But these basic ideals must ultimately be accepted by an act of faith. Hence, we are arriving at an impasse. To believe in something means to be convinced that the things really are as the given belief expresses them. One cannot accept certain axioms as the basis of ones world-view out of pure convenience or necessity. Religious truth (and every fundamental ideology is a kind of religion) cannot be accepted or discarded at will like a scientific hypothesis. We observe that even in science, although the hypothesis can be rejected, we always believe in the validity of the scientific method itself. It is the scientific method, accepted ultimately on the basis of a set of beliefs, which constitutes our ultimate faith in all scientific investigation. Even on purely pragmatic grounds we cannot accept a fundamental set of beliefs solely because of their usefulness. If we do so, then our real fundamental faith is not the one which we accepted but is contained in the belief in the validity of pragmatic philosophy. Hence, we are again accepting something because we believe in it and not just because it is useful to accept it. Thus, on the one hand we know that all-pervading and commonly shared faith is a matter of life and death for any civilization (Communist societies are no exception, as the Communist ideology has all characteristics of an all-embracing religion), and on the other hand we cannot create such a faith artifically, unless we intend to cheat outselves.

The only way is to search for such principles as would be genuinely acceptable in the climate of our times, and this we will try to do, in a very sketchy manner, later in the book. The above remarks should not be considered as antagonistic to any of the revealed religions. On the contrary, in the light of the foregoing anybody who has a deep faith in a revealed religion can be considered as privileged, because he has at least a firm anchor in life. That the influence of revealed religions is on the wane at present, particularly in Western societies, is a fact that has to be faced. The lack of a religious background is undoubtedly one of the reasons why the Western world cannot stop the advances of Communism. In addition, many of the fundamental issues of today cannot be convincingly answered by the revealed religions. The preferences for a static or a progressing society seem to be equally acceptable on purely religious grounds. Social conditioning or even outright slavery can well exist in an atmosphere of religious fervour, as many historical examples clearly prove, and as South Africa is demonstrating today. The life of an individual or of a society is an integrated affair and none of its major aspects can be treated separately from the others. Nevertheless, the division between the secular and religious spheres of competence and jurisdiction has been one of the cardinal features of Western civilization. Although several attempts at the unification of the State and the Church had been made, they were never really successful, and in the modern epoch the division became universally recognized by both sides. In consequence, the soul of Western man has been torn apart. The lack of ideological integration resulted in the development of many powerful social phenomena without reference to the basic religious doctrine. It is useless to say that religion is concerned with the salvation of the soul alone, and that it is not interested in the form of government, industrial developments, laws of property, remuneration etc., so long as they do not interfere directly with religious dogmas. Perhaps the fanatical and inconclusive wars in the period of the great Schism, threatening the total collapse of our culture, made it imperative to proclaim religion as a private matter of each individual. Perhaps only be excluding religion effectively from many basic social and political issues could broad agreement be achieved, and the universally acceptable basis for the development of the society be built. But if it was so, then a heavy price was paid for this division.

The modern epoch transferred the aim of life from the other-world to this in which we happen to live. The life of modern man became centred around problems of social organization, industrialization, science, enrichment and other such worldly affairs. If religion can offer no decisive leadership in such spheres then it becomes irrelevant, so far as the majority of men are concerned. As no all-embracing secular ideology has managed to provide a satisfactory lead either, Western societies have been left spineless and empty. Hence the search for basic axioms for the conduct of life is imperative in the highly industrialized and rapidly progressing communities of today.

CHAPTER 10

Planning or Wrangle?

THE post-modern epoch is being born among terrific social and political upheavals. The old ways of living are crumbling under the pressure of new forces, which are fighting among themselves for supremacy in the new age. One of the basic aspects of this ideological struggle is the controversy between the protagonists of the planned development of the society and the supporters of the opposite view. Because of the materialistic climate of our times, it is being fought mainly on an economic plane although it also extends to other domains of social life.

Believers in free economy point out the apparent inefficiency of bureaucratically run large economic units and the associated neglect of the consumer's needs and desires. Most important of all they argue, supported by the large mass of evidence available from present-day totalitarian régimes, that complete control of the economy by the state leads apparently to the suppression of freedom in all other fields.

It is the contention of this book that large-scale and long-term planning is inevitable and absolutely essential in the environment of our extremely complex society. Humanitarian planning, far from leading to slavery, is in present conditions the best safeguard of personal freedom. It is the lack of planning which brings the greatest restraint of freedom, because if the complicated network of relationships and mutual dependencies, growing continuously with the development of industrialism, is left to itself, it engulfs the individual like an octopus. An individual's theoretical legal freedom is of little use if he is effectively immobilized by the powerful grip of the tentacles of an industrialized society. On the other hand, planning, if it is to be beneficial, must be flexible and above all non-doctrinarian. We must plan for freedom and not against it, we must restrict planning only to the cases where the existence of the plan is obviously better than the lack of it, and we must never plan just for the sake of planning. All this is very difficult to achieve but the only other alternative is chaos, anxiety and wastage of men and materials.

The machine was introduced on a large scale at the end of the eighteenth century in conditions of economic laissez-faire, and disastrous social consequences followed for lack of foresight and planning. It is often argued that a free market constitutes the best environment for an enterprising businessman and that he has more incentive for promoting his privately-owned company than any salaried state official, in charge of a comparative unit, could possibly have. It follows then that the total sum of the activities of all entrepreneurs, conducted in the optimum conditions of a free market, results in the maximum benefit for the whole community.

Although this is arguable, let us concede for a moment that the privately-owned company is more efficient. However, the losses resulting from the lack of a rational plan for the use of the total available resources are much greater than the questionable loss of efficiency of each contributing unit. It is well known from general principles of the analysis of complex systems that the separate optimisation of each contributing unit, or sub-optimization, to use a technical term, is generally incompatible with the true optimization of the whole. What is the good of having ten companies very efficiently competing in a market where only a couple can ultimately survive? Apparently this leads to the victorious emergence of the most efficient organization. Whilst not denying the strength of that argument, one must not forget about the terrific waste inevitable in such an economic wrangle. And why have the state-controlled industrial units to be necessarily less efficient anyway? The majority of managers and many of the directors of the privately-owned companies are salaried officials, similar to the administrators of nationalized industries. Assuming the choice of the right men and competition for positions of power carrying high remuneration, the necessary incentive can be provided equally well in the nationalized industry. Also, the managers of state-controlled enterprizes need not have any less freedom than their counterparts in the privately-owned companies. They ought to be given only broad directives, leaving plenty of scope for personal initiative within the established framework.

What one has to condemn in unmistakable terms is centralized bureaucratic planning aimed at the determination of all the minutest operational details in every unit, in the absence of knowledge of local conditions, and restricting the creative powers of lower echelons. But planning does not have to be of this nature. All one requires on the top level is the gross, rational plan for the deployment of the total resources available. This should not be left to the hazardous judgments of independent organizations, guided solely, in the last analysis, by the motive of maximum profit. How can anybody seriously suggest that that would be the optimum in conditions of an extremely complex network of mutual economic relationships?

The doctrinaire attitude expresses itself in the belief that there exists an economic system, optimum in any conditions. This is manifestly not true. When a society is relatively primitive and its economy is mainly agricultural, the individual ownership of land may be truly the most efficient arrangement. Work on a primitive farm is hard, demanding much effort, and a direct tie between one's exertions and the crop available is the best incentive. Little planning of total resources is necessary and the poor performance of an individual farmer is unlikely to affect anybody else but himself and his family. In such conditions the nationalization of land may easily lead to laziness and reduced efficiency. Nevertheless, with the growth of industrialization individual people and human groups become increasingly interdependent and the consequences of any activity become more widespread and enduring. Hence, more and more central planning and co-ordination become necessary. This does not mean necessarily a dictatorship, because the central planning and executive organ can still be chosen by common consent and held responsible to the electors. In conclusion, different proportions of planned and unplanned activities are likely to be the optimum at different levels of technological development.

It is the contention of the followers of laissez-faire that in the conditions of a free market the customer gets what he wants, and that this is unlikely to happen in the planned economy, where he gets what the planners have made available. The argument seems plausible at its face value, but becomes less convincing after a closer look. If we were ants, with an immutable set of reflexes, then indeed the best way to make us happy would be to give us whatever our inborn instincts desired. But human beings are not insects and almost all their attitudes and wishes can be influenced and altered. The best practical proof of this is the enormous sums spent on advertising of all sorts. The manufacturers claim to produce in response to popular demand, but first they spend billions on telling the public what it should demand. Now, it is commonly known that to appeal to the lower human desires is much easier than to please the more subtle and more noble desires. Any educator, preacher or sociologist who would make use of human mediocrity for his own ends, would be severely and universally condemned. But the manufacturer and the salesman are free from these constraints. The customer gets what he wants, which means the satisfaction of his elementary needs and emotional urges of a trivial nature. It is much easier to entice an average man to buy a flashy tie than a good book. Hence the tremendous production of easily saleable non-essentials. The huge supply of such goods lowers the prevailing taste and influences the choice of banal aims in life. These lead in their turn to even more demands for irrelevant goods. The whole regenerative process is strongly enhanced by high-pressure advertising, influencing further popular preferences towards a purely utilitarian outlook. As a result, the major part of the capital and labour resources of the community are allocated to the production of non-essentials.

How the principle of profit, which is ultimately the guiding aim of every private business organization, is supposed to lead to the maximization of total happiness and creation of the conditions for the highest development of every man and woman, remains a mystery. From the beginning of the industrial revolution machines should have been introduced for the improvement of life, for the elimination of drudgery and for the creation of a world where every individual could attain a truly human stature. The economic factor is very important for such development, but is far from being the only one which matters. Yet the perfectly free market forces every company to concentrate almost exclusively on maximum profit or to go out of business. All other factors must be subordinated to this end and any activity of an educational, recreational or social-relationship nature may only be sanctioned if it contributes directly or indirectly to achieving an economic target. Automation and A.D.P. are now being introduced because of various direct and indirect benefits, described in the earlier chapters and expressible finally in monetary terms. The motive of eliminating inhuman and degrading jobs in the office and on the shop-floor is most definitely not the principal reason for the employment of computers. Yet, in the long-run the question of making work fit for the high potential abilities of human beings is the most important thing for general happiness—far more so than a rise in the standard of living by a few points. But the present masses of workers are so strongly conditioned to the performance of their inhuman tasks that they would be amazed to look at automation from any other point of view than economic. In fact, the people engaged on the dullest tasks, of the kind which turn men into automatons, usually protest most strongly if they are relieved of their drudgery. These are the very people who would be most likely to break the machine. It is little wonder, for in an unplanned economy, with 'every man for himself', the human robots replaced by their mechanical counterparts are likely to suffer most. Is this the sort of society we want to perpetuate?

To aim at a profit is quite legitimate in any sort of economy, if by that one understands the recuperation of the capital employed, insurance against the risks involved in any kind of venture, and the gain of resources necessary for the extension of activities for some useful purpose. But when profit becomes an end in itself, as is always the case in any private company, however hard some people are trying to veil this fact, the whole activity becomes distorted. In such a situation salesmanship becomes more important than design and manufacture. A persuasive salesman is worth his weight in gold because he can even sell a mediocre product, while the best design and most efficient production methods can bring little profit if the salesmanship is poor. This fact is amply confirmed by the remuneration of salesmen as compared with designers and producers. For the same reason, huge sums are spent on advertising. The customers must be informed, of course, of what is available in any kind of economy, but from their point of view a simple catalogue, quoting objectively the features of the wares on the market, would be not only sufficient but immensely superior to the thousands of expensive advertisements, consisting mostly of packs of lies, better or worse concealed. The latter only tend to confuse the potential buyer and make him chose on the basis of distorted, if not false information. The cost of promoting sales and advertising is in many cases greater than the total cost of research, development and production. The money so spent must be recovered by an increase in the price of the product, hence it is the customer who pays in the end for all this stupendous waste. Yet, when everybody advertises heavily, the best product has no chance of success on the market without an expensive sales promotion.

An efficient distributive network is essential, as the Russians, who badly neglected this sector of their economy, are now learning. The more complex an industrial society becomes, the more involved the network grows, hence the number of people engaged in it is likely to increase. But this does not justify the spectacular rise in the ratio of middle-men to productive workers which has taken place during the last fifty years, out of all proportion to the real needs of efficient distribution, and caused mainly by the fact that in present conditions an enter-prizing man, with the gift of persuasion, has a much better chance to make quick money by engaging himself in some sort of selling activity than by doing anything else. In a planned economy the tremendous waste of massive advertising and sales promotion would be reduced to the minimum, and whole armies of middle men, often very industrious and intelligent, could devote their energies to more useful tasks than to pulling wool over other people's eyes.

The unplanned and unco-ordinated endeavours of thousands of closely interdependent and competing units are bound to result in wide fluctuations in the levels of activity of each unit and of the whole system. The dynamic feedback model of the national or world economy demonstrates with mathematical clarity how the levelling-off of the demand in one sector affects adversely activities in other adjacent fields. The stagnation spreads, the faith in the profitability of future ventures dwindles, and credit becomes less readily available. Unemployment and short-time lowers the incomes of the mass of the population, resulting in a still smaller demand and reinforcing all these ill-effects. Then things liven up in some section of the economy, often due to the purposeful intervention of the Government (much against the principles of economic liberalism!) and the whole chain-reaction leads to 'boom' conditions, only to be followed again by another depression. What sort of mass madness possesses us to consider this sort of arrangement as an optimum? A planned economy could avoid all these fluctuations, although, due to planning imperfection some difficulties would obviously arise now and again. But their severity and spread would be much more limited. The fluctuations in the level of activity in a truly free economy, in the present extremely complex conditions arising from the high technological standard of industry, would be extremely severe, as the Great Crises of 1929 amply demonstrated, if it were not for the readiness of Governments to intervene. Thus, free economy is being saved repeatedly by its very antithesis: planned action. The outlook of 'every man for himself' flatters men in the time of boom, as it gives them a feeling of pride in personal achievement, although they are more often the consequences of a favourable conjunction of circumstances. This attitude changes quickly during depression. The most stalwart believers in governmental non-interference begin to complain that the controlling executive organ 'is not doing anything about it'.

It has been seriously suggested for many years that a true 'relaxation' of the present international tension, leading to large-scale disarmament, would probably result in an almost uncontrollable economic crisis, lasting perhaps for years. If so, then what sort of economy is it which needs the mass-production of the means of destruction to keep it going?

Business cycles, although of much decreased severity due to the planned intervention of Governments, are still with us and cause a lot of unnecessary anxiety and frustration. In periods of boom the economy of the Western world is still developing in a topsy-turvy fashion and increasing measures of control are applied in times of depression, when something seriously goes wrong. If these means are successful in difficult times of trouble why should they not be even more beneficial during the trouble-free period?

Every individual is encouraged through his educators to find a set of targets for his life. Young people are told that whilst taking advantage of the opportunities presenting themselves at any time, they have to be clear about their final aims. Drifting through life is certainly not recommended, and purposeful and planned activities are thought to be the best means for creative development and success. On the level of the human group, companies are introducing more and more planning. The allocation of progressively larger resources for planning and co-ordination of present and future activities, particularly by big companies, is a phenomenon well known to any industrial consultant. The augmenting of intuition and experience by the high-powered mathematical methods of investigation and planning is gathering strength. Automation and A.D.P. are bound to increase this tendency manyfold.

Every top level expert in administration and management is now advocating more and more planning for almost any kind of large industrial unit. Yet, as soon as the logical extension of this trend is proposed, up to the level of the national economy, hosts of arguments to the contrary are advanced. But it is just at this highest level where efforts towards the co-ordination of all important activities are likely to prove most rewarding. The bigger the unit, the longer it can afford to wait for a return on the capital resources employed, hence it can embark on worthwhile schemes which the smaller units, working on relatively shorter periods of turn-over, are not capable of supporting. This refers most of all to educational activities, basic research, development of means of communication and transportation, building of settlements and capital investments in various sections of industry.

The most unprejudiced observer cannot help feeling that contrary opinions are expressed more because of the vested interest of certain powerful groups, or because of ideological fanaticism, than for any other reason. There is, for instance, a curious argument about decentralization, the success of which apparently proves the fundamental undesirability of far-reaching central control. In fact, it proves nothing of the sort. If the central organ could receive the information about all detailed happenings in the branches as quickly as the branch executives do, if the orders emanating from the centre could be equally quickly transmitted, if the centre had the data processing capacity and intelligence equal or superior to the sum of those of branch administrative organs, then it would be best, from a purely organisational and economic angle, to plan and direct everything in detail from the centre.

However, due to delays in the receipt of relevant information and in the transmission of orders, and to the limited data processing facilities at the centre, and because of the necessarily limited mental capacity of the central management, it is often best to give the branch managers a considerable degree of autonomy. But this neither proves the fundamental failure of central planning, which can be much increased in scope and depth with the advent of high-powered computers and rapid data-transmission networks, nor means that decentralization implies loss of control over the branches. In fact, if any board of directors of a large industrial empire were to fail to establish and enforce the co-ordinated plan for all subordinate companies they would rightly be accused of negligence. But on the level of a national or world economy the opposite of planning is supposed to be the most beneficial.

Perhaps the best proof of the necessity of economic planning is that in spite of all arguments for a free economy and attempts to maintain it, the latter is slowly but surely disappearing. With the growing complexity of human societies an increasing degree of planning is unavoidable. The present policies of even the most liberal or conservative governments in the Western states would have been considered raving socialism only fifty years ago. The true free economy no longer exists on a large scale. It is obvious that a fully planned national or even world economy is the next step in the historical development of human societies. Its advent can be delayed, probably with detrimental consequences, but it cannot be avoided. As any other social process, the ascent of planned economy does not occur at a constant gradient. There are ebbs and flows but the general trend is unmistakable.

Concerning the view that planned economy leads to planning in all other aspect of social life, and results finally in totalitarian slavery, it must be admitted that this danger does exist. But it is avoidable. First of all, planning need not be done by a despotic oligarchy; all citizens can participate through their chosen representatives. There seems to be no basic difference between a democratically chosen government favouring laissez-faire and an equally democratic giovernment supporting social planning. Secondly, although planning of all aspects of social life can lead to ossification of the whole society into the rigid structure of laws and rules completely suppressing personal freedom, there is no compelling reason why it should necessarily happen. The planned life of an individual does not lead inevitably to the suppression of his creative abilities. It can lead equally to the greater development of his natural capabilities, enable him to reach a greater stature, to acquire more influence and wealth, all of which result ultimately in a greater measure of effective personal freedom. Other things being equal, it is a drifter who wastes his potential abilities, stultifies the development of his mind and ends with little freedom because of the poverty of his inner life and the limitations ensuing from his humble position in society. It is not enough to be free to think and to speak as one pleases, but in order to exercise the freedom of speech one must have first of all something to say. It is not enough to have freedom to travel, but one must have also the money to buy a ticket. The complex interpersonal and intergroup relations limiting perfect freedom of action will arise in any case, planned or unplanned, with the advancement in technology. This mesh will be much more stifling if it is left to grow uncontrolled. The maximum real freedom of the individual, compatible with the industrialization and development of social relationships, can be achieved only when the whole structure is planned accordingly, but never in conditions of chaotic expansion.

Perhaps the greatest difficulty in social planning is that men change with altered conditions. Often planners forget about that and assume that what men want today they will also want tomorrow. But, as if to confuse the planners, human nature is very flexible, often in a manner difficult to predict. So solutions acceptable in a certain set of conditions may be unpalatable for the men living in the environment altered according to the plans initially plausible.

Planned society is a novelty in Western civilization and therefore it is little surprising that its methods and techniques are still rather rudimentary. It often brings undesirable results, but in time a planned society may reasonably be expected to provide the conditions for a happy life, for personal advancement, and for the development of creative human powers to a degree never achieved before. Planning must be flexible and always ready to change, even basically, in view of new developments. It must avoid at all costs the construction of rigid frameworks built on foundations of dogmatic principles. It must be ready not only to accommodate new currents but also to provide the conditions for their encouragement. It should furnish the base for the highest development of human creative urges, but

M

never to try to suppress them in the name of some commonly accepted axioms.

The disastrous limitations of personal freedom in Communist countries stem more from their historical traditions of slavery than from planned economy. There were concentration camps and secret police in Russia long before anybody dreamt of Communism. China was hopelessly entangled in a web of tradition and custom before it had ever made effective contact with the Western World. Political freedom of the masses cannot be achieved overnight, but requires centuries of appropriate historical developments. Nowhere is this more evident than in England. The personal rights of an Englishman are based fundamentally on the traditions of ages and only to a smaller degree on the democratic social institutions of this country. The latter are merely the consequences of the former. The English react adversely and almost automatically to any form of potential dictatorship and in this attitude lies the best guarantee of their freedom.

The world is moving unmistakably towards the planned society. If the freedom of the individual, perhaps the greatest achievement of Western civilization, is to be preserved in the coming historical phase, Western societies should readily adopt this new form of social structure. Adherence to outdated political ideologies can only cause the gradual loss of Western influence, passing the leadership of the coming world civilization over to other cultures, often built on traditions of slavery and despotism.

Supporters of unrestricted capitalism are now fighting a losing battle and are in a position similar to the Royalists at the time of the French Revolution. They are out-of-date, clinging to a system which is no longer suitable in present technological and social conditions. Their downfall will probably be gradual and many temporary successes will perhaps be put to their credit. Monarchy survived the French Revolution and new ideas were apparently suppressed by the Holy Alliance. But only for a while. The new ideas spread all the same and the aristocratic form of government was wiped out of Europe or degenerated into a powerless façade. Now it is extinct over practically all the world. Similarly, full blooded capitalism will still flourish, probably for a long time in many parts of the world. Nevertheless, in the end it will be superseded by socialism of one brand or other, whatever the official label of the latter may be, only to survive as an economic curiosity in some remote regions, as today the Arab sheikdoms echo the dynastic splendour of eighteenth century Europe.

The present ideological struggle between East and West may be compared to the religious wars of the Reformation. In either case both sides have proclaimed coinciding aims: salvation of the soul in one case and economic advancement, freedom and democracy in the other case. Each side assumes its own immense moral superiority and sees the other side as the very reincarnation of evil. During the Reformation both the Catholics and the Heretics claimed the guidance of the Holy Ghost. Today, both the capitalists and the communists claim that historical laws are on their respective sides. The struggle is so intense that it is almost impossible to form a balanced view while living in the midst of it. In the leading countries of both camps, United States, Russia and China, the atmosphere approaches religious fervour. It is almost as dangerous to declare oneself a Communist in the U.S.A., as it is to be an anti-Communist in Russia.

In the politically divided countries of Western Europe an individual is requested to declare himself positively on one side. If he prefers to remain impartial, he is suspected at once by both camps and is likely to be persecuted directly or indirectly by the followers of either. It is almost impossible to realise the gigantic waste of effort and material resulting from this tragic division of the human race. The lack of global co-operation on an economic and political plane, the fantastic sums spent on useless armaments and the upkeep of large armies are only the most obvious consequences. Worst of all, fanatical ideological strife stifles freedom of thought and creates an atmosphere where any true ideological advance is impossible. Even the highest intellectual representatives of both sides seem to dismiss the ideological achievements of the other half of humanity. What makes the whole situation so very dangerous is the fact that now, unlike the age of the Reformation, both sides possess weapons capable of total destruction and perhaps even the complete extermination of the human race. No rational men could possibly use such a weapon if they knew that a few hours later they would be at the receiving end. But the fanatics may.

Belief in the righteousness of one's own way of living may easily become so obsessive, that one can come dangerously close to the conclusion that it would be better not to have humanity at all than to have it living according to the opposite ideology. In time of excitement, due to some minor incident, such a fanatical attitude may easily give the spark necessary for the destruction of the world. The position is dangerous and idiotic in the extreme. What makes it so funny, if anything can be funny when the whole future of humanity is at stake, is the fact that both sides proclaim, often sincerely one feels, the same aims. Very broadly speaking, the difference is mainly in the methods of achieving the similar targets.

Religious dogmas were a matter of life and death during the period of the Reformation, as millions, slaughtered on the battlefield, dead from starvation or pestilence caused by incessant wars, or tortured to death, found to their disadvantage. The inconclusive results of religious wars and the danger of the total collapse of European civilization forced the opponents to sheath their weapons and to try to co-exist. Later generations made such a good job of religious co-existence that today such religious strife is peacefully buried and we cannot comprehend what our ancestors were really fighting about. We pay far less attention to religious dogma and estimate other people in terms of generally accepted social ethics, concentrating rather on actions than on declarations of intentions. It is more than likely that future generations will find the present struggle equally futile and incomprehensible. If it is true that the optimum political system depends mainly on the level of the technological development, then in the presence of technical near-parity it may be expected that finally both apparently irreconcilable camps end with the development of identical, or nearly identical, social and political systems. Signs that this is happening are already present. Western countries cannot help introducing an increasing amount of economic and social planning. Communist countries learned the lesson that high mental achievements and an efficient development of creative human power are incompatible with slavery. In order to compete with the West they have to give a higher education to a sizeable proportion of their people. These people will in future become politically and socially a very important stratum, and having learned to think they are unlikely to limit their thoughts exclusively to technological matters. They will demand greater individual freedom, a higher standard of living and security from atomic war. This sort of development is the only hope for the human race. Otherwise, sooner or later the big explosion of nuclear war is almost bound to happen.

In all fairness, the present tragic political situation is mainly due to the policies of the Communist countries. The West made tremendous concessions to Russia at the end of the war, sacrificing all Eastern Europe and, judging by information available, was quite prepared to co-operate and co-exist with the Communists. Unfortunately, this attitude has been interpreted as a sign of weakness and the relentless Russian pressure began. How can one co-operate with somebody who openly and repeatedly declares that the destruction of the rival political system by any means is the basic tenet of his policy? Militant Communism attacked Western societies at all levels: by direct military threat, by subversion, espionage, propaganda, etc. In order to defend itself the West had to reply in kind. Many socialist politicians of Western Europe, criticising the admittedly deplorable witch-hunting in U.S.A., certain activities of the C.I.A. or the flights of American planes over Russia, etc., would be well advised to remember that all these things are predominantly the self-defensive acts of a community which feels itself mortally threatened. In the long run, one is almost invariably forced to deploy the same weapons as one's opponent, or otherwise he will gain an advantage. The stifling of the intellectual climate, the fanatical and uncompromising attitude towards the inimical ideology, the large-scale anti-espionage activities (often ridiculous), the frantic development of weapons of mass-destruction, were all easily predictable in the West, right at the beginning of the 'cold war' imposed by the Russians.

Whether Marxism is right or wrong, one thing remains clear: as applied today in Communist countries it is certainly unacceptable. Even if one believes the declarations of Communist leaders that their aim is the future happiness of man, which is open to doubt because the motive of personal power seems, at best, equally important or even predominent, the sacrifice of whole generations is inexcusable by any standards. Of course, we have duties to our descendants and it would be, for instance, very unfair to them to use up now all the material resources of the planet and leave them high and dry. Nevertheless, it is not the mass which feels but an individual human being, a little self-contained cosmos, which has the right to demand a certain measure of happiness and an opportunity for the realization of the aims in his own life. The brutal extermination of political opposition, running into tens of millions of victims in Russia and China, the inhuman destruction of other tens of millions in concentration camps, the sacrifices of the happiness and labour of whole generations for the sake of creating an industrial base—these cannot be accepted. Above all, Marxism as applied today has all the features of a fanatical and all-embracing religion, disallowing any opposition. While claiming scientific support, it is rigid and dogmatic in the extreme and completely unwilling to modify its basic tenets. It declares that all the basic truths have already been discovered by Marx, Engels and Lenin (and Stalin when he was alive) and further progress is only possible within this framework. Even biology and physics have sometimes had to conform under the threat of persecution. Such an attitude is the very antithesis of science and brings us back into the dark ages.

Trying to be objective, certain excuses can be offered. One must not forget that Western industrialism was also built through the miseries of the exploited workers of the nineteenth century. Apparently the swift creation of the necessary basic capital for industrialization is very difficult to achieve without extreme measures in savings, leading to austerity and to a deplorably low standard of living. Also, the expediency of political orthodoxy is sometimes necessary in times of great effort. Discipline must often come before freedom, if only temporarily, as for instance in the army. Further, the history of Western states is by no means free from large-scale atrocities and murders, committed either at home or in the colonies. Nevertheless, the blood of the destroyed millions will forever stain the Communist systems, which ironically claim to fight against the oppression of the common man.

In the long run a rigidly and totally planned system leads to the extreme specialization of society, comparable to the biological specialization of the species. Although such specialization usually brings extinction, because of the loss of adaptability to a changing environment, it also offers some immediate benefits. Hence, although a perfect totalitarian state is likely to be a dead end for human development, nevertheless it may achieve a temporary advantage over more liberal societies and thus conquer and destroy them. This is one of the dangers of the present day.

Some people maintain that the human spirit could not be contained within the rigid framework of a totalitarian society and kept forever in slavery, but that it would liberate itself sooner or later. Let us hope sincerely that it is so, but such an experiment on a world scale would be too dangerous. The insight gained during the studies of the principles of the control of extremely complex systems, the better understanding of the working of the human mind on psychological and physiological levels, the advances in genetics and biology of the cell, the gradual discovery of the social laws governing human societies, all represent wisdom which can be used for good or evil like any other knowledge. It is quite feasible that sometime in the future a ruling group could condition and manipulate a whole society with the minimum use of direct physical force. The means could be so subtle and their application so well-planned and co-ordinated that no resistance would arise, because hardly anybody would be aware of being induced to act in a given way. Every member of the community, apart from a few oligarchs and their scientific advisers, would be so perfectly conditioned and relatively happy that he could conceive no other way of living and would therefore lack the incentive to rebel. Psychologists could do better than Hitler did in appealing to the subconscious urges of the masses. This is the reason why his methods, although very successful, were earlier referred to as amateurish. The subtle and continued propaganda through schools, books, newspapers and the all-pervading means of communication like radio and television would prevent the majority of individuals thinking on any other but orthodox lines. The counterblasts of different ideological movements would be absent in a world-wide state. The widespread use of drugs, under the name of vitamin pills, for persuasion during light sleep or in state of drowsiness, through tape-recorded messages, applied under the pretext of a scientific method of teaching, and the early conditioning in schools and many other techniques now available could certainly turn the great majority of people into docile followers of official ideology. For the more resistant there would be brain-washing, applied presumably under the excuse of psychiatric treatment, or even brain surgery like leucotomy, which could turn even the most rebellious and mentally vigorous men and women into obedient automata, still capable of performing useful functions.

Some conclusions drawn from the heroic Hungarian uprising or from events in Poland of that time are unfortunately unconvincing. These happenings do not necessarily prove that the human spirit is unbreakable but rather that the methods employed by the ruling Communist parties were inefficient. But this is no guarantee that in, say, twenty years time the truly totalitarian governments, if there are still any of them left at that time, will not be able to apply much more powerful and scientific means of mass-persuasion.

On the other hand, awareness of the existence of a developing body of scientific knowledge which could be employed by the potential oligarchs of the future, should not throw us into the panic state of regarding every attempt at organized life as a diabolic plot for the enslavement of humanity. Such an attitude, if generally prevalent, would be an ideal environment for the clever groups of operators to make certain views and ways of living predominant for their own purposes. Such attempts would be much more difficult in a planned society, organized by men well aware of possible dangers. Of course, the question which immediately suggests itself is: *Quis custodiet ipsos custodes*? But to this we return later.

For the present let us see how much conditioning we already have in our supposedly free society. As said already, civilization can only develop around a certain dominant religion or ideology, the existence of which is indispensable to the cohesion of the whole group. Through laws, traditions, customs and ethics this dominant ideology pervades all aspects of life, shapes mental attitudes and thus conditions to a large degree the whole growth of a given culture, and consequently, of every individual belonging to it. Assuming that man has a certain degree of essential freedom of choice, which is itself controversial as we are well aware, this freedom is limited both externally and internally. The external limitations are obvious to see. Every man lives in a certain environment and this together with the set of laws and the attitudes of other people limit severely his freedom of action, even if his inner life were entirely unrestrained. Whether we like it or not our actions are restricted by the law of gravity, the criminal law and the attitudes of our supervisors and neighbours. It is for instance, hardly possible to ignore the driving habits of other road users. The internal limitations of our freedom are perhaps less obvious. The mind of a new born baby is almost a complete blank. In contrast to animals man has very few, if any, truly inborn instincts and ways of behaviour. Hence, his tremendous potentialities for learning and his enormous flexibility of development. Within certain limits, which are genetically determined, man can develop almost into anything.

The external world acts on a baby with millions of sensorial impulses which the newly born mind attempts to arrange into patterns, forming a certain mental model of the environment. It acts on the basis of this model and corrects the latter and adds to it according to the results of his actions. Thus, from the very beginning the environment influences the self-organizing process of the brain and mind. Human attitudes and desires are not given *a priori* but are learned and acquired during life. For instance, the primary drive may be the satisfaction of hunger; but this requires him to behave like a 'good boy', meaning obedience to parents, otherwise, he is sent to bed without supper. In time, to be obedient becomes an end in itself and the original reason for this attitude is forgotten. To be obedient may mean in turn to practise good table manners, according to the wishes of the parents. Again, in time good table manners become an aim in themselves and one may be shocked by observing anybody acting otherwise. This extremely simplified example is intended to stress the fact that in order to find out why an adult likes certain things and dislikes others would mean unwinding the history of his whole life. The same applies if we wanted to trace the origins of his opinions and his way of perceiving the world, or in other words, if we wanted to investigate his mental model of the environment. In general, the brain manages to organize itself into a sort of system which is useful for the individual's survival.

However, one has to observe that many attitudes developed by the human mind are not immediately connected with survival, or at least the connection is difficult to see. To this category belong, among others, artistic activity in a very broad sense and many kinds of intellectual endeavour. It seems that the systems constructed in our brain are so complex and rich that it has plenty of spare capacity for non-utilitarian ends. Also, the given world-model and a set of emotional drives connected with it may be useful in a certain environment, but quite useless in another. Hence, the great danger of sudden basic changes in an environment as, for instance, the rapid industrialization of backward nations.

Sometimes things go wrong and the brain organizes itself into a system which cannot secure the survival of the individual. Instead of coping successfully with the environment, it collides repeatedly with it. This leads to unbearable stresses and a neurosis develops. But even the examples of people who are considered to be mentally healthy, and who are held in the highest esteem, prove that the brain can produce attitudes which are very harmful to the individual. Consider a volunteer who is sacrificing his life for the group without being forced or induced by unbearable social stresses to do so. However much we may admire his attitude, it must be admitted that, object-ively speaking, his choice is most harmful from the viewpoint of his own survival. The possibility of a calm and balanced repudiation of the very will to live, shows how immensely rich are the potentialities of the self-organized human brain.

Conditioning is characteristic of every kind of social life. Through nursery rhymes, school, church, family life, books, communication media and social pressure, certain ideas are repeatedly being inserted into the mind of an individual. He has only a limited number of roles which he can assume in the community and consequently perceives himself as the per-former of some of them, with all the limitations involved. One could object that any kind of education by definition implies propagation of certain ideas. However, we shall call educational activities of all kinds as they are exercised today a conditioning, because in present society ideological upbringing is not objective. Anything widely differing from prevailing ideology is suppressed or ignored on the excuse of removing undesirable influences. The atmosphere in England is perhaps freer intellectually and ideologically than that of any other large country, but even here the establishing of an institute for the scientific analysis of propaganda, designed to deal with the Nazis' ideological offensive, was discouraged because of the opposition of various religious and educational groups. These obviously feared that the rational and analytic methods used to expose the venomous rubbish poured out of Dr Goebbels's department could be also used to undermine 'respectable' views. Hence, the battle for minds is nowhere being conducted in an honest and truly objective manner. The individual is not being helped in his free choice because the facts are not being presented in an impartial manner according to the knowledge available at the time. Even if facts are not directly distorted, some of them are conveniently omitted, with the object of creating the desired impression. We are all far more conditioned than is generally realized, and the better the conditioning the less visible it becomes to the people affected by it.

The remarks concerning the distorted reporting of facts, without obvious falsehood, apply very aptly to large sections of the popular press, and above all to advertising. Advertising consists almost entirely of cleverly concealed lies, with a few true things thrown into the stew to make them more digestible. It shamelessly takes advantage of human subconscious urges and desires of a low nature to profit the manufacturers. It is not concerned with truth or beauty or progress or anything else, but has one single objective in view: to sell by every available means. It even uses simple songs and nursery rhymes to reach children, in order to influence the parents, or even to create the life-long 'brand loyalty'. This mass-cheating, even if everybody comprehends it as such, is bound to lower the value attached to truth. In fact, it tends to make purposeful lying a respectable profession. Mass advertising may be necessary for the success of mass-production in our kind of economy, like a form of automation in selling, but this does not make it any more acceptable. On the contrary, it merely charges our chaotic economic system with another sin.

The concepts of planned economy and of the planned society evolve almost automatically in our minds the vision of a small group, firmly entrenched in positions of power and autocratically directing the whole life of the community according to their own wishes, while disregarding those of others. At present the West is not generally receptive to the argument that it would be perfectly possible to establish working controls that make the rulers responsible to the whole nation; that supreme power could be divided into the legislative, executive and judicial functions in order to maintain the balance, much as at present; and that in the final analysis the freedom of the individual depends more on the cultural atmosphere of the given society than on the nature of its legal institutions. Perhaps the idea of the planned society would be more generally acceptable if two things were clearly realized. Firstly, democracy, in the commonly accepted sense of the word, meaning an equal participation of every adult in the effective ruling of the society, does not exist and could not possibly exist within the framework of the large industrial state under present conditions. Secondly, even if by some miracle such an arrangement was, in fact, possible, it would be far from an optimum social system.

The first fundamental condition for the existence of democracy in the above meaning would be the equality of people, not in the legal sense of course, but in all their essential real qualities. Otherwise the more gifted individuals, 'the born leaders', are bound to assume effective leadership under one guise or another. While the quality of leadership is not an inborn capacity, it can be learned, and which individual becomes the leader of the group depends on circumstances; nevertheless it is quite true that in a given environment certain men are readily accepted by the group as its leaders. In fact, without an effective leadership the group is unlikely to perform well. People are manifestly not equal; they differ considerably in their innate potential abilities, magnified further by the influence of environmental factors and efforts at self-improvement. Hence, depending on the social conditions of the environment, certain people are bound to exercise a much greater influence than others, whatever the system.

It might be objected that in democratic society they will do so only with the free consent of the others, but this holds only in a small and relatively primitive community. If every citizen knew all the important state problems closely, and if speech were the only effective means of mass-communication, then it might be accepted that the oratory effort is a fair tool of persuasion. In an extremely complex society like ours, the average man or woman is comparatively uninformed about affairs of state, hence he or she can hardly offer advice in that field. Secondly, the flood of information pouring incessantly from television, radio and newspaper moulds the wishes and opinions of the individual. It is true that the human mind is resistant to such pressures and that the citizen is not yet completely conditioned. But to a large degree his opinions are made of the propaganda stuff of powerful social groups. Political candidates are promoted by advertising techniques very similar to those used for washing powders or other goods. As the citizen could not possibly understand the real issue at stake, elections are fought often on the level of irrelevant matters, and the party which wins is not the one which can offer superior solutions to the fundamental problems of society, for very few people realise that such questions exist at all. The winning party is the group which can capture the support of the mass through plausible promises, and above all the party which commands a superior propaganda machine. Hence, while there is every reason to believe that in the great Western democracies the actual counting of the votes after the ballot is absolutely honest, elections are largely reduced to a battle of propaganda machines. A vigorous attack by a party on an ill-informed, gullible electorate bears hardly any resemblance to the noble principle of a choice of rulers by free consent of politically conscious citizens. It hardly needs adding that in totalitarian countries the elections are an outright comedy.

The intricacies of an industrial society create favourable conditions for people possessing the quality of leadership, whose powers may be considerable. This is inevitable whatever the political system of such a society. But in the present conditions of chaotic social development and unrestricted accumulation of wealth, the people who control the community are often either demagogues or plutocrats. The effective influence of the man possessing millions is obviously incomparably greater than that of a pauper, even if legally they are both equal. In a planned society the intellectuals and scientists would presumably attain a relatively greater measure of influence. The common man fears the 'egg-heads' and the 'boffins' because he does not understand them. The business-man, motivated by a simple aim of profit or a trade union leader from the ranks are more acceptable to the common man because of a smaller gap in the mental make-up.

In the final analysis we have to trust somebody, despite the controls we establish. Would it not be more reasonable to trust that class, which by the very nature of its occupation was more strongly conditioned to impartial judgement and object-ivity? All through history noble and progressive ideas, including our Christian religion, were creations of the intellectually leading groups of the time, even if the latter sometimes wore rags and were apparently powerless. Great concepts, from which the whole of humanity ultimately benefits, were born in the minds of a numerically very small class of gifted men. These advanced ideas were hardly the products of the combined efforts of millions of dull brains or of the wealth-grabbing activities of the plutocrats.

A democracy of highly educated and socially conscious citizens would be unquestionably the most noble system. But today is does not exist and cannot exist. The clear realization of this truth and the alternation of the present system in accordance with sober facts, far from restricting the freedom of the individual, would actually increase his effective liberties. At present, due to the unquestionable acceptance of democratic principles, the bulk of the population shares the illusion of their applicability to present conditions. The difference between the real and the theoretical state of affairs gives to the various operators a wonderful chance to promote, for their own ends and under cover of democracy, practices which are its very antitheis. By recognizing the limitations of a purely democratic form of government, a system more realistically adjusted to the environment could be designed. Only such a system could furnish the optimum conditions for the development of the individual and of the nation.

Coming now to our second question, let us assume that a true democracy, in the sense previously stated was, in fact, possible within the context of a present-day industrial society. Would this be an optimum political system?. The answer is, No. Modern industrial society breeds the dull type of man, standardized and conventional in thought and action. Monotonous and simple work, the utilitarian outlook, the chaotic production of non-essential goods, the lack of any visionary ideology prevents the great majority from attaining a truly human stature. If this colourless mass ever gained effective control, fortunately impossible, we could say farewell to human progress. Leadership by the masses could only be desirable if they consisted of fully developed human beings.

Mythical faith in the 'people' is as fanciful as belief in the divine rights of kings. Before we can even think of a true democracy we must first give every citizen the chance of better

and wider education, far exceeding present technical specialization. We have to make all work fit for human beings. We
have to provide conditions for the development of creative
human abilities. We have to inspire the masses with the idea
that life is something more than making money and caring for
rudimentary pleasures. Such people could then be entrusted
with the fate of the human race.

From early neolithic times the common man has been
ruthlessly exploited by his rulers, hence little wonder that he
has rebelled against his masters whenever he has had a chance.
Any just social system must guarantee the fundamental rights
and freedoms of everybody, but this is not synonymous with
an arrangement whereby every member of society has an
equal share in governing. Why the latter state should be the
most just is not easy to see. Would it not be fairer to give
greater powers to those who make greater contributions? The
danger is, of course, that any ruling class has the tendency to
entrench itself in its position of power and to attempt to transmit its privileges on a hereditary basis. However, hereditary
privileges can be abolished, as modern societies demonstrate,
and this could be extended to the inheritance of riches, which
gives today many mediocre people an unfair advantage over
their contemporaries. The greater influence of the aristocracy
of talent and effort could be perhaps the best hope for society.

The inheritance of privilege in the aristocratic form of
government is bound to lead in the long run to a rigid system,
where the privileged minority, no longer worthy of their status,
defend themselves against the new leading class arising from
below. The struggle is usually fierce and long as the old aristo-
crats are helped by their better educational facilities, the
command of large physical resources, by customs and traditions,
and an occasional resurgence of former ability. The new class has
only its personal abilities to rely upon, but they are tough and
selected by the survival of the fittest; in the end it invariably
wins the struggle, degenerating centuries later and giving
way to yet another group. The influx of new blood into a ruling
circle is essential and the aristocracy of talent would amply
satisfy this condition.

It is just that all should have a say in government. In any
complex system a certain measure of feedback is usually very
useful. But the measure depends on the structure of the system

and on the purpose of its performance. The aristocratic governments of the past were invariably incapable of maintaining their supremacy for very long for reasons stated. But a ruling mass would be large enough biologically to avoid weakening, and thus could rule forever. Its rule could be more oppressive, all-pervading and intolerant than any despot could ever dream of. We are already tasting the vulgarity and boredom of 'mass culture', for instance, the present forms of mass-entertainment. It would be catastrophic if this sort of influence extended to other sectors of life.

CHAPTER 11

The Principle
of Progress

WE have previously expressed the belief that the growth of
civilization needs some central idea, which alone can provide
the basis of a common attitude to life for all the members of
that society, and permit the integrated development of social
relationships, laws and aims. Without such an idea, or religion,
the community cannot achieve the necessary coherence of
action to create the inspiring vision of the future, the target of
all endeavours, which are essential for fruitful development.
History demonstrates that the guiding ideology can be of more
than one kind. The conquest of other tribes and nations, the
salvation of the soul and happiness in the other-world, the
accumulation of riches, the conquest of nature, all seem to be
able to provide the driving force for the growth of great civilizations. Provided the common idea is widely shared and ardently
believed, civilization can grow. If, however, the former fades,
and becomes an empty symbol, no longer with the power to
inspire human minds, the whole structure withers and finally
disintegrates.

The drive for the accumulation of riches and the utilitarianism
of modern Western civilization furnished sufficiently strong
motives for spectacular growth, until the very results achieved
on these lines made further progress nearly meaningless. When
one has to work very hard for mere survival, and lives in
poverty, any material achievement is a blessing contributing
substantially towards the increase of happiness. But when the
level of abundance of everything which really matters is reached,
a further rise in the standard of living brings little additional
satisfaction. This is happening in the richest countries of the
world today and will happen tomorrow in all human com-

N

munities, provided that there are no atomic wars, that population growth is controlled, and that there is continuous economic progress on a world scale. Although such a statement may sound a grim mockery, at a time when two thirds of the human race suffer from perpetual undernourishment, it must not be forgotten that the technical means exist for creating world-wide abundance in no more than fifty or a hundred years. Assuming that these means will be used, we would be well advised to start a search for ideological principles for the new epoch now, if we are to get real benefits from material riches, and to avoid degeneration, boredom and the futility of satiety. An ideology must grow and strike its roots deep down into the very hearts of men to become the guiding force.

The prevailing mood of technical and scientific civilization is unfavourable to any ideology formulating its final aims in terms of other-worldiness. Religion in its conventional sense is now generally considered a private and individual matter, and has no longer the power to inspire the community. This trend is likely to increase with the further mechanization of many aspects of life and the even deeper penetration of technology and science into human minds. The *homo technicus* is unwilling to orientate his whole life towards the goals which are to be realised only after death. Whether he believes in God or remains an atheist, he places the greatest emphasis on his real life and searches for aims in the world in which he happens to live. Of course, such an attitude does not automatically imply an inevitable collision with any of the revealed religions. The two domains are simply separated, for better or worse. But this does imply the absolute necessity of an ideology which could inspire the actions of the whole country. If does also imply the clear statement of targets acceptable to the men and women of coming ages to orientate their lives.

As mentioned already few people would be reluctant to accept the principle that the supreme aim in human life is to achieve the maximum measure of happiness. Although this may appear to some nobler souls as an exceedingly low and unworthy aim, it all depends on how one defines happiness. In fact, by suitably extending the definition, it is debatable whether a human being can act in any other way than that which leads to the satis-faction of the desires of the moment. It can be easily argued that a dedicated scientist or artist, renouncing many of the obvious pleasures of life in order to concentrate more of his energies on reaching the aims of his intellectual pursuits, does so because in the end he derives more pleasure from that course. *Mutatis mutandis*, the same can be said of a hermit, or the hero who sacrifices his life for others. In fact, anything that we are doing is the result of our volition. When we say that we do not want to do something, but we have to do it because of some compelling reason, external (physical) or internal (moral), what we really mean is that we deplore the unfavourable circumstances arising from the environment or from our own psychological conditioning, but as we cannot change them, we choose to do just what we do, because, taking everything into account, this is what gives us most satisfaction, or least dissatisfaction in the given situation. In other words we always either maximise the pleasure or minimise the pain, which is the same thing.

When all the everyday needs of human life are abundantly satisfied, we have to ask ourselves seriously what are we really living for. The answer is: to develop to the maximum all our natural faculties, and by employing them fully towards gaining more understanding and mastery over our environment in the broadest sense, to achieve the greatest measure of happiness.

This does not at all mean that in future all material and human resources should be concentrated solely on scientific ventures, although they will undoubtedly account for a sizeable proportion of the total efforts available. The internal world of human emotions, feelings and thoughts is just as real as the world of physics. The poet, the painter, the composer, together with the scientist, endeavour to create patterns expressing certain relations of the external or internal worlds. The internal world of the human mind is, so far, almost exclusively the domain of the humanists. The external world of physics belongs only partially to the field covered by the scientist.

Great paintings, sculpture, poetry and music express certain relations existing in the physical world in a manner no less impressive and important than that appearing in the equations of the physicist. The finding of physicists may be more useful for gaining mastery in manipulating the environment, but they do not necessarily give a truer representation of the reality. In some distant future all human thoughts might be expressible in terms of equations governing the neural processes in our brains. Perhaps so, but we are very far from this, and we do not know whether it will ever be reached. For the foreseeable future we have to treat the humanities and science not as opposites, but as mutually complementary ways of understanding the physical universe and ourselves.

It is not at all true that the higher flights of the mind are only accessible to the privileged few. They could be shared by almost everybody, if the education and general climate of our society were favourable. As it is, it can be said that at present certain people manage, in spite of all impediments, to pierce intellectually the straight-jackets into which our culture is squeezing all of us. Observe the joy any normal child gets from the satisfaction of curiosity. Curiosity, which is also evident in young animals of the higher species, may be basically a trait having a survival value, because it leads to indispensable knowledge of the environment. But in the case of human cubs, their immense curiosity also has other potentialities apart from serving as a survival tool. Yet it invariably happens that orthodox education and social pressure gradually limit the child's natural curiosity. He learns slowly that is is unseemly to inquire into certain matters, and useless or futile to think about others. All his energies are progressively directed into channels approved by the society he lives in.

The belief that maximum happiness is synonymous with exercising every human capability and, while not neglecting the more elementary pleasures, aiming at the fullest understanding of the universe including ourselves, is not only intuitively rather obvious, but it seems also to coincide with the evolutionary development of life.

The tendency for the creation of progressively more complex forms is evident in nature even below the level of living matter, though this statement may appear to contradict the second law of thermo-dynamics. However, if we assume that the universe, as we now know it, arose from an amorphous mass of elementary particles, then the patterning of the latter into the complex structures of atomic nuclei, atoms and molecules evidently represents steps towards greater organizations. Of course, it can be argued that the first stages of creation, during which the degree of organization of the universe apparently increased, were caused by the intervention of a supernatural force acting against the natural properties of matter. Hence, the first stages were comparable to the winding up of a clock which has since been gradually running down. Such questions are the subject of hot debate and the recent theory of continuous creation throws still further light on the whole problem. Leaving this problem undecided, we will limit outselves to the unquestionable observation that in certain parts of the cosmos the degree of organization is manifestly increasing and that the process of life is, for all we know, the most outstanding example of the latter tendency. Thus a collision with the law of progressive disorder or the increase of entropy is avoided because the increase of organization in certain parts of the system (or decrease of entropy) does not contradict the decrease of order-liness or increase of entropy in the system as a whole.

Incidentally, if we do admit the views expressed in Chapter 8, the initial winding of the clock seems unnecessary as the matter-energy-mind entity can 'wind itself up' because of its twin tendencies towards order and disorder. Also, life does not appear in this light to be the brave, but ultimately hopeless, struggle against universal chaos, but rather the most intense manifestation of a tendency towards order. Further, it becomes possible to assume that this tendency is prevailing on a cosmic scale, thus constituting a belief in a true progress of the universe.

The formation of inorganic molecules into extremely complex organic molecules, capable of interaction with the environment by absorbing parts of it and exchanging matter and energy, while perpetually maintaining their specific forms and possessing the ability to create other similar molecules, is still much hidden. But there is little doubt that the creation of living matter from inorganic compounds took place at a certain period; otherwise we would not be here. The single living cell already represents an extremely complex system of interacting physico-chemical processsses, but it is only a building block for the creation of integrated, multicellular systems. The evolutionary development of the latter again exhibits progress towards the more complex forms. As mentioned previously, it is not size or direct physical strength which appears to have the supreme survival value; the successful species are those which possess more efficient and more involved internal structures, so that they are capable of a wider range of responses to environment and more appropriate reactions to a situation. Their processes of homeostasis are superior, leading to survival in wider brackets of environmental conditions. Their perception of the external world is also superior and their mental patterning of the environment mirrors the latter more truly, with consequently more intelligent responses. The possession of an integrated nervous system, co-ordinating all reactions into a coherent whole, seems to be an essential step in development. This process culminates in the growth of the brain, where the layers progressively added during the hundreds of millions of years of evolution result in increasingly more versatile and complex performances. The higher forms of life are more independent of environment and command the greater part of it, man being a supreme example of this principle.

The tendency towards increased organization does not stop at the level of multicellular organisms but extends itself to co-operative groups. The classical examples of these are the great communities of ants, bees and termites characterized by the extreme biological interdependence between their members. Such a community is really one living organism, the limbs of which are the individual insects. The latter are completely helpless individually and cannot survive alone. Although the 'couplings' between the members of human communities are much looser, nevertheless the degree of interdependence and organization in modern societies is stupendous and swiftly increasing.

Evolution does not proceed at a constant gradient, but rather in jerks and steps. Moreover, the major advances seem to consist of developing the traits which could be seen only very dimly in the rudimentary forms. This is perhaps the most important of all features of evolution, because it makes the whole process infinitely wonderful and proves that the potentialities of life are almost unlimited. Who would suspect, when looking at an amoeba, that this tiny creature could develop into being capable of creating an inter-planetary rocket? Yet man is the product of endless chains of mutations which has an organism as simple as an amoeba as one of its links. Who could see the potentials for performing thousands of immensely complicated activities of a living cell in the relatively simple, rigid structures of the inorganic compounds? Who could think that the descendants of fishes would live comfortably on land, fill the air with the flutter of their wings and survive in almost completely waterless deserts?

Each successive major evolutionary stage exhibits new laws, new ways of living, new abilities which could not be suspected in previous forms. It is a long way from an elementary photo-sensitive cell to an eye capable of the three-dimensional perception of environment in the full richness of colours and hues. Yet life is capable of even greater feats. It has the ability to transcend problems in that it does not limit itself to the perfecting of already existing features, but finds the correct solutions by creating entirely new traits, changing radically the equilibrium between the organisms and their environment.

Yet the purpose of the evolutionary process is unknown. Maybe this is because the very notion of purpose, which is after all a creation of the human brain, does not mean anything at all when applied to nature. Maybe the notion of purpose is only a peculiar category of human thinking. As things are, although the evolutionary tendencies described above are unmistakable, the higher forms of life do not get any special favours from nature. On innumerable occasions they succumb to the on-slaught of the lowest forms of life, such as viruses and bacteria. The fantastic wastage and immense amount of suffering which exist in nature makes one ponder. The apparently senseless cruelty, waste, blundering, the extinction of whole classes due to evolutionary blind alleys, the destruction of superiors by their inferiors, is all rather a macabre spectacle. Peaceful nature exists only in the minds of poets. In reality everything fights against everything else. The serene meadow flooded with the golden rays of the sun, which appears to be the very essence of heavenly tranquillity and peace, is in fact a tremendous battle-field where millions of living creatures are locked in mortal combat. Insect fights against insect, a blade of grass against other blades; each flower tries to overshadow another and starve it of light, each root tries to displace other roots and grab all the minerals for itself. The stakes are life and death and no quarter is asked or given. And the winners are not always the superior forms of life. It is true that a wonderful interlocking exists between living creatures, but apart from the obvious cases of co-operation like symbiosis, pollination of flowers by insects, the raising of young, and some others, interdependence between the various forms of life is predominantly of a pre-datory character, with one species feeding on another. It is a relationship based on strife and fear, or hate, when the capacity for emotional feeling exists. Certainly the foundations are not love and tolerance. Nature does not seem to care at all about the individual, but only about the species, and its most effective tool is the ruthless elimination of the individuals less adapted to the struggle.

With the advent of a rational mind which could consciously strive for the realization of its aims and transmit the knowledge gained to later generations, a new, fundamentally different kind of evolution came into being. In biological evolution progress is being achieved through random mutations and the selection of desirable features based on the survival of the fittest. These features are transmitted from generation to generation through the hereditary mechanism based on genes. Only small changes associated with each mutation are generally possible, hence the whole process is relatively very slow and tortuous, lacking a clear directing force. Everything that the animal learns during its life is lost as far as the next generation is concerned, and the latter must start again to learn from the beginning, as only the potential abilities of the organism are transmitted through the genes (the elementary 'teaching' of animal cubs by their parents—hunting and certain other activities—is relatively neglegible). When, however, the transmission of knowledge gained during life became possible through speech, the situation radically changed. A further advance was the invention of writing, enabling the storage of a vast amount of information, and its accurate transmission, capable of being passed from generation to generation. The extraordinary human capacity for learning and for rational thinking, coupled with the means of storing and transmitting to future generations the knowledge once gained, resulted in a fantastic acceleration of the evolutionary process on a cultural plane. These are the reasons why in a very short time, as compared with the hundreds of millions of years of biological evolution, we have advanced from the level of anthropoidal apes to the stage of advanced philosophy, arts and science. During the cultural evolution man adjusts consciously his aims and skills to the environment. Hence such an evolution is of a Lamarckian type, meaning that the environment directly causes the development of certain cultural features, as opposed to the genetic type of inheritance where the effect of the environment is only indirect, through the elimination of the less fit. In other words, in genetic evolution the instructions for the development of an organism are handed over, unmodified, directly through the environment, whereas in the cultural evolution the instructions for behavioural patterns are modified by the environment, in the sense that the latter determines the type of experience gained by the previous generation. It matters little that genetically we are similar to our cave-ancestors of the paleolithic era. The final stage of development reached by any self-organizing system depends on both the in-built capacities and the character of learning or self-structuring. With man the inborn potentialities are transmitted through the genes, while the learning process is determined to a large extent through the cultural inheritance obtained from past generations. Hence, although their genetical equipment is similar, an adult caveman of the past and a highly educated man of today represents two very different beings. The genetic evolution of mankind is, of course, still slowly going on, but the cultural evolution superimposed on it is immensely faster.

The influence of cultural evolution makes the idea of survival of the fittest a cruel anachronism in human societies, where this law simply does not apply in such conditions. The cultural value of an individual can be considered in terms of his intellectual activity during his whole life. Thus he adds his contribution to the common pool of knowledge. However, from the point of cultural evolution, there is no reason for eliminating the intellectually weak individual since he will not appreciably affect the total cultural heritage of the race. Moreover, his mental inadequacies will be transmitted in but small amounts to his progeny, the latter being mainly affected by the general atmosphere of the given civilization based on the total amount of information available. Similarly, ignoring for a moment the problem of genetic transmission of undesirable traits, a weak and chronically ill but mentally powerful individual can make greater contributions for the development of the human race than thousands of perfectly healthy but intellectually mediocre men.

The appearance of the self-conscious mind marks the beginning of a great new epoch in the evolution of life. Man is part of nature, hence, his self-awareness and fully conscious perception of the environment are like a mirror in which nature sees itself for the first time. Taking life as a whole, man's

massive activities, affecting progressively greater domains of
nature, and based on conscious perception of the latter, provide
a powerful feedback link in the system, changing essentially
its character. Hence, to advocate the modelling of human ways
of living on those observed in a mindless sector of nature, or
even on traditions developed during early stages of human
civilization is to be entirely missing the point. The large-scale
activities of the mind transform the whole system of life,
bringing it to another, higher level. The laws stating what is
right or wrong in mindless nature are not necessarily valid in
the new stage of mindfulness. What was good for the fishes
did not apply to the land-based reptiles, and in turn the ways
of the latter were not those of the mammals. Mind frees itself
now from the bounds of old evolutionary ways and is becoming
able to control its own evolution to an increasingly greater
degree. In place of ruthless competition and elimination of
the individuals less fit for surival in particular circumstances,
the mind appears to substitute the principle of co-operation.
If this is true then the change brought by the mind into the
evolutionary process could not be greater. Perhaps the idea of
universal love expressed or implied in all great religions, was a
prophetic insight into the trend which can now be supported by
scientific arguments. The human mind seems to employ only
a portion of its energies on the activities directly connected with
survival. The rest is used for the search towards the understanding of the universe, through arts and sciences in their
broadest meaning.

One can only guess where this whole process will take us,
but tremendous and unimaginable advances and changes in
ways of living are certainly to be expected. What today appears
as unnatural to us as living on sand dunes would appear to the
fishes, tomorrow may be the common experience of everybody.
Whether man will develop finally into a more intelligent animal,
endowed with a higher degree of consciousness and a superior
capacity for rational thinking, we do not know. But taking into
account the tremendous speed of cultural evolution as compared
with its biological counterpart, one would venture to guess that
fantastic changes will take place in human ways of living,
based on correspondingly great advances in our understanding
of the universe and in the control of the latter, before we change
appreciably in the biological sense. In spite of the lack of con-

certed action, continual erring, and hundreds of rigid ideological inhibitions impeding the mental development of the
race, we have made tremendous progress in relatively a very
short time. What the concerted action of the whole human
race could achieve in conditions where machines already
magnify a thousandfold our physical forces and soon will be
augmenting in a comparable degree our mental capacities, is
difficult even to imagine. The conquest of the solar system, the
spread across the galaxy, the complete elimination of illnesses
and even of death itself seem almost inadequate aims to absorb
the energies of our race. While taking the environment into
account, our alienation from mindless nature will progressively
increase. When the mind is weak the animal needs of the body
naturally come first. But when the mind, capable of probing
into the deepest secrets of life, aims at complete control new
factors come into existence.

The rate of change is continuously increasing and in future
we will be confronted with a growing number of revolutionary
changes. When considering the applicability of each of such
major steps we will have to be guided by the principle of whether
the proposed change adds to human betterment and increases
our understanding and control of the universe. These seem to
constitute the very essence of the activities of the mind; and
only by following them to the utmost of our abilities can we
hope to fulfil our true destiny and, incidentally, achieve deep
personal happiness.

CHAPTER 12

The Pointers
to the Future

OUR previous deliberations lead us to the conclusion that there exists at present a disparity between our technological and scientific achievements on one hand, and our sociological progress on the other. Scientifically we are like gods when compared with any previous civilization. Sociologically we are still barbarians. Although we pay lip service to the ideas expressing higher types of relationships in human communities, and although some of our aims are compatible with the advanced stage of our biological development and with our unique position among living creatures, the cave mentality brought from our animal past has still a powerful grip on us and orientates our lives. We think that strife and fight are natural ways of living, and co-operation and love are impractical fancies. But the plain truth seems to be the opposite. It is love and co-operation which are the natural modes of existence of mindful creatures, living at the stage of development where the effects of cultural evolution prevail over their purely biological counterparts.

Similarly, we still tend to think that the satisfaction of primary needs is the only real aim in life. Our insatiable greed for the accumulation of material goods is based on the traditions of our past, where the fulfilment of basic desires was invariably achieved by the command or possession of material objects. The latter is true for any animal, plant or primitive human being. But the satisfaction of elementary urges does not seem to be the supreme aim of the emerging mind and it becomes relatively insignificant in the era of general abundance. A higher achievement is the natural aim of human brains. Witness the joy and immeasurable happiness which creative work brings to a painter, to a composer or a research scientist. This is true for the whole human race. By concentrating on purely material improvements and viewing the humanities, science and art as superfluous luxuries, we do not build on sound foundations in accordance with so-called human nature, but we pervert the latter and distort it. This is the essential reason of the ideological bankruptcy of Western civilization and it leads to a weak social and political structure unable to support the weight of scientific and technical progress.

If we are to survive and to use our technical knowledge for the creation of a paradise on this planet, instead of turning it into a mechanized version of hell, we have to find the aims and ways of living fit for human beings. Only on this basis shall we be able to introduce and employ the machines of growing complexity for the benefit of humanity and not for its enslavement. The problem is immense and cannot be solved on the superficial plane of economics and our outdated ideology. We have to gain a thorough understanding of the nature of the human being and of a machine, of the essential features of our bodies, brains and minds, of the structure of the societies in which we live and of the general laws applicable to the dynamics of large human groups. Also we have to state our targets clearly and design the means for their achievement.

Any new mechanical gadget must be considered in the light of all its consequences and not only from the angle of increased production. The effects of the machine on the mind of the operator, in the broad sense, on social relationships of all kinds, from the family to the political structure of the nation, on morals and ways of living, on educational requirements and leisure and thousands of other facets of social life, must be taken into account. The increase in production and in the standard of living is only one of the many consequences. In the 'affluent society' any new machine must be viewed principally as the means to augment our physical and mental powers, to eliminate drudgery and to increase the material standard of life, in that order.

It is plain that the introduction of any new type of machine into the complex framework of our industrial society is bound to have manifold effects. If this process is to be generally beneficial, rational and far-reaching, planning is imperative, though it may mean a compromise between the rules of the society and the freedom of the individual. As stated before, it is believed that the effective freedom of the individual, as opposed to his theoretical legal freedom, will in fact increase in the humanly planned society, because the strangling jungle of chaotic relationships and restrictions, which develop spontaneously in highly industrial societies, will be effectively pruned. By removing the profit motive from its pedestal and putting human happiness and progress in its place, both related to the basic properties of homo sapiens and of evolutionary life, every activity could be planned to give maximum satisfaction and optimum conditions for developing a truly human stature. This refers to education, work, means of communication, development of settlements, transportation, social ethics, etc. Perhaps the construction of a firm basis for the growth of future societies demands an initial period of rigid planning, with restrictions on the freedom of the individual. Perhaps totalitarianism is an unavoidable historical phase. One would hate to think so and there seem to be no compelling reasons for such pessimistic conclusions; nevertheless a phase of rigid planning is one which may honestly have to be faced. Western societies managed in the past to maintain a modicum of individual freedom under various social régimes and they should be able to do so even in a transition phase from the chaotic to a humanly planned society. But by delaying this transition and clinging to the forms of social structure which are outdated and unsuitable in the present stage of technological knowledge, existing social tensions are increased and transition into the new epoch is made more difficult. Such ideological stubborness is also the easiest way to lose our magnificent cultural heritage, by allowing world leadership to pass to other groups tainted with traditions of slavery and disregard for human dignity.

If one still fears that a planned society would impose a physical and mental straight-jacket on the individual, and that increased mechanization may reduce human intelligence and resourcefulness, perhaps we may point out that the spectacular growth of science and technology following the second world war actually raised the minimum acceptable mental standards for a research worker. This trend is likely to increase in future.

The importance of the type of mind capable of embracing several highly specialized fields is becoming increasingly greater. Such minds can only develop in the intellectually free climate where the natural curiosity of human beings is encouraged to the utmost. But they could hardly flourish under conditions where too rigid planning obtained. Hence, a robot society could not survive for long at the stage of high technological development, which imposes a very complex network of relationships and problems, both in the field of natural sciences and human activities. Such a society would be unable to breed the men to run it, and would eventually disintegrate.

The necessity of keeping the brain at full throttle is probably nowhere more apparent than in modern scientific research. The importance of the ability to synthesise increases relatively to the capacity to analyse and dissect. It is a well-worn cliché that the age of universal geniuses, flourishing during the time of the Renaissance, is gone for ever, since the body of knowledge is now so great that a mind even of the order of Leonardo da Vinci, could embrace no more than a minute fraction of all things known. Yet there remains a paramount need for men capable of forming a bird's eye view on many advancing branches of science, if we are to avoid a disintegration of the scientific process. Today we observe at many scientific meetings that people working in different fields hardly understand one another's technical language, and are only partially aware of the discoveries made in domains other than their own. Narrow specialization is unavoidable when it needs many years of intensive study to grasp even a restricted segment of the knowledge available.

Yet at the same time somebody has to correlate the advances and bring together various disciplines. Knowledge is an integral entity and cannot be indefinitely divided without becoming finally meaningless and useless. The discoveries in one field lead very often to most important advances in some other domain, very often apparently little related. Fruitful developments occur often in between the recognized disciplines, like the growth of cybernetics which incorporates elements of mathematics, physics, biology, psychology, logic and others. Then the mental climate of the epoch, perhaps the most important factor conditioning progress, must be necessarily bred on the synthesis of all knowledge available at that period.

In the present state of affairs, a man trying to form a necessarily superficial view covering several fields is likely to be criticized by the specialist whose total knowledge may be less. Yet the synthetic exposition, even if inadequate in many respects because of the limited capacities of even the best brain, is often of more value than the faultless piece of work which lacks reference to the broader fields of human endeavour. Fortunately, there is every hope that in future machines will be able to help very appreciably with the burden of storing a rapidly swelling amount of information. It is interesting to notice that printing, which ranks among the earliest methods of automatic data processing, helped us to store and disseminate information ages ago. Today, techniques far more powerful are available. If this book was stored in the binary notation on a magnetic tape, the modern computer would read it in perhaps one minute. At present any research worker embarking on a new investigation knows that the perusal of literature relating to the subject will be a major task, perhaps consuming more effort and time than any other stage of his research. By suitable techniques of extracting and indexing it ought to be possible to arrive eventually at the stage when a gigantic library could be searched by a computer for the relevant information within minutes or even seconds.

Hence the wisdom of generations, stored now in books, will be in future transferred to magnetic tape or to some other storage medium convenient for giant processing machines. In view of a real flood of new publications outpouring in almost any domain, the problem of rendering the relevant pieces of information quickly available becomes a major technological undertaking. It is absolutely essential to master it if we are not to become buried under mountains of paper, and the machine offers the only possible line of approach.

The growing complexity of relationships and dependencies in modern co-operative groups—for instance, in large industrial concerns—forces us to consider the administrative and organizational problems in more precise terms, with the extensive use of mathematics and statistics. Here again the computers can offer great help in the massive calculations involved, and their role in the era of automation will be even greater. Although the idea of a ruling computer, which alone will be able to take into account millions of essential factors and co-ordinate the functioning of our complicated future society, belongs perhaps to science fiction, nevertheless, the use of self-organizing computers or cybernetic controllers in the automatic factories of tomorrow is already seriously considered. Although none of the hardware required is yet available, they will probably become quite feasible and assume great importance in one or two decades. Curiously enough, machines can even help in education and are already employed for the individual tuition of various kinds. Although a 'mechanized teacher' is perhaps a rather repulsive idea, the former is undoubtedly the more trustworthy and reliable than 'comics', daily papers or other means of mass communication which tell us so many things that just 'ain't so'. Sensationalism may be helpful from the sales point of view, but it has a negative educational value.

While speaking about education one has to emphasize that for full mental development wide interest in both natural sciences and humanities must be maintained by each individual, apart from professional specialization. Owing to almost unprecedently swift progress in the majority of fields of mental endeavour, knowledge gained during school years and academic studies soon becomes out of date, if it is not being continuously revised and added to. A large proportion of graduates now work in fields which did not even exist when they took their degrees ten years ago. Today, a university degree is more significant as a proof that its holder is capable of learning and has acquired the correct ways of thinking. In conditions of continuous and rapid changes, we have to keep on learning all our lives. To stop doing so means inevitably the progressive loss of professional standing. Fortunately, the human mind is admirably suited for the continuous absorption of new knowledge. Although the young brain may be somewhat superior in the rate of absorbing information, the ability of selective reception, or of being able to learn and remember what really matters, improves with age. The mature mind, if continuously exercised, can maintain a very high level of efficiency almost until death. Perhaps this is the main difference between mental and physical development. When almost any athletic powers must inevitably decline with advancing years (some relatively very early, like the capacity for fast short-distance running), intellectual prowess, if properly cultivated, may persist and even increase.

The balance between sciences and humanities must be maintained throughout. Endless discussion about which is more

o

important, so popular these days, often forget that both science and art are essentially different means for the attainment of the same ends. The scientist and the artist are both engaged in the discovery and representation of certain relationships or patterns existing in the universe, comprising inorganic matter, living beings and mental life. The scientist works through experimentation and rational thinking and represents his discoveries in forms of logical or mathematical statements, which apart from expressing certain truths in the sense previously discussed, are also useful for the manipulation of things. The latter is the realm of technology. The artist works mainly from the subconscious level, where his mind is capable of forming certain patterns which mirror those existing in nature or represent his inner life. In doing this he depends on his insight, imagination and inspiration although, of course, he uses a great deal of conscious thinking in arriving at the final form of his creations. He then expresses his findings through a certain medium, producing the patterns which can be seen or heard. Again he does not appeal, in general, to the rational faculties of the mind but tries to achieve the desired effect on the subconscious or emotional level. Hence his language is very different from that of a scientist. Even if his medium is the normal spoken word, he does not concentrate on rational meaning, but uses words mainly for the creation of certain mental states and images, not amenable to rational definition. Any artist has to work hard to achieve proficiency in the techniques of expression. But once the language of any art is mastered, the rest depends on the degree of perception and the level at which the artist is able to comprehend and express the relationships in nature or in his own mind. The superb craftsman has mastered the language of art but has little to say; the true artist not only knows the grammer and the dictionary of his preferred medium but also has some ideas worthy of communication. To discriminate between the ideas expressed in a certain piece of artistic work and the language in which they are conveyed is extremely difficult. The work of art speaks to our subconsciousness and either it has the desired effect or it does not. If it does not, then it may be that the artist had nothing much to say, or that we reject his ideas, or that we do not understand his language. To perceive an object as beautiful means the subconscious comprehension of the patterns it represents and the acceptance of these patterns. In fact, one suspects that the intensity of feeling awe or beauty depends on the degree of resonance between the mind of the observer and the pattern of the object of art, hence in the lasts analysis, on the mental similarity between the creator and the perceiver. It is not surprising therefore that standards of beauty are very different in various human groups. Certain modes of artistic expression are more easily understandable in one civilization than in another. The extremely difficult language of abstract arts accounts mainly for the small appreciation by the general public.

Returning now to the balance between science and the humanities, it must be said that in all fairness the humanists are in general much more ignorant of the natural sciences than the scientists are of the humanities. Scientists are usually self-conscious of their inadequacies in the humanities and often apologize for it, but only on rare occasions does one hear a scientist ignorantly dismissing summarily all other fields of human endeavour but the sciences. Not so with the humanists. The total disregard of science as a sort of craft is almost fashionable in certain circles. It is about time that some people understood that natural sciences contribute very substantially to our understanding of the universe on a basic level and have nothing to fear from comparison with the humanities. The reason for this unfortunate state of affairs is probably not very difficult to find. The predominant type of education received in the past by the intellectually and politically dominant classes was mainly of a humanistic character. Through the strength of traditions and because of the fear of losing their elevated positions in more than one sense, many powerful groups insist still that science, although very useful at the applied level, is nevertheless inferior in a fundamental sense as compared with other intellectual activities.

There are also other factors. The triumphant progress of science during the last few centuries has, one after another, demolished traditional concepts and completely changed our outlook on the world. However, some large fields remained only superficially affected by science; among them the basic features of living beings and the mental abilities of the human mind. The most complex machines of the past were so rigid and pre-determined in their functioning, that by comparison even the simplest living things appeared to be much superior.

Even less explicable or imitable were the powers of the human brain. Machines could not perform even the simplest mental tasks. Great feats of leadership or artistic ability have been so utterly beyond any mechanistic explanation that any attempt to find one seemed futile. As administration and leadership are most important for the existence of large communities, and as the ability to cope with every-day life is essential for the survival of the individual, and as art and religion could not be discussed in the language of science, scientific method could not form the basis of the *weltanschauung* in the proper sense, but had to remain a tool applicable in certain situations only. The subordinate position of the scientist in society bears witness to this situation. Even the great industrial revolution, which was basically the creation of the scientist and the technologist, was directed by men entirely lacking, in general, any scientific knowledge. And today, in highly industrialized societies, how many leading personalities in public life, politics or industry know the bare fundamentals of science?

Although the considerations of the problems of religion lie beyond the scope of his book, the relation between science and revealed religions cannot be ignored. It is most unfortunate that the clash appears to be on the basic level. Any revealed religion accepts certain unalterable dogmas concerning the basic problems of the universe and human life. Thus no progress on a basic level is possible because the framework is fixed and future discoveries must be accommodated within it. On the other hand, science is always willing to modify its basic theories and never claims their final validity. Thus a genuine fundamental progress is always possible. These two systems of thought, one immutable, the other continuously altering, must clash from time to time. It is no use saying that religion and science concern themselves with different matters and are therefore independent.

Any religion, however abstract or centred on the after life, must be translated finally into a set of rules, applicable to the conduct of the individual and society, or it loses all significance. The very meaning of religion implies a group of fundamental beliefs governing the behaviour of the faithful as an all-embracing ideology and pervading all fields of human activity. The divorce of religion from many fundamental social issues in recent times has led to the progressive loss of influence by Christian Churches. Similarly science, though in the early stages concerned only with rather simple physical phenomena, from which it was not possible to draw conclusions concerning more general matters, in the more advanced stages establishes certain theories which have a definite bearing on the conduct of life and on the fundamental problems of the universe. In fact, at a high stage of development, which has not yet been reached, science is bound to become as all-embracing as religion; hence science and religion act in overlapping fields. Clashes between the two are unavoidable.

One can easily verify that in the past scientific discoveries conflicted many times with religious views; the heliocentric system of Copernicus and the theory of evolution being only two of the most notorious examples. In each case, after a period of struggle, the official position of the Church was modified in face of a mass of evidence which could not be ignored. A temporary and uneasy truce was reached only to be broken again by disagreement at some other point. If in the future theologians persist in their obstinacy, it is difficult to see how a further decline of church influence can be avoided. This would be regrettable, because the spirit of Christianity, as distinct from dogma, is, if anything, supported by modern scientific discoveries.

These views certainly do not imply the advice to incorporate all new scientific theory into one's world-view. There are few things more ridiculous than a sudden change in one's basic opinions because of some newly announced hypothesis, usually of a tentative nature initially. Great theories rarely appear suddenly, but are usually, a crystallization of views apparent for a long time. Basic scientific theory can only be accepted as a part of a world-view if the former has been demonstrated beyond reasonable doubt.

Certain findings of modern social science seem too hastily and uncritically accepted. It must be remembered that the psychology of the individual human being and of the interactions in human groups is extremely complex, and we have so far only scratched the surface. There are few things in this field about which we can be dogmatic. It must be stated bluntly that most theories in psychology and social science simply cannot be called scientific in the full meaning of the term, because experimental evidence is highly inadequate, often almost non-existent. For instance, the social scientist as a rule studies the relationships existing only in a certain type of society, hence he is not entitled to regard his conclusions as universally valid. Also the social sciences are, as any other science, amoral in themselves and can be applied only with reference to the universal set of human values accepted at a given period. It is rather unfortunate that a majority of psychological observations are made on mediocre or defective individuals, neglecting by comparison, the gifted and outstanding human specimen. This is perhaps because as a rule a psychiatrist comes in touch with the former as because they present greater immediate problems, though from the long-term view it is the gifted individual who constitutes the greatest asset to the community and deserves the maximum care. As a result, the solutions proposed today in psychology aim at the creation of conditions favourable to the mediocre specimen of our race and, *eo ipso*, encourage mediocrity. Hence the stress on adjustment to the environment, on making popular views easily acceptable, on removing all obstacles and on the perfect fitting of the individual to the group. Such other-directed or organisationally-minded mental posture is obviously easily acceptable by a mediocre individual, but it is stifling and crippling to the development of creative powers. Related to the above is the very evident tendency to absolve the wayward individual from all his misdoing by abolishing the concept of personal responsibility. On the less sophisticated level this idea expresses itself in the very evident popular tendency not to condemn crime on moral grounds but to treat it rather as an exciting game. Guilt becomes associated with the fact of being caught.

Discussion of these matters obviously brings us to the old problem of free will and materialism and, as we know, the answer is far from simple. One thing must be clearly borne in mind. The great influence of environment on the behaviour of the individual is beyond question, and while judging any sort of generally disapproved activity, it is the duty of society, acting through its representatives, to take into account all factors having a bearing on the case. Ideally, the whole life story of the accused should be examined in the minutest detail, but this is an unattainable perfection. On the other hand, summary condemnation without consideration to the circumstances, is unjust and stupid. Nevertheless, certain areas of free choice, however limited, must be admitted, and the idea of moral guilt cannot be entirely abolished. It is an observable fact that the behaviour of people living in roughly similar circumstances varies widely from person to person. Not all children reared in slums become thieves and prostitutes, most develop into fairly decent citizens.

The counter-argument is, of course, that the circumstances of each such child are not exactly identical and secondly, that there exist vast differences in the genetic equipment or innate tendencies. However, if we admit that the behaviour of, the individual is entirely dependent on his innate features and on the influences of the environment, leaving no room for free choice, then we are *eo ipso*, turning human beings into machines. This is very much what some psychologists and social scientists imply. But it is only one further step to the idea that a human being should therefore be treated like any other complex machinery. Hence, the apparently benevolent and humanistic approach to the criminal or the anti-social individual, if carried to its logical conclusion, paves the way for most tyrannical ideologies leading to the complete conditioning and regimentation of society. In the end it is the criminal himself who would suffer most from the widespread acceptance of such tendencies. If he is completely irresponsible, then his readjustment and conversion into a useful member of the community must be considered mainly from an economic point of view, like the overhaul of a car. If the 'modification' proves too expensive, then the evil-doer should be scrapped. There is nothing fantastic in such considerations, as the tragic extermination or the brutal enslavement of countless millions under certain régimes testify only too well.

There is no definite rational argument that human beings have no free choice because, as we have seen previously, the admission of intrinsic freedom of very complex systems, however limited, is not only permissible but plausible. Also, even if a human being were only a machine, it would be very stupid to make him aware of that fact. It would be silly to programme a computer for useless or erratic performance. The apparent wide-spread irresponsibility of teenagers, if really true, could very well be attributed to the fact that these young people are continuously being told that whatever wrong they do—negligence, laziness, sex crimes, stealing or violence—there is always something or somebody else to be blamed for it. The actual delinquent is almost invariably represented as a misguided being, deserving all the sympathy in the world. The victim usually gets much less consideration, let alone any sort of compensation. Admittedly, if human beings were only machines, then to blame them in the moral sense for their misbehaviour would be a deception, but perhaps a very useful deception.

Finally, let us not forget that there is usually a considerable time-gap between pure science and its practical applications. This applies also to psychology and social science. Both are most important and vital disciplines from the point of view of happiness and the development of the individual and society. But this does not imply the rash application of any tentative hypothesis. On the contrary, as the consequences are in this case all-important, let us be very cautious. We ought to allocate far greater resources to basic research in these fields, but we ought also to apply the findings only when we really know what we are doing. Above all, these powerful techniques should not fall into the hands of unscrupulous groups, who might apply them for their own ends. The totalitarian régimes are not the only culprits in this respect, scientific propagandists of various sorts, and the sales promoters of our so-called free world, being strong contenders for the title of 'experts in brain-washing'.

Among the many fundamental sociological issues of our times is that of the welfare state. Briefly, while some people consider it the most advanced social structure so far developed by man, others insist that it leads to general laziness and the decline of the individual resourcefulness, because the satisfaction of basic needs is assured even in the absence of effort. As some form of welfare state is now generally accepted by industrial societies, it is obvious that this kind of social arrangement is one of the historical phases of the development of our civilization. It is also in agreement with the principle of co-operation embodied in the cultural evolution of mankind. It is beyond question that any temporarily or permanently handicapped individual ought to receive a full measure of help from society and the idea of 'every man for himself' belongs to the Dark Ages. However this does not imply that everybody should get the same share of the national cake, irrespective of his or her contribution. The concept of equal income is unjust and promotes laziness and disinterest among all members of a community, especially the more gifted. At present, remuneration for work performed is mainly of a financial nature, and although this kind of reward is not the only one possible, we have to live with the facts as they are, at least so far as the near future is concerned. The fact that nearly equal pay, achieved both by the progressive reduction of differentials in salaries and wages and by taxation, leads to less intensive work is so obvious that it needs no discussion. But that the above policy is also basically unjust is perhaps less evident.

Some people suggest that because some are naturally more gifted than others, earners should be rewarded according to their efforts and not according to their contributions, as apparently more could be expected from abler individuals. But this is unfair. Men are unequal not only in their working capacities but also in many other respects. Compare a physically well-developed man of excellent health and looks, but mediocre as a worker, with an anaemic, unattractive individual whose only assets are a high mental ability or great manual dexterity. It is obvious that, other things being equal, the former has much better chances to enjoy a pleasant life. Then why rob the latter, by paying the same salary to both, disregarding their unequal contributions in work. Everybody should get a good living wage as a minimum and people seriously handicapped mentally or physically are fully entitled to all the help necessary. But anything above this minimum standard should depend on the individual's contribution, resulting from both his efforts and his natural endowment. The inequalities which should be abolished are those stemming from an income based on the possession of capital inherited or gained by various kinds of speculations.

The social group which suffers most from the tendency towards equalization is the middle class of professionals and experts. This relatively small group of men and women, representing the most valuable part of the community, is at present caught between the grindstones of big capital and organized labour. Big business, although now much more humane in its methods and restricted by the State and by the activities of trade unions, still occupies a dominant position in Western countries. On the other hand, the attitudes of trade unions, especially in this country, have too much of the character of grab-and-charge-it-to-the-public to be regarded as true socialism. But they are immensely powerful by virtue of sheer numbers and organization. Because of its traditions, the middle class generally abhors the idea of organizing for political and financial gains, hence it remains powerless and its dwindling social and economic statis, is the best proof of the situation. Yet the development of any civilization is largely due to the contribution of a small creative minority, which the mass follows by sheer imitation or coercion.

The professional middle class is the very backbone of a nation. It was this class that the Nazis and Communists singled out for destruction in the conquered countries. The upper class, once stripped of its power, was too small numerically to bother about, and the working class, when deprived of leadership, was powerless. Hence, by the same argument political power belongs to the middle class for the asking. All that is needed is to close the ranks, and to unify purpose and action. It is sheer nonsense to insist that the political organization of the middle class would interfere with the professional performance of its members; this is the sort of myth which certain circles are careful to cultivate. The professional man is supposed to do his job to the best of his abilities for a relative meagre reward, and leave the rest to those who own and run the business by virtue of their mysterious qualities of leadership, unattainable by average mortals. It hardly needs saying that the political supremacy of the knowledgeable people would be most beneficial for the nation and those who would probably most fiercely oppose it (for instance, organized labour), would in the end certainly benefit. But perhaps in any case, in the coming age of automation and automatic data processing, the ranks of the middle class will so swell much with specialists that it cannot finally fail to take the leadership of the nation into its hands.

In the automized welfare societies of tomorrow, with short working hours and an abundance of goods, the problem of leisure will become very important. To those men of past ages, exhausted by hard and incessant toil, the very idea that leisure can be a problem would appear just as far-fetched as the possibility of contacting intelligent extra-terrestrial beings is to

THE POINTERS TO THE FUTURE

us. Spare time gained through mechanization is only of value if we know how to spend it enjoyably and constructively. Existing forms of popular entertainment are both moronically simple and increasingly passive. Instead of offering scope for fulfilment, a chance for self-expression and the joy of exercising mental and physical powers, they tend towards the simple forms of escapism. Far from enabling people to get a wider outlook and experience of things outside the field of their professional work, they create continuous and senseless distractions. This may be incidentally very helpful to the ruling classes, because it makes the mass more docile and more manageable, but it is hardly likely to bring the real satisfaction that results from the achievement of certain aims, from a sense of purpose and from decision-making activities. True, the masses want the present forms of entertainment, but the wishes of the people are fixed no more in this field than in any other, and they can be altered by education.

Because of equalizing tendencies in remuneration, the importance of the more educated groups as customers has dwindled. The common man, by virtue of sheer numbers, is now commercially speaking the most important customer everywhere. Hence the general decline of taste in almost everything commercially available, entertainment included. But by giving the common man exactly what he wants a great dis-service is being done him. He is by virtue of his natural endowment just as good as the people at the top, and what he really needs is education in the broadest sense. Only then will he be able truly to enjoy his increased material prosperity and the leisure which the shrinking working week will offer him. It is hard to believe that millions of people, gazing every evening at their television, are really enjoying themselves.

On the political plane, one of the most important problems facing our epoch is the massive help required for the underdeveloped countries, together with the related problem of population control, and also the burning issue of abolishing nuclear weapons. The latter constitutes, of course, one of the many facets of the global struggle between West and East, or between capitalism and communism, and may be meaningfully considered only in this context. The division of the world between the 'haves' and the 'have-nots' was probably never greater than it is today. While the consequences of over-abundance of material goods are becoming a serious issue within the richer industrial societies, appalling poverty is the lot of two-thirds of the human race.

There is something incredibly parochial and ironical in the fact that while the tendency towards the equalization of salaries and wages is, if anything, exaggerated in the Western countries, very little is being done to improve the desperate economic position of the industrially backward nations. The worn-out and outdated ideologies of soveriegn states, of nationalism, racialism, imperialism and cultural parochialism prove still stronger than the feeling of brotherhood of *all* men. While welfare activities, the levelling up of the standards of living, and the idea of social justice are now being increasingly accepted within the industrial states, almost perfect egoism rules international relationships. While obesity is a serious medical problem in the Western societies, malnutrition and often outright hunger is the normal experience of hundreds of millions of human beings. The privileged economic position of the white man is not entirely due to his own efforts but is largely the result of the favourable combination of several really incidental factors, like geographical position, the currents of world history, climate, the richness of soil, and mineral deposits.

When a single man or a group becomes extremely rich and refuses to share the riches with other men or social groups, we usually blame them on ethical grounds and finally force them to share by revolution or legislative action. But apparently everything is in order if a very rich nation refuses to part with even a relatively small portion of its total income, although a small sum would provide enough capital for the development of a poorer country.

But moral considerations apart, it is obvious that complex relations in world economy between the extremely rich and the extremely poor is harmful to both in the long run. By withholding help to the poor countries, we may momentarily preserve a few points in our living standards, but we are also doing a great dis-service to the economic future of the world. When economic ties are as closely knit as now, and when everything points to an even closer interdependence, it is obvious that progress cannot be made unless the whole planet is developed in a harmonious and integrated manner. Hence, it is not only the moral duty of the rich countries to help the poor; by doing so they also foster their own interests. Further, apart from purely economic considerations, the tremendous inequality in living standards creates great political tension. The hungry and disgruntled man is an easy prey for the demagogue. He has little to lose, and the mere destruction of the wealth of the envied nations may prove an attractive proposition. We have to realise finally that all men belong to the same species, and that the idea of every man for himself is incompatible with the cultural evolution of mankind. Egoism may be natural for a solitary, predatory animal, but it is destructive for a social animal, for whom co-operation, at least so far as his own species is concerned, means survival.

Co-operation within a species is often evident even in the brutal struggle for survival experienced during its evolution. The very creation of multicellular organisms can be considered as a supreme example of the co-operation of millions of cells, each of which is a basic and complete unit of life. In the realm of cultural evolution co-operation becomes imperative. It is the basis of the whole process. Unfortunately, the opposite can be observed. Although the prophecies of Marx about the rich getting richer and the poor becoming poorer did not materialize so far as industrial societies are concerned, nevertheless the Marxist view is not entirely pointless. Disparity in the standards of living between rich and poor countries, is actually on the increase. This is due mainly to the lack of capital and education in the underdeveloped countries. Although some people maintain that the concept of an underdeveloped country is a matter of definition, because even in the richest states further economic progress, is always possible and in this sense every country is underdeveloped, yet the distinction can be made. Industrial development is a threshold phenomenon. It does not take place at all, or at the most it proceeds at an extremely slow rate, until a certain amount of investment capital is accummulated. Hence, we can say that an underdeveloped country is the one which is below this level. But once the starting capital is available, either as savings or as gifts from outside, industrial progress proceeds by leaps and bounds. Hence, what is needed is the provision of this basic capital and of the technical help.

The problem of the underdeveloped countries is intimately connected with the unrestricted growth of population. The numerical strength of pre-scientific communities has been limited by high mortality rates, especially during early infancy. Sporadic epidemnics have sometimes destroyed half of a population. But enormous advances in medical science have led to the practical abolition of mortal epidemic disease in the West and have increased the expectation of life very substantially. This has obviously been a blessing to Western societies, where the increase in population has been matched by a corresponding increase in productive capacity. But in underdeveloped countries an increase in medical care caused a population explosion without any corresponding advance in food production. So by giving technical help to produce more food and by abolishing at the same time the major causes of high mortality, we reach the situation where in a poor country, instead of X millions of starving and disease-ridden people, live 2X millions of relatively healthy but still starving inhabitants. Obviously, this is not really much better than the earlier situation, so population control is the only possible solution, if both external help and internal effort to create the basic capital for industrial expansion are not to be swallowed up by the swarming millions.

Population control is rejected either on religious grounds or on the basis of fundamental human rights, one of which is supposedly the freedom of begetting an unlimited number of children. It is also pointed out that, if all the resources of our planet were rationally developed, a population many times greater than the present could be comfortably supported, but this would require the development of technologies which at present do not exist, although scientifically feasible, the creation of a world state and the redistribution of the existing population. Taking facts as they are, such schemes are impractical in the foreseeable future. Further, even if they were realisable, even if every ounce of food, which it is possible to grow or manufacture by artificial means were in fact produced, it is obvious that there is a limit somewhere. Even into taking account the present rate of population increase, in a relatively short time there would be not even standing room for everybody alive, and some centuries later the total mass of living humanity would be greater than that of the earth itself.

Over-population is incompatible with conditions favourable for the full development of human capacities and the enjoyment of life. It must lead inevitably to over-organization and rigid planning, not for freedom, which would aim at providing every individual with maximum facilities, but a planning with the sole object of keeping the whole structure going and preventing a collapse under the pressure of numbers. The freedom of the individual would become a relatively trifling matter in such conditions. In fact, freedom could hardly exist at all, and wars that aim at exterminating other competitors for the limited resources, vital for survival, would be more likely.

As in many other fields, a compromise between the rights of the individual and the welfare of the society must be achieved also in the control of population. The right to an unlimited number of children must finally produce universal slavery. How control can be achieved is another matter. If some people are capable of restricting their sexual life on religious grounds, all the better, but taking a sober look at the present ethical and cultural level of mankind, the use of some simple and cheap contraceptive measure seems to be the only practical solution.

Limitation of numbers, however, is not the only issue. We must also devise some means of preventing the genetic transmission of undesirable traits. At the prehistoric stage the law of survival of the fittest was operative, pruning ruthlessly the grossly detrimental heriditary features. But in the conditions of advanced medical science and of the welfare state, many physically or mentally defective individuals survive and beget progeny. Thus the total genetic pool of the race is likely to deteriorate, and medical science must devise a substitute to prevent the race from degeneration.

The subject is extremely complex and is still only very imperfectly understood. Among the influential factors are: the social habits of choosing a mate, the average age of men and women on entering marriage, social discrimination, family planning customs, the extent of medical care, mortality and many others. It has also been pointed out that the meaning of fitness is a relative concept. For instance, resistance to a given disease is irrelevant when that disease is eliminated, and an illness like diabetes becomes relatively less important if the supply of insulin is plentiful. The majority of the population in civilized countries is probably basically less fit for survival in extremely primitive conditions than the races accustomed to

such habitats. On the other hand primitive people can withstand hunger, cold or heat, yet prove must less resistant than
'soft' city dwellers to the civilized 'germs'. However, some
defects are obviously quite undesirable; as, for instance,
proneness to mental illnesses or severe physical malformation.
In the end, the whole race could degenerate to such an extent
and the number of people depending on continuous medical
care of one sort or another would be so great, that the whole
structure could come to a grinding halt or even collapse under
its own weight, especially during some major social, political
or natural catastrophe.

If agreement on effective measures for preventing the hereditary transmission of gross mental and physical defects was
reached, the question which would naturally suggest itself is:
Could we go one step further and by suitable combinations of
constraints and encouragements promote the breeding of those
human strains which we consider most desirable and superior?
The laws of genetics tell us that harmful mutations are predominant and lead to the degeneration of any organ or feature,
in conditions where the latter have no continuing survival
value. The greatest fears in this connection are expressed with
regard to the average human intelligence, where some social
factors not related directly to survival may be influential. For
instance, lower-class families, which are supposed to be less
gifted mentally, are usually larger. But the evidence of intelligence tests in school is so far inconclusive. Be that as it may, the
possibility of developing superior races of human beings by
genetic control appears possible.

One is, of course, fully aware of the existence of very strong
social and moral taboos surrounding this subject. Any step
towards the artificial breeding of human beings, however
benevolent and limited, is almost certain to evoke universal
disapproval. Nevertheless, restrictions on the choice of mate are
already very strong and plentiful, but as they have developed
mostly in an uncontrolled fashion, apart from laws prohibiting
marriages between closely related persons, they are apparently
socially acceptable. In theory, apart from the above mentioned
exceptions, any mature, single man or woman can enter into
matrimony, if they desire to do so. But in practice, the differences of race, class, age, religion, economic status, educational
level and hundreds of others, very effectively limit the choice.

Additional restrictions of equal strength, scientifically designed to develop desirable characteristics, could go a long way towards achieving the result. But to do so, a rational attitude to the subject has first to be developed. Today, a man who would most violently decry any suggestion of genetic control, will neverthe-less forbid his daughter to marry the man she loves, probably quite desirable, because his income is inadequate. It must also be remembered that some kinds of artificial human breeding has been going on for centuries e.g. among the aristocracy. The higher the status of the person concerned the more limited was the choice, and amongst royal families there was often no choice at all. Yet these people were most proud of their lineage. So why could we not also be proud of belonging to a genetic line of mathematicisns, painters or weight-lifters?

However, objections to closer genetic control other than the elimination of obviously undesirable characteristics are stronger on scientific grounds. The traits genetically transmitted seem usually to be connected in groups. Hence, by eliminating certain undesirable traits we might also abolish some features of possible greater importance. Similarly, by enhancing the development of certain positive traits we might also promote the growth of some very detrimental factors. Not only is our knowledge of the laws of genetics still very incomplete, but we cannot even decide which traits are relatively more import-ant. Is it better to be very intelligent or to be resistant to certain kinds of illness? To be tall and slim or sturdy and muscular? To have a highly rational mind or artistic abilities?

In this connection it is clear that any sort of racialism is invalid. First of all, the spread in the intensity of any important, measurable feature among the members of any race generally swamps the relatively small differences between the racial averages. Secondly, even if we allow that the obvious physical differences, e.g. colour of skin, correspond to certain differences in physical and mental fitness, the answer is still: so what? The values attached to the majority of mental and physical features are largely arbitrary and,to speak about social superior-ity or inferiority is therefore sheer nonsense. The political, cultural or technological supremacy of a certain nation or race in a given period proves almost nothing, so far as the apparently superior natural endowment of this race is concerned. During the half million years or more of human history, various races

P

and nations have gained and lost advantage over others.

In conclusion, if we ever decide to embark on a developed form of genetic control we will have to be exceedingly cautious. The breeding of animals shows clearly that pure strains are very vulnerable and easily die out. The heterozygot or a mixed strain is more resistant to an adverse environment than the homozygot or pure strain. The best safeguard of the species in being able to cope with unforeseen changes in the environment is avoidance of specialization, thus retaining plenty of capacity for development of the traits necessary for successfully meeting the environmental challenge. Evolution demonstrates clearly that the highly specialised species have smaller chances of survival than the unspecialized ones. Once the species achieves specialization there is no way back. It is arguable what degree of specialization, biologically speaking, has been reached by the human race so far, but some potential for further development and adaptation to the altering environment is still clearly present. It may be safer to preserve it.

The existence of nuclear weapons constitutes one of the most fundamental problems of the present time and therefore has a bearing on almost any general social or political issue. In fact, because these weapons, used indiscriminately, could wipe out the whole human race, they are probably the most important physical factor existing. The widespread tendency to ignore this danger, is simply self-deception. The existence of atomic weapons means for every individual a very appreciable increase in the possibility of sudden death, together with all he loves and cares for. Such fundamental facts cannot fail to affect the activity of any thinking human being. On a purely rational basis it decreases the value of any sacrifices made of immediate benefits for the sake of future gains, because it diminishes the probabilities of their realization.

The existence of nuclear weapons raises two issues: first the problem of testing them, and second, a stop to their production and the destruction of existing stocks.

Humanity today is divided into two gigantic blocks, both at a comparable scientific and technological level, commanding tremendous manpower, industrial capacities and natural resources, and thus creating a planetary balance of power. But it is an uneasy balance, because both sides are fiercely inimical to each other and apparently irreconcilable ideologically. Hence, the resulting situation has many features of a titanic religious struggle. As pointed out previously, the basic issues of this struggle are clouded by cultural and social parochialism and by a misunderstanding of the forces and tendencies present in advanced industrial societies. It seems likely that the contestants are fighting shadows and that the way of living, based on science, industrialization and progressive mechanization of physical and mental work, inevitably leads to the parallel social developments in both groups. At the moment, the mutual hatred scarcely lessens; hatred is being deliberately spread through each camp, and the populations are indoctrinated accordingly. Huge strategic forces are poised for instant use. Each side appears to be ready to fight to the end, even if it means mutual annihilation, rather than surrender. There exists also a third group of nations which are not directly committed, although hardly anyone of them can claim real neutrality. In any case, these nations are generally under-developed, weak industrially and militarily, and cannot immediately affect the balance of power, although they may well do so in the near future.

A few hundreds of 'clean', well-placed hydrogen bombs could kill a sizeable part of the population in the 'industrial belt' (U.S.A., Western Europe, Russia) and many more millions would eventually die through the delayed effects of radioactive fall-out, through epidemics and starvation, due to the disruption of organizations and transportation. Civilization would be crippled, and considerable genetic damage to future generations would be inevitable.

A few thousands of 'dirty' bombs in the multi-megaton class may well kill the majority of the human race, either directly or through fall-out. They also could increase the general level of radiation to the point where all the highest species, including human beings, would eventually perish because of the resulting excessive rate of mutations. The latter are as a rule detrimental, hence there is a maximum rate of mutation which any species can withstand. Even if the number of 'dirty' bombs exploded was not big enough to wipe out the human race, the adverse genetic consequences would persist for thousands of years.

There also exist—in theory, if not in fact—certain types of bombs, like the cobalt bomb, which if used in sufficient quantities could almost certainly destroy all forms of life. Even if this statement is at present perhaps controversial on scientific grounds, there is little point in arguing about it, because in any case the construction of weapons of complete annihilation will be technically feasible in the next decade or so. One must remember that the power of nuclear bombs has increased about a thousand-fold within one decade.

Both sides have large stocks of nuclear weapons and the means of their delivery, against which no effective defence exists. Taking into account the possible failure of the weapon, losses from defence measures, adverse atmospheric conditions, and all other factors diminishing statistically the efficiency of nuclear weapons, a large percentage of the total number put into action could still produce results within the specification.

The above facts are certainly true in the qualitative sense. There is no point at all in arguing whether it is ten or one hundred bombs which are necessary to destroy a given country, whether missiles are more effective than planes, whether existing stocks are already as high as the figures mentioned above or whether anybody makes 'dirty' hydrogen bombs or even cobalt bombs. All that matters is that the weapon systems exist, capable of destroying the civilization, or even destroying the human race and all other higher forms of life. Bearing in mind the stakes involved, the question of tests, if considered separately from the main problem of total disarmament, fades almost into insignificance. The few hundred thousand deaths due to increased leukaemia and other illnesses caused by fall-out from the tests, are not very important, if the preservation of national independence and of the way of living of half of the human race is involved.

The weapon which has not been tested experimentally is not reliable on technical grounds, hence, the deaths of innocent people affected by nuclear fall-out, however regrettable, are a relatively small price to pay, if the possession of nuclear weapons is the essential means of preventing enemy attack and forestalling defeat. But, if the end of tests is considered mainly as the first step towards total disarmament, its importance increases immensely.

In the long run total disarmament seems to be the only practical alternative to total destruction. In conditions of extreme political tension, of the very complex interaction of two opposing systems, and in face of fanatical communist ideology, the explosive spark is bound to come sooner or later. It may result from the action of some neurotic commander at a relatively low level, because of a mistaken radio signal, or because of some relatively unimportant matter in which neither side is prepared 'to lose face'. But it is also conceivable that one side will reach a temporary advantage over the other and therefore start a 'preventive war' in the hope of wiping the opponent out before he can retaliate. It suffices to say that, taking everything into account, the chance of an all-out atomic war with all the consequences described above, does exist and, assuming the continuance of present conditions, the possibility of an eruption sometime in the future is very substantial. So, the means leading to total disarmament must be found, or we will all perish. It is very unlikely that the actual contestants, with their populations partly extinct and the remainder heavily contaminated by radioactive products, will spare the neutral countries. By entering the all-out nuclear war, the belligerent nations will demonstrate that they prefer to die rather than allow an alien way of living to conquer the world; therefore they would be rather inconsistent, if, after having almost completely destroyed themselves, they should leave any other powerful country untouched. As the country, or group of countries, which escaped annihilation would naturally dominate the world after the atomic war, it would mean to at least one contestant that he is dying in vain. Is it reasonable to think that he would allow it to happen?

Total disarmament may be effected in two ways: as a unilateral disarmament by one side or as the negotiated gradual disarmament by both sides simultaneously.

Unilateral disarmament would certainly abolish the possibility of total destruction through an atomic war, but at the same time it would mean complete surrender to the other side. One has to be quite clear on this point as the suggestion that a good example set by one side would influence the other side to act likewise deserves the attention of a psychiatrist rather than a serious discussion. The very idea that men in the Kremlin, or in the Pentagon could be brought to tears of repentance and to mutual benevolence by somebody destroying his nuclear stock-piles is just too ridiculous to be seriously entertained.

The unilateral renunciation of nuclear weapons by one side

would be most certainly interpreted as a sign of weakness by the other. Also, the atomic disarmament of a minor power in either group, for instance, of Great Britain, is very unlikely to make for greater safety. The opposite would be true, because the additional deterrent power would be lacking and the enemy would destroy such a country during a major war in any case, whether it possesses atomic weapons or not. It is too naïve to think that Russia, when almost totally destroyed by the U.S.A., and having itself almost totally destroyed the latter, would allow an intact Western Europe to take over the leadership of the world. A similar argument applies to China.

The surrender of the West at present would mean the total extinction of the ideals in which we rightly or wrongly believe and the physical extermination or imprisonment of many millions of people, mainly from the upper and middle classes, as in Russia, China and Eastern Europe. Various Western idealists who suggest unilateral disarmament, no doubt with the best intentions, cannot apparently admit that the consequences would be a world totalitarian state, based on Asiatic traditions of slavery and disregard for the individual's right. Or do they believe in the survival of Western ideals even under a totalitarian rule? The blood of Hungary should convince them about the ruthlessness and determination of the men in the Kremlin. And the merciless suppression of the uprising was effected at a period when world opinion is extremely important for the masters of the Soviet Union. How much more ruthless could they afford to be if they ruled the whole planet and independent opinion no longer existed. Many people believe that Christianity and humanistic ideology will always win in the end, whatever the forces trying to suppress them. In other words they believe in the ultimate triumph of an idea, no matter what physical forces are pitted against it. This may be true, if the idea is based on the elementary urges of human nature (one has to be very careful with such an interpretation) and expresses the natural tendencies in the development of the society. But it is also true that an idea can be suppressed for a very long time, perhaps for thousands of years, if it is not defended by force against physical violation. For instance, it is very doubtful whether Christianity would have survived the onslaught of Islam, if it had not been defended by the swords of medieval knighthood.

One could also add here that proposals aiming at the organization of passive resistance and of an armed underground movement in the surrendering countries are equally impractical. Such movements could not survive for long in the absence of support from outside.

However, from the long-term point of view, the millenial rule of even the most oppressive system would be obviously preferable to total extinction. No system lasts for ever, and one would reasonably expect that after a sufficiently long time even the worst conditions would improve. The principles lost would be rediscovered and reinstated, so either of the two blocks can rest assured that if its ideas are really valuable they would eventually re-appear, even if the other side managed to suppress them. The ideals of civilization would only be lost if there were no longer any normal human beings left alive.

The chief drawback is, however, that hardly anybody is prepared to sacrifice everyting for the benefit of future generations. A given human being lives only once and a capacity for very intense suffering is one of his many faculties. He perceives himself as a separate entity and however strongly he may feel compassion for other people and for the world at large, he is never entirely submerged by his environment to the point where he forgets his essential and unique personal distinction. He may be persuaded to take the interests of his distant descendants into account, but he cannot be expected to sacrifice his freedom and happiness for their sake. And this is just what the advocates of a unilateral disarmament advise. Their proposals mean that a nuclear holocaust will not happen, but the price to pay for it would be extermination, slavery and suffering for many millions in the Western world. No doubt, the leading classes in the communist camp could put their case in a similar form. Hence, the price for unilateral disarmament, although relatively small, if the alternative is total extinction of the human race, simply could not be paid. One could hardly expect to persuade the ruling circles, in the widest sense, to adopt an attitude of total self-sacrifice. And the alternative to surrender is not the certainty of total destruction, but a substantial risk of it. There is some possibility of a gradual disarmament of both sides by means of a negotiated agreement.

Mutual understanding and tolerance between East and West is essential not only because of the existence of nuclear weapons threatening our total destruction. Even if atomic bombs did not exist at all, and if expansionist tendencies were absent in either camp, the closest international co-operation is needed to develop the world's resources for the benefit of all. Then the possibilities resulting from the closer interplay of Western civilization and Eastern culture are immense.

All through history we observe the coalescing of human groups into progressively greater units. Their sizes depend among other things, on means of transportation and communication. It seems that when it is physically possible to travel to any spot on the planet in a matter of hours and to make instant contact with people thousands of miles away, we are obviously entering the stage of world civilization. Hence, the nationalism and sovereignty of the state become out-dated, and in the presence of atomic weapons, are very dangerous ideas. At the stage of tribal communities, supreme loyalty to one's tribe was the highest virtue. A man capable of perceiving the possibility of a supra-tribal or national loyalty would have been considered a traitor to his tribe. But when the tribes merged into a nation, national loyalty then became the true loyalty, and to put the interest of one's tribe before those of the nation could well become a crime. Similarly today, a man who has genuinely stronger feelings of loyalty to the whole of humanity than to his own nation, might make, in certain situations, a choice which would brand him a traitor to his own community. And yet from humanity's point of view such a choice could be correct on ethical grounds, for it puts the interest of the whole before that of its parts.

The merging of cultures could be fruitful only in an atmosphere of common tolerance as otherwise the prevailing culture would swamp and destroy the cultural heritage of other human groups. Any civilization tends to consider itself not only as better than all the others, present or past, but as a final stage of human progress. Even in this age of fantastic changes, which take place from year to year, the above attitude still persists. We talk about great future technological developments, but we often state explicitly or implicitly that our basic ideology will persist for ever. The American way of life, the British way, the Russian way—all these are tacitly assumed to be eternal. Is it perhaps because the people are afraid to probe too deeply into issues which, while basic and all-important, are after all a matter of opinion? Do they fear to find that the foundations of their world-view are far less solid than is usually assumed? If so, then all our ideologies are based on deception.

Cultural parochialism is also harmful in many other ways. It stands to reason that as human races are broadly equal, although not necessarily identical in all features, the civilizations developed in various parts of our planet all possess certain good and bad traits. Hence, maximum tolerance is necessary, and the ability to understand other points of view is essential. Moreover, it is supreme nonsense to assume that any culture could be the final and optimum stage of the development of mankind. On the time-scale appropriate to the existence of man on earth the creation of great co-operative communities is only the very last invention, existing for a relatively short period. The human race is trying to develop a way of living suitable in the conditions of division of labour and technological progress. Many experiments have been conducted, some of them lasting thousands of years. The knowledge and experience thus gained have been partly lost and partly transmitted to the following generations. Glimpses of certain universal laws and ways of living, suitable for human beings, have been reached at various times and in various places, but all this is only a beginning. Many fundamental mistakes have also been committed. It is not only individuals who make errors but also large human groups; in fact, whole civilizations can be wrong. New societies arise in place of the old and try again. It is well to remember this, when holding views opposite to the majority of people in any group. The argument that 'everybody thinks like that' does not carry much weight and the individual must have the courage of his convictions, even if they run contrary to accepted opinions. One may well be right and millions may be wrong. This has happened many times in the past.

Any future world civilization must give every type of man a chance for development. There could hardly be anything worse than standardization of personality and of the way of thinking and living. This would automatically lead to ideological stagnation and to the suppression of the creative powers of man. A standardized civilization tends naturally to treat the non-conforming individual unkindly, thus rejecting often the best the human race can produce. There is no ideal type of man and no single, ideal way of living. Humanity can achieve full development only by consciously fostering the multitude of different kinds of human types and ideologies, exploring all possible avenues of social, cultural and scientific development. The whole structure must be designed in such a way as to be able to accommodate change and progress. In fact, the element of change must be the essential part of future world civilizations. With the rate of change increasing, progress in all fields must be harmonious and co-ordinated.

All these problems are immensely difficult. To grasp the idea that man can consciously direct his destiny, not only on a cultural, social and technological level, but perhaps even in a biological sense, is not easy. To level the barriers of out-dated ideologies and of national loyalties, and to substitute tolerance and the feeling of belonging to the human race is even more trying. To approach rationally many of the basic problems, all charged with high emotional content, and, while permeated with life-long indoctrination, to challenge the very basis of one's own world-view is almost superhuman. And yet it has to be done. The periods of upheaval, the fall of idols thousands of years old, and the erection of new signposts for future generations has occurred several times in the history of mankind. There are times when man must live and think like a giant or perish, and ours seem to belong to this category.

The future is unknown but one thing is certain: There is no way back and no permanent stabilization at any level. Man broke with mindless nature a long time ago and is now on his own. He has to face the universe, to find a way of living suited to his present condition, and to take control of his destiny. He has made so far only a few steps on the long road, full of dangers and challenges, often passing close to the precipices of annihilation. The emerging mind pushes relentlessly forward, fulfilling its eternal destiny; and the choice lies between the star-ship and a return to the animal state. There is nothing between.

BIBLIOGRAPHY

C. ALLEN. *Modern Discoveries in Medical Psychology*. Macmillan 1949.

L. A. ALLEN. *Management and Organization*. McGraw-Hill 1958.

H. ARENDT. *The Human Condition*. Cambridge University Press 1958.

R. ARON. *The Century of Total War*. Verschoyle 1954.

R. ARON. *The Opium of the Intellectual*. Secker & Warburge 1957.

W. R. ASHBY. *Design for a Brain*. Chapman & Hall, London 1952.

W. R. ASHBY. *Introduction to Cybernetics*. Chapman & Hall 1956.

A. J. AYER, *The Problem of Knowledge*. Macmillan 1956.

J. BARZUN. *The House of Intellect*. Secker & Warburge 1959.

W. S. BECK. *Modern Science and the Nature of Life*. Macmillan 1958.

S. BEER. *Cybernetics and Management*. English University Press 1959.

D. A. BELL. *Information Theory and its Engineering applications*. Pitman 1956.

N. J. BERRILL. *Man's Emerging Mind*. Dobson 1958.

N. J. BERRILL. *You and the Universe*. Dobson 1960.

P. M. S. BLACKETT. *Atomic Weapons and East-West Relations*. Cambridge 1956.

I. M. BOCHENSKI. *The Contemporary European Philosophy*. Trans. D. Nicholl & K. Afchenbrenner, University of California 1957.

H. M. BOODISH. *Our Industrial Age*. McGraw-Hill 1949.

L. BRILLOUIN. *Science and Information Theory*. Academic Press Inc., New York 1956.

D. E. BROADBENT. *Perception and Communication*. Pergamon Press, London 1958.

I. BROSS. *Design for Decision*. Macmillan 1953.

Intro. B. H. BROWN. *The East and West must Meet*. Symposium, Cora Dubois and others, Angus and Robertsons 1959.

J. S. BRUNER, J. J. GOODNOW, G. A. AUSTIN. *A Study of Thinking*. Chapman & Hall 1956.

A. J. BURTON, R. G. MILLS. *Electronic Computers and the Business applications*. Penn 1960.

R. G. CANNING. *Electronic Data Processing for Business and Industry*. Chapman & Hall 1956.

R. G. CANNING. *Installing Electronic Data Processing Systems*. Chapman & Hall 1958.

F. P. CHAMBERS and others. *This Age of Conflict*. Harrap 1950.

S. CHASE. *The Proper Study of Mankind*. Phoenix House 1950.

C. CHERRY. *On Human Communication*. Wiley 1957.

C. CHERRY (Ed.) (Symposium)—"Information Theory". London 1955. Butterworths Scientific Publications 1956.

E. CONZE. *Buddhism*. Oxford Cassier 1951.

J. COHEN. *Humanistic Psychology*. Allen and Unwin, London 1958.

S. A. COBLENTZ. *The Long Road to Humanity*. Yoseloff 1960.

P. COUDERC. *The Wider Universe*. Arrow Books 1960.

L. T. CHRISTY, D. LUCE, J. MACY. "Communication & Learning in Task-Oriented Groups'. Technical Report No. 231, Research Laboratory for Electronics M.I.T. 1952.

C. W. CHURCHMAN, R. L. ACKNOFF, E. L. ARNOFF, J. WILEY. 'Introduction to Operations Research' 1957.

C. E. CHURCHMAN, R. J. ACKNOFF. 'Purposive Behaviour and Cybernetics'. Social Forces 1950.

C. G. DARWIN SIR. *The Next Million Years*. Hart-Davis 1952.

S. DEMCZYNSKI. 'Computers in Business'. Automation Progress, September 1961.

K. W. Deutsch. 'Communication Theory and Social Science'. Amer J. Ortho-psychiot 1952.
K. W. Deutch 'Mechanism, Organism and Society'. Phil. Sci. July 1951.
K. W. Deutch. 'Mechanism, Teleology and Mind'. Phil. Phenom Res. 1951.
E. Dimnet. 'The Art of Thinking'. Fawcett. Thersons 1958.
M. Djilas. *The New Class*. Thames and Hudson 1957.
Dostoevsky, T. M. translated by D. Magarshak. *Crime and Punishment*. Penguin Books 1951.
Drucker. *The Practice of Management*. Heinneman 1955.
R. J. Forbes. *Man and Maker*. Constable 1951.
C. Frankel. *The Case for Modern Man*. Beacon 1959.
S. Freud. *Outline of Psycho-analysis*. Hogarth Press 1949.
S. Freud. *Totem and Taboo*. Routledge & Kegan Paul 1960.
J. K. Galbraith. *The Affluent Society*. Hamilton 1958.
M. Gardner. *Logic Machines and Diagrams*. McGraw-Hill 1958.
K. W. Gatland. *The Inhabited Universe*. Wingate 1956.
E. Gellner. *Words and Things*. Gollancz 1959.
F. H. George. *Automation, Cybernetics and Society*. Leonard Hill 1959.
L. Goodman. *Automation and Man*. Pelican Press 1957.
C. C. Gotlieb, N. P. Hume. *High Speed Data Processing*. McGraw-Hill 1958.
E. M. Grabbe. *Automation in Business and Industry*. J. Wiley 1957.
G. Hardin. *Nature and Man's Fate*. Cape 1960.
R. Harre. *An Introduction to the Logic of the Sciences*. Macmillan 1960.
R. F. Harrod. *Foundations of Inductive Logic*. Macmillan 1956.
F. H. Heinemann. *Existentialism and the Modern Predicament*. Black 1954.
W. Heisenberg. *Physics and Philosophy*. Allen and Unwin, London 1959.
W. E. Hocking. *The Coming World Civilization*. Harper 1956.
F. Hoyle. *Man and Materialism*. Allen and Unwin, London 1957.
A. Huxley. *Brave New World*. Chatto and Windus 1953.
A. Huxley. *Brave New World Revisited*. Chatto and Windus 1959.
J. Huxley. *Soviet Genetic and World Science*. Chatto and Windus 1949.
J. Huxley. *New Bottles for New Wine*. Chatto and Windus.
H. B. Jacobson, J. S. Roucek (Ed.). 'Automation and Society'. New York Philosophical Society 1959.
K. Jaspers. trans. by E. & C. Paul. *Man in Modern Age*. Routledge 1951.
F. Kant. *Critique of Pure Reason*. Macmillan 1929.
G. F. Kennan. *Russia, the Atom and the West*. Oxford University Press 1958.
H. A. Kissinger. *Nuclear Weapons and Foreign Policy*. Harper 1957.
J. W. Krutch. *The Measure of Man*. Redman 1956.
A. M. Lassek. *The Human Brain*. Lackwell Scientific Publications 1957.
I. Leclerc. *Whitehead's Metaphysics*. McMillam 1958.
H. F. Levin. *Office Work and Automation*. Chapman & Hall 1956.
F. A. Lindsay. *New Techniques for Management Decision Making*. McGraw-Hill 1958.
A. C. B. Lovell. *The Individual and the Universe*. Oxford University Press 1959.
S. Madariaga. *Victors Beware*. Cape 1946.
J. G. March, H. A. Simon. *Organizations*. Chapman and Hall 1959.
K. Marx. *Capital* Vol. 1. Lawrence & Widdell 1954.
P. B. Medawar. *The Future of Man*. Methuen 1960.
F. O. Miksche. *The Failure of Atomic Strategy and a new Proposal for the Defence of the West*. Faber 1959.
R. H. Macmillan. *Automation Friend or Foe*. Cambridge University Press 1956.
C. W. Mills. *The Sociological Imagination*. Oxford University Press 1959.
G. E. Milward (Ed.). *Organization and Methods*. Macmillan 1959.

L. Von Mises. *Theory and History*. Cape 1958.

M. J. Moroney. *Facts and Figures*. Penguin 1958.

V. H. Mottram. *The Physical Basis of Personality*. Penguin 1944.

L. Mumford. *Transformation of Man*. Allen and Unwin, London 1957.

L. Mumford. *The Conduct of Life*. Secker and Warburge 1952.

G. R. G. Mure. *Retreat from Truth*. Blackwell 1958.

G. Murphy. *Human Potentialities*. Allen and Unwin, London 1960.

J. U. Nef. *Cultural Foundations of Industrial Civilization*. Cambridge University Press 1958.

J. Von Neumann. *The Computer and the Brain*. Yale University Press 1958.

T. M. Newcomb. *Social Psychology*. Tavistock 1952.

G. Orwell. *'1984'*. Penguin 1954.

L. Paul. *'Nature into History'*. Humanities.

J. Pfeiffer. *From Galaxies to Man*. Gollancz 1960.

M. Phister. *Logical Design of Digital Computers*. Wiley 1958.

J. A. Postley. *Computers and People*. McGraw-Hill 1960.

F. H. L. Poynter (Ed.). *The History and Philosophy of Knowledge of the Brain and its Functions*. Thomas 1959.

Reed. *The Meaning of Art*. Faber and Faber 1931.

B. Remsch. *Evolution above Species Level*. Methuen.

J. H. Reyner. *The Universe of Relationships*. Stuart 1960.

R. E. de Ropp *Drugs and the Mind*. St. Martins 1957.

B. Russell. *The Impact of Science on Society*. Allen and Unwin, London 1952.

B. Russell. *History of Western Philosophy*. Allen and Unwin, London 1946.

B. Russell. *Scientific Outlook*. Allen and Unwin, London 1949.

B. Russell. *Mankind so far*. Allen and Unwin, Lpndon 1951.

B. Russell. *New Hopes for a Changing World*. Allen and Unwin, London 1951.

B. Russell. *Common Sense and Nuclear Warfare*. Allen and Unwin, London 1959.

B. Russell. *My Philosophical Development*. Allen and Unwin, London 1959.

B. Russell. *Wisdom of the West*. P. Foulkes (Ed.). Macdonald 1959.

V. Samuel. *In Search of Reality*. Blackwell 1957.

M. W. Sasieni, A. Yaspan, L. Friedman. *Operations Research*. Chapman and Hall 1959.

E. Schroedinger. *Mind and Matter*. Cambridge University Press 1958.

E. Schroedinger. *What is Life*. Cambridge University Press 1944.

A. Schweitzer. *An Anthology*. C. R. Joy (Ed.). Blackwell 1952.

R. Seidenberg. *Posthistoric Man*. Beacon 1950.

E. Shannon and J. McCarthy (Eds.). *Automata Studies*. Oxford University Press 1956.

M. Sheriff. *An Outline of Social Psychology*. Harper 1956.

C. Sherrington. *Man on his Nature*. Cambridge University Press (2nd Ed.). 1951.

A. T. W. Simeons. *Man's presumptious brain*. Longmans 1960.

E. W. Sinnott. *Matter, Mind and Man*. Harper 1957.

W. J. H. Sprott. *Social Psychology*. Methuen 1956.

R. Strehl. *The Robots are Among Us*. Arco 1956.

A. E. Stevenson. *Call to Greatness*. Hart-Davies 1954.

A. Steward. *You are Wrong Father Huddlestone*. Bodley Head 1956.

A. J. Toynbee. *A Study of History*. Oxford University Press 1949.

A. J. Toynbee. *A Historian Approach to Religion*. Cambridge University Press 1956.

G. Viand. *Intelligence: Its Evaluation and Forms*. Arrow Books 1960.

K. Walker. *So Great a Mystery*. Gollancz 1958.

K. Walker. *The Unconscious Mind*. Ryder 1961.

P. A. F. WALTER. *The Social Sciences*. Macmillan 1949.

W. G. WALTER. *The Living Brain*. Duckworth 1953.

H. G. WELLS. *The Mind at the End of its Tether*. Heinneman 1945.

A. N. WHITEHEAD. *Adventures of Ideas*. Cambridge University Press 1938.

W. H. WHYTE. *The Organization Man*. Cape 1957.

N. WEINER. *Cybernetics*. Chapman and Hall 1948.

N. WIENER. *The Human Use of Human Beings*. Eyre & Spottiswoode, London 1955.

M. V. WILKES. *Automatic Digital Computers*. Methuen 1956.

J. S. WILKIE. *The Science of Mind and Brain*. Hutchinson's University Library, London 1953.

F. WILLIAMS. *Magnificent Journey: History of the trade unions*. Odham Press, London 1954.

C. WILSON. *The Outsider*. Gollancz 1956.

C. WILSON. *The Age of Defeat*. Gollancz 1959.

W. P. WHITCUTT. *Rise and Fall of the Individual*. S.P.C.K. 1958.

T. WOODS. *Poetry and Philosophy*. Hutchinson 1961.

G. H. WRIGHT. *The Logical Problem of Induction*. Blackwell 1957.

GEORGE ALLEN & UNWIN LTD

London: 40 *Museum Street, W.C.*1

Auckland: 24 *Wyndham Street*
Bombay: 15 *Graham Road, Ballard Estate, Bombay,* 1
Bridgetown P.O. Box 222
Buenos Aires: Escritorio 454-459, *Florida* 165
Calcutta: 17 *Chittaranjan Avenue, Calcutta* 13
Cape Town: 68 *Shortmarket Street*
Hong Kong: 44 *Mody Road, Kowloon*
Ibadan: P.O. Box 62
Karachi: Karachi Chambers, McLeod Road
Madras: Mohan Mansions, 38c *Mount Road, Madras* 6
Mexico: Villalongin 32-10, *Piso, Mexico* 5, *D.F.*
Nairobi: P.O. Box 4536
New Delhi: 13-14 *Asaf Ali Road, New Delhi* 1
São Paulo: Avenida 9 *de Julho* 1138-*App.* 51
Singapore: 36c *Prinsep Street, Singapore* 7
Sydney, N.S.W.: Bradbury House, 55 *York Street*
Tokyo: 3 *Kanda-Ogawamachi,* 3-*Chome, Chiyoda-Ku*
Toronto: 91 *Wellington Street West, Toronto* 1

THE FLAMMARION BOOK OF ASTRONOMY

Translated from the French by BERNARD AND ANNABEL PAGEL

The first Russian Sputnik was indirectly responsible for a great many things, including an increase in the number of popular books on Astronomy. But it was not responsible for Flammarion's *Astronomie Populaire*, first published in 1880. This is a classic, with a tone and flavour of its own, a popularization in the style of the giants of the nineteenth century, to whom H. G. Wells was perhaps the latest successor.

Science, and astronomy in particular, have of course advanced beyond recognition since Flammarion wrote. His book has increased in length by over one third and now offers a singularly full account of man's entry into space. Yet what Flammarion wrote remains the framework and inspiration of this thoroughly modern book. It retains a classic quality. For it is more than another clear exposition of an intricate mass of knowledge. Flammarion provides this too, but he offers more than workmanlike explanations.

He has those qualities which give greatness to a popular account, namely the ability to write literature, an understanding of the social background and an ability to transmit the awe and wonder of the subject—a nineteenth century characteristic maybe, but one which is not displaced in the study of astronomy and without which we are the poorer. He also makes no demands on the reader's mathematics. The illustrations of today's books on astronomy are generally admirable, yet few can hope to do more than stand comparison with the 921 superb illustrations with which his widow, his successor in France and his family firm of publishers have made it a point of pride to endow *The Flammarion Book of Astronomy*.

The fact that the English translation reads like an original English book is due to the unusual success of two years of work devoted to it by Dr Bernard and Mrs. Annabel Pagel. Dr Pagel, an astronomer at the Royal Greenwich Observatory, has added considerable new material to the latest revised French edition. He has also contributed an original survey—perhaps the first popular survey—of what rockets and artificial satellites have contributed to astronomy.

Large Quad. Medium (11½ins. x 8¾ins.)   £5 net

LONDON: GEORGE   ALLEN   AND   UNWIN   LTD.